THE NEXT
DEVELOPMENT
IN MANKIND

THE NEXT DEVELOPMENT IN MANKIND

Lancelot Law Whyte

With a new introduction by
Gary David and **Brian Rothery**

Transaction Publishers
New Brunswick (U.S.A.) and London (U.K.)

This book is printed on acid-free paper that meets the American National Standard for Permanence of Paper for Printed Library Materials.

Library of Congress Catalog Number: 2002073282
ISBN: 0-7658-0162-0 (cloth); 0-7658-0969-9 (paper)
Printed in the United States of America

Library of Congress Cataloging-in-Publication Data

Whyte, Lancelot Law, 1896-1972.
    [Next development in man]
    The next development in mankind / Lancelot Law Whyte ; with a new introduction by Gary David and Brian Rothery.
       p. cm.
    Originally published as: Next development in man. London : Cresset Press, 1944. With new introd.
    ISBN 0-7658-0162-0 (alk. paper) — ISBN 0-7658-0969-0 (pbk. : alk. paper)
    1. Civilization—Philosophy. I. Title.

CB19 .W5 2003
901—dc21   2002073282

Contents

Introduction to the Transaction Edition

We, Brian Rothery in Ireland and Gary David in the U.S., found each other on the Internet through our mutual interest in unity and participation. But the nodal point of our interest which drew us together was the name Lancelot Law Whyte. We had each read Whyte's *The Next Development in Mankind* in the 1960s. We, (Brian, a much-published book author and science journalist, and Gary a musician and Ph.D. in epistemology), had been so moved by what we read in the scrawlings of Whyte's soul that thirty years later, from two different continents, we converged, saying, "How could the works of one of the most important observers and commentators of science and society go out of print?" Over the years, the profundity, clarity and passion of his writing have been a guiding map for us, and for many others, both scientists and non-scientists alike. We did not want to see such important, hard-gained, and still relevant work go forgotten and unavailable in the twenty-first century. Whyte himself wrote in his autobiography, "Very general ideas may have to wait long before their importance is recognized."

We decided to so something about it. We started a website called Philosphere to promote the works of Whyte and other authors who had creative ways of seeing the development of civilization in science, art, religion, and in everyday life. Shortly after, we found that Boston University was the trustee to Whyte's literary work. We had scanned in the first titles from dog-eared paperbacks, and begun to advertise our intentions to publish under Philosphere Publishers (www.philosphere.com). Brian went to Boston University where he studied the archives of Whyte's legacy, including his personal diaries. Eventually, it brought us to Transaction Publishers, whose chairman of the board and editorial director, Irving Louis Horowitz, was also an avid reader of Whyte. They agreed with our goals to republish his work, and together, we are proud to begin a process that will bring the major works of L.L. Whyte back into the mainstream of public communications and let, you, the reader, see for yourself if these are not some of the most profound, unique, and creative insights into our times.

Our first offering is Whyte's most widely read book, *The Next Development in Mankind*, the ideas of which were started in 1937, and eventually published in 1943. It was the book that brought him to worldwide attention, especially in the United States where, just before his death, he was listed in *The Last Whole Earth Catalogue* as among the father figures of a new generation.

L.L. Whyte's Intellectual Passion

Lancelot Law Whyte (1896-1972) the son of an Edinburgh clergyman, became a physicist, business manager, and philosopher, and lived most of his life in London. He was driven by a passion that grew out of an insight he had at an early age—his vision of unity. He sought to explore principles of that insight in each of his sixteen books, and in many papers, articles, seminars, and interviews. One of his contemporaries, Teilhard de Chardin, wrote, "Stage by stage, my initial faith in the world has taken a definite shape. What was at first a vague intuition of universal unity has become a rational and well-defined awareness of a presence." Those words could have been written by L.L. Whyte.

Whyte was trained in physics under Ernest Rutherford at the Cavendish Laboratories in Cambridge, and he became as well-versed in biology, astronomy, psychology and philosophy as in physics. He was among a handful of philosophers and scientists who conveyed an overview of civilization that was clear, profound, and still rings with relevance today. He was part of a stream of thought that could be called *organic holism*. Others of his time were Alfred North Whitehead, J.S. Huxley, Jan Smuts, Joseph Needham, Alfred Korzybski, J.S. Bois, David Bohm, Gaston Bachelard, Silvan S. Tomkins, Pierre Teilhard de Chardin, Henri Bergson, and Kurt Goldstein.

One thing that distinguishes Whyte from his peers is that, although he knew in a professional and comprehensive manner all of the fields mentioned above, he maintained the aesthetic sense of experience usually associated with artists. He was similar to

Bachelard in that respect. Paul Goodman and Fritz Perls called him the major theoretician of Gestalt therapy. Allen Watts and Arthur Koestler became admirers and associates, and he, along with Lewis Mumford, and Patrick Geddes were the champions of organismic philosophy of the time. Theodore Roszak called him, "a significant thinker, certainly one of the most gifted natural philosophers of our century."

Yet, some saw him as a "marginal man," a maverick who functioned as an observer and critic of science with no institutional strings to control him, and only his obvious and deep understanding of what he observed to give him credibility. In his last book, *The Universe of Experience* (1972), Whyte wrote of himself in a chapter titled, "Who Has Written This And Why,": "He [Whyte himself] is a scientific frontiersman who has spent fifty years, not tied to a chair, but using his free time to canter around the no-man's-land of science along the frontiers where physics, biology, and psychology face the unknown, with an eye also on philosophy . . . . He is a *metaphysicist* in search of unity." Elsewhere he wrote, "I have made myself an amateur specialist in the history, present, and near-future of three ideas: atomism, organic co-ordination, and unconscious mental processes."

But Whyte always thought of himself as a theoretical physicist, foremost. His diaries revealed something withheld from the books: he had spent the best part of fifty years working on a mathematical/geometric unified theory, which appears to reveal more great potential for us in the use of electromagnetism, and also had some theories that stand in contrast to Einstein's theory of relativity. He appears to have been on the threshold of expressing it mathematically just before he died, suddenly, at the age of seventy-six. How seriously one can take this is underlined by the fact that he studied under, or worked, or talked with, Rutherford, Bohr, Born, Heisenberg, and Einstein. His theory also embraces psychology and biology. In the case of psychology, he wrote about Freud and talked with Jung. In the case of biology, he anticipated the problems and opportunities presented by human cloning, forty years before such cloning became a real possibility.

He was a great admirer of Goethe of whom he wrote, "Goethe is a unitary man, living in the eighteenth century. . . . [He] stands beyond the range of a personal or literary criticism because, like

Socrates and Jesus, he unhesitatingly followed a vision of life which bore within it the germ of centuries to come." In 1949 Whyte put this quotation of Goethe's on a Christmas card that he and his wife Eve sent out: "*Nobody understands that the formative process is the supreme process, indeed the only one, alike in nature and art.*" He added the following: "In this prophetic intuition Goethe points to the most general principle in nature and the basic urge in human nature, lying beneath the apparent division of matter and mind. The main limitations of exact science and of dialectical materialism arise from their neglect of the formative aspect of process, in physical nature and in the human personality respectively. This was the heart of Goethe's single view of nature and man."

It was also the heart of everything Whyte wrote; it was the lens through which he lucidly explored all avenues of life. He vigorously explored the idea of a pervasive unity-in-diversity, a tendency towards order underlying the inorganic world, organic nature, and human life. He called it the "Unitary Principle, by which asymmetry decreases and gives place to symmetry." He sought to bring into closer relation the scientific conception of the forms of external nature and his personal sense of the forms of experience. He proposed that the formative tendency represents internal factors of evolution. (He authored a book by that title in 1965.) He prophetically wrote in his autobiography, "The decades from 1950 onwards will be recognized as marked by a change in evolutionary philosophy: the gradual discarding of an unduly narrow view of the mechanism of the evolution of species as due only to the external or Darwinian adaptive selection of matured forms resulting from haphazard mutation." In light of the current controversies surrounding "evolution," "creation," and "intelligent design," a view such as Whyte's, even from his early perspective in 1943, is a breath of fresh air in the smog of semantic confusion.

The Next Development in Mankind was written in the depths of the Second World War in London in the face of overwhelming evidence of the triumph of Nietzsche's nihilism and certainly that of a collapsed European tradition of reason and enlightenment. It was also a dark period in the life of "Lance," as he was known to family and friends. Two great adventures had just ended. The British government had taken over his spectacularly successful "Whittle engine" project, in which he had been managing director of the company that had developed the world's first jet engine, the acknowledged prototype for all the great passenger jet engines which followed, and then in June 1941, two weeks later, his beloved wife Lotte died. Lance moved to a new wartime job in the Ministry of Supply, beginning four years without a life partner. Apart from his daytime job, he did occasional nighttime fire watching.

Whyte was a generalist in the best sense of the term. His was an historical way of thinking shaped by careful induction, and not wild generalities asserted with dogmatic assurance. His vision was fused with the fundamental fact of hierarchy in nature. While some great historical thinkers have discussed many forms of process, historical and personal, Whyte saw that none of them had made clear the essential character of change, at least not with the degree of precision attempted by what he called "unitary thought." His 'unitary method' is an attempt to carry forward and clarify a great tradition, by making a clear assumption regarding the general form of all processes.

Unitary thought is based on a recognition of a universal formative process present in every phenomenon, and underlying all dualisms. Matter, life, and mind are ultimately to be interpreted as different aspects of this underlying process. He later called this formative tendency a "morphic" process that not only underlies our universe and drives evolution from within, but is also a force that each of us can harness to change our lives for the better. It opens our minds to a new vista of forms, and regions that have seemed to be separated by a metaphysical abyss are rediscovered in their true unity because the characteristic of any particular process by which its continuity is recognized is called "form," but by that Whyte is not referring to the static images of form. He calls it the recognizable continuity of any process.

As the text for *The Next Development in Mankind* was being scanned in for republication in late February 2001, we noted that day's newspaper headlines announcing the completion of the human genome sequencing, and looked back at Whyte's words: "There is no drama to compare with the attempt of the human race to understand its destiny, to understand external nature and human nature. The entire human race now for the first time faces a single collective challenge. During the next few decades it must decide what kind of man and community is to survive on this planet."

Key Constructs of *The Next Development in Mankind*

On page 21 of the introduction, Whyte wrote, "The main theme of the book is the conviction that nature is a system of formative processes, that the static concepts and dualisms of other systems of thought represent aspects of nature which are secondary to this basic form, and that this principle can be applied to the diagnosis of the condition of a society which is suffering from its failure to recognize it."

Whyte called his book *a spiritual history of the West.* He said, "I dislike that heavy Hegelian title. But it states the theme in three words: next—development—man." It is an example of historical method of reason, as opposed to analytical reason. Not a history only of events, but one that takes into account all of the known functions of a human being: electro-chemical, motoric, affective, cognitive, memory, time, and environment. He called it "unitary thought."

The book is a "Unitary Manifesto," a declaration of his conviction of a universal formative process. Unitary thought is based on a recognition of a universal formative process present in every phenomenon, and underlying all dualisms. Matter, life, and mind are ultimately to be interpreted as different aspects of this underlying process, functionally similar to what David Bohm would later call an "implicate order."

How did we come to this place where such a unifying construct was vitally necessary? In *The Next Development In Mankind*, Whyte gives the most compelling historical account that we have ever read of how our *methods of thought* led to what he called the "European dissociation" which eventually became an organic "lesion" in the human nervous system. His account of this should be fundamental reading for every student of the West. He describes it as a dissociation of the ability to long delay our responses (deliberation), and the spontaneous instinctual and instinct-like responses. Our methods of thought shaped these coordinated functions into dualism. "The accumulated results of this dual tendency of thought had hardened into a metaphysical dualism which reinforced the tendency for conflict to develop between deliberate and spontaneous behavior." He shows that this is not a mere dualism of categories, but one that has biological effects and consequences.

Any process which displays one general form of continuity is called unitary, whereas a process which appears to display two incompatible forms is called dualistic. From this Whyte developed his conviction about the dualistic nature of the European tradition producing a kind of distortion he described as dissociation. We became fragmented, tortured. Our very social systems maintained the dissociation at the expense of organic development, and it is such organic development which is natural and healthy within both the individual organism, and the greater society, in a complex process which never reaches complete and static symmetry, but continues in development through continuing adjustment.

We have fallen from organic harmony and undivided thought, and European culture and civilization have deepened the dissociation. Great thinkers such as Descartes hardened the division by promoting intellect and static concepts as fundamental, and although we have a "deep preference for the static," Spinoza, Goethe, Hegel and others have shown the way. Only unitary thought, and only a community, which is already in course of a corresponding change, can guide the further development of humankind. When we also read his next book, *The Unconscious Before Freud,* we may have a way of seeing that the change is indeed underway.

Whyte says, "Isolation is death; life is the developing conformity of the whole" and we think of the God-forsaken who do not interact with others. He goes on: "The individual cannot cure himself of a distortion, which is of social origin. Mutual aid is indispensable and one kind of person may complement or repair the deficiencies of another kind." In his prognosis, he assigns a key role to the feminine: "The European dissociation is primarily a male distortion, and man has the opportunity of recovery, or at least of compensation, through woman."

Another key term is co-ordination—the organization of specialized processes. The dissociation he writes of explicated itself in separation of body-mind, mind-matter, and intellect-emotion. In the latter split, intellect based on memory and recording processes, depended on separating language from emotion. The intellect became more and more specialized and abstract and disguised the disappearing of the formative aspect of mental process. At the other extreme, he describes how when sense discrimination and memory recording cease, the mental process loses all specific form and dissolves into a "formless passion like the fury of a beast." His view was that intellect and emotion cannot be separated, that each performs a function in determining behavior: "The intellect is therefore mainly related to special local stimuli and specialized responses. The emotions on the other hand are related to the sustained coordination of behavior, and express states of polarization of the system as a whole, which maintain the integration of activity along one general course by facilitating some modes of behavior and inhibiting others." A contemporary of Whyte's, Silvan S. Tomkins, who was later to discover the basis of the biological affect system within the brain, confirmed Whyte's formulation. In speaking of the affect system as the amplifying, motivational aspect, and cognition as the transformational, he wrote, "Amplification without transformation would be blind; transformation without amplification would be weak. The blind mechanisms must be given sight; the weak mechanisms must be given strength."[1] In a unified human being, a new kind of emotional maturity would be reached.

He chooses nine representative thinkers to particularize the general developments of the European adventure and the part played by special individuals in the social process: Heraclitus, Plato, Paul, Kepler, Descartes, Spinoza, Goethe, Marx, and Freud. These thumbnail sketches "illustrate the continuous development of the structure of European thought, and where appropriate a suggestion is given of the personal response of each to the role which he found was his."

In the appendix, Whyte carefully lays out his "Glossary of Unitary Thought," with each term defining and related to the next in a hierarchy of interdependent meanings. A key construct is that of "facilitation." Every system displays a formative tendency, which is realized if it is consistent with the tendencies of all the larger systems of which it is a part. Facilitation is the tendency of structures to extend their form by repetition of the process by which they were formed. In general, the formative process tends to develop structures which facilitate further development. Process has a self-developing tendency; it facilitates its own development.

If systems did not facilitate their own development there would be closed systems only. The concept of facilitation asserts that the universe is a cosmos in which there is the degree of ordered unity which is implied in the existence not only of discrete physical systems with definite characteristics, but of organisms and of thinking organisms.

One of the central paragraphs of the whole book sums up the biological imperative implied by unitary thought: "I suggest that one conviction alone can serve as the central principle of the reorganised tradition, the conviction that a formative process pervades nature. Man needs this principle to organise his thought. He needs it equally to organise his feeling, and through his thought and feeling his action. This conviction is on all grounds indispensable to the recovery of man. It is a biological need, which once recognised cannot be denied. Man can understand himself only by viewing himself as a system in which a dominant formative process organises an organic hierarchy of such processes in an environment of similar processes."

He believed that we are now entering a period in history, which will be characterised by the individual's awareness of the formative process, which unites him or her with nature. And this will be the mark of the coming unitary individual—the conviction of a universal formative process. The coming period in history will be thus characterized by our awareness of the formative process, which unites us in thought to our unity with nature. This unitary human principle also means that the individual becomes mature only through a recognition of his or her being a component in the unitary system of nature and in the developing system of their community. In support of this we can point to both the huge increased interest in mental well being and environmental integrity. The distinguishing mark of a period dominated by a constructive trend is that the interest of the individual and of the community can no longer be separated: "Unitary thought says to every individual: to know yourself is no longer adequate, because static knowledge is not possible. You can realize yourself only as a developing component of the community."

He predicted a coming end to the distortions and injustices caused by the abuse of quantity. We have since seen the curbing of the kind of financial madness which caused the 1929 crash, and also the acceptance of international standards for trading quality and 'fitness for purpose' as well as greatly improved environmental probity and public safety. But we still experience the "toll gate" piracy of major corporations operating cartels and monopolies, and we are threatened with a new war between "the common people" and the powers of globalization. Some individuals in the West are as rich as small third world countries, and everywhere we see corrupt politicians and state officials who put private gain over public good and integrity. If we are to see the public honesty and integrity associated with the emerging unitary unifying form, we may still have to wait some time.

Another distortion sorely needing repair is in the area of human sexuality. The European dissociation in particular expressed the spiritual as "more legitimate" than the sensual appetites. This biased discrimination prevented the integration, which is essential, if we are to continue in development. Whyte admitted that there had been a relaxation of the inhibitions: after all he lived through the trials of Oscar Wilde, Radycliffe Hall, and D.H. Lawrence and suffered his own private trials. When in his own sixties he experienced the permissive 1960s, and saw the beginnings of global pornography. He wanted the emotional honesty required for our coming reorganization and unity, but saw the dangers also: "The relaxation of the inhibitions on the instinctive life, which maintained the dissociation without the substitution of any adequate novel co-ordination expressing the integrity appropriate to human nature, has resulted in a new emphasis on the animal needs of man."

Above all perhaps, in the book is the haunting dream, the promise that so many of us recognize: "Within the pageant of daily life, and beyond the reach either of religious tradition or personal introspection, there lies hidden the promise of an important truth, like the memory of some forgotten experience or the anticipation of one not yet known." It is also a promise of the possibility of a process of development, and this process itself, not its apparent aim, is its justification, for achievement brings with it new tensions and new opportunities. It could be that the dissociation is a stage along the way in a development seeking emergence.

A reading of *The Next Development in Mankind* reveals that almost everything he forecast has, in fact, since happened but at a slower pace than he had anticipated, but even that criticism may be made redundant by growing evidence that more and more people are thinking in process or unitary form, whether or not they use such expressions to describe it, and they are acknowledging the power of the unconscious. Whyte's notion of the "unconscious" was a bit narrow at the time in that he ascribed consciousness to reasoning processes. He corrected that restriction in later work, and made more plausible his statement that *the world awaits a conscious expression of something its unconscious already knows.*

"Today the only hope of social order lies in the establishment of a valid universalism, a doctrine true to the nature of *homo sapiens* and, so, acceptable to all peoples. The blunt fact is that the species must now think harder and better than ever before if civilization is to be saved from progressive decline." Many have been infused with the dream of a unity that already exists but not within our systems of thought which have yet to catch up to our intuitive sense of that unity.

Yet, this idea is already operating within the minds of millions of us, so that, as he forecast, we may indeed be entering an age when we can begin to bring about the wholeness of self and society he was so sure could be achieved.

Brian Rothery and Gary David

Note

1. Tomkins, Silvan S., *Affect, Imagery, Consciousness, Vol. IV*, Springer Publishing Company, New York, 1992.

1

Introduction

Thought is born of failure. Only when action fails to satisfy human needs is there ground for thought. To devote attention to any problem is to confess a lack of adjustment which we must stop to consider. And the greater the failure the more searching is the kind of thought which is necessary.

At no previous period in human history has there been such widespread examination of the nature of man and his present situation. This is partly because the race has become more self-conscious than ever before, more aware of its own failures, and partly because it faces problems which are unprecedented both in gravity and extent. The blunt fact is that the species must now think harder and better than ever before if civilization is to be saved from progressive decline. The situation calls for a unique effort of courageous, realistic, and imaginative thought. What is necessary, as we shall see, is better thought about nature as a whole, and in particular about human beings and the kind of society they require.

The entire human race now for the first time faces a single collective challenge. During the next few decades it must decide what kind of man and community is to survive on this planet. In the past, regional civilizations have come and gone, but now we are all involved together and share a common future.

This does not imply a uniform standardization of human life throughout the globe in the coming years. It means simply that without some *universally acceptable ideas* about nature and man there can be no stable world order. The world is now one; we are entering a period of universalism. From now on only universal ideas can be effective. The great world religions and ideologies of the past have sought universality but failed to achieve it. Commu-

1

nism fails because it offers too narrow a view of man, and Christianity, at least as known up to now, does not meet the needs of countless millions in Asia and elsewhere. Today the only hope of social order lies in the establishment of a valid universalism, a doctrine true to the nature of *homo sapiens* and, so, acceptable to all peoples.

Such a universal doctrine can only emerge from the broadening of science. We are in a scientific age, and science alone has the technique to discover, and the authority to present, a view of nature and man which can be accepted by men and women everywhere. Science has been prejudiced by its departmentalism and excessive attention to the inanimate realm, but its unique authority remains. The next step is for science to become so truly scientific, so comprehensive and humane that instead of damaging man it can teach him how to live by showing him the truth about nature and himself.

Or to express it another way: the present condition of man demands the formulation of a universal method of thought at once true to nature (so that the structure of all natural processes can be understood) and appropriate to present-day human nature (so that men and women everywhere can find a common ground in using it). This is much to ask, but it seems that nothing less will do. The establishment of such a method of thought would be no more remarkable, in relation to present knowledge, than Isaac Newton's *System of the Universe* was in relation to the knowledge of his time.

Great advances can be made only if many are ready to dare much and to fall by the wayside if necessary. Even in failure, the fun is in the daring as much as in the achievement. This is particularly true for the scientific mind, since science advances mainly by its ability to prove certain assumptions *wrong* and to cast them aside. This book is an experiment in thought based on certain clear assumptions. Be it proved a failure, that too may be useful.

The principal assumption is that only what is here called a *unitary* system of thought can satisfy the contemporary mind, reflect the true structure of nature, and show man how to think. The term "unitary" is used for a system of thought which:

(1) Emphasizes process, development, and transformation. This is a perpetually changing universe, and conceptions of unchang-

ing permanence must play no part in the basic formulations of the system.

(2) Is capable, at least potentially, of bringing all facts into relation with one another. This implies that it recognizes no absolute dualism, such as *mind/body*, or *good/evil*. These and similar dualities must be interpreted as referring to pairs of aspects of one underlying phenomenon: the process of the universe in all its forms.

(3) Recognizes at the start a *universal formative process* in nature, a process in which regular spatial forms (symmetrical patterns) are developed and transformed. Nature is not a chaos of particles, but a process which consists in the development and transformation of patterns (such as are evident in the structure of molecules, crystals, tissues, organs, and in organisms and their behavior patterns). If there were no patterns in the world, the mind could make no sense of it

If these assumptions seem arbitrary, they can be accepted provisionally as the basis of an intellectual experiment. The pages which follow apply the unitary method to the interpretation of the present historical situation and to suggesting a possible way forward. In fact, the argument suggests that care of the greatest needs today is precisely the development and application of a unitary method of thought in all fields from physics and biology to sociology and social and political thought.

This would be a preposterous suggestion if unitary thought were wholly new. But the reverse is the case. Unitary thought is nothing but one step in the further clarification of ideas which have been emerging in Western thought, and all in science, for a very long time.

For Plato, only the permanent is real. The contrary view, that *change* is real, is represented in Western thought by a long line of thinkers who have emphasized process, from Heraclitus in ancient times to Vico, Schopenhauer, Hegel, Marx, Spencer, and Nietzsche, and to Bergson and Whitehead in this century. These thinkers have discussed many forms of process, historical and personal, but none of them has made clear the essential character of change, at least not with the degree of precision attempted (whether successfully or not) by unitary thought. The unitary method is an attempt to carry forward and clarify the great tradition represented by these names, by making a clear assumption regarding the character of change, i.e., the general *form* of all processes.

In another, more specific, sense the unitary method is the continuance of an old outlook. For in its attempt to transcend all absolute dualisms the unitary method follows the lead of the great monistic thinkers, and particularly that of Spinoza and Goethe, for whom man and his thought were part of universal nature. Many religions have proclaimed the unity of God and all his works. The attitude reappears within the scientific context of unitary thought as the attempt to interpret all natural phenomena as parts of one pattern, or more precisely, as expressions of one universal form of process. When dualistic terms have to be used, this must be so because we have not yet recognized the single underlying phenomenon of which the dual terms represent pairs of aspects. In its monistic emphasis, unitary thought is anything but new.

Finally, in its postulation of a formative process, i.e., a process in which regular patterns are developed, the unitary method is the culmination of a tendency which is evident in much of the scientific thought of the last forty years in physics, biology, psychology, and sociology. It appears that the utility of "atomistic" ideas may be provisionally exhausted, and that as a result science is being led to concentrate more on the study of pattern and symmetry, and on the emergence of new patterns. In many fields the crucial task of scientific inquiry is now to identify the *structure* of each phenomenon, i.e., the changing pattern of relationships (which determines its character). The unitary method seeks to ease this task by pointing to a formative process, a tendency towards the clarification of form and pattern, in every phenomenon.

Thus, in all these respects, unitary thought is a development of well-known ideas. Its novelty lies only in the emphasis on a universal formative process present in every phenomenon, and underlying all dualisms. Matter, life, and mind are ultimately to be interpreted as different aspects of this underlying process. Moreover, it is suggested that only by developing and perfecting such a method of thought can man properly understand either nature or his own historical situation, and so overcome present confusions.

There is no drama to compare with the attempt of the human race to understand its destiny, to understand external nature and human nature. This work is an attempt to advance that supreme adventure by one minute step. If its main theme is valid, and the unitary method is indeed timely, then the next generations may experience the resolution of some of the harsh conflicts which frustrate human lives today. If it is wrong, then its failure may contribute to human enlightenment. The reader will judge for himself which result appears more probable. The years to come will decide.

2

Development

A unitary method of thought is indispensable to the interpretation of the history, of the West. The pervasive dualisms which distort the thought of Western man are an element in his general condition, which therefore must be diagnosed in a language which does not take these dualisms for granted. No interpretation of Western man in traditional terms can bring the truth to light, any more than the color-blind can know their own deficiency. A language is needed that does not beg all the questions on which the Western mind has long been made up. This language must express a form of reasoning based on unitary premises. A new and more general concept of man, capable of throwing light on the peculiarities of Western man, only can spring from a new concept of nature.

The intellectual system introduced in this chapter may be regarded as a special development of the English language, a general method of thought, a philosophy, or the anticipation a new kind of law of nature. The languages which contemporary Western communities have inherited carry implicit assumptions regarding the general form of nature, and one of the main tasks of unitary thought is to bring these out and to show where they are invalid. This demonstration would be of small importance if it were an arbitrary or isolated intellectual analysis. If dualistic thought were still appropriate, the formulation of unitary thought would achieve little. But if the further development of man can be guided only by unitary thought, then one of those rare moments has arrived when an intellectual system may appear to have the power to influence men's habits. For the change from dualistic to unitary thought can be accepted only by a community which is already in course of a corresponding but more general transformation.

Unitary thought claims to offer a way of thinking which, when developed, will facilitate correct inference about everything. If the method is applied with understanding and without prejudice it will eventually lead to correct inference.

Moreover if nature has the general form postulated in unitary thought, then certain conclusions follow at once regarding the human species, the history of man and the state of contemporary man. Unitary thought is a guide to correct thought because it organizes knowledge in conformity with the forms of nature. Knowledge is already vast, and more than ample for the solution of many pressing problems. Unitary thought provides that minor but all-important re-orientation which eliminates the prejudice that has hitherto obscured our vision of the facts. A slight change of position, and the interrelations of everything are transformed so that a simple order is revealed.

My purpose here is to apply that re-orientation to the interpretation of certain aspects of the history of Europe and the West. I must therefore develop the language of unitary thought before coming to grips with the main task. All readers may not welcome so radical an approach, and a more superficial interpretation may be obtained by passing directly to chapter 2 or chapter 4. On the other hand anyone who wishes to convince himself of the self-consistency of unitary thought can use the Appendix as a supplement to the present chapter. There he will find a glossary of the primary concepts of unitary thought arranged in logical sequence.

We are now to look below the traditional frame of thought. An ancient prejudice has been discarded and nature guides the forms of our thought so that her own forms may be seen as they are. There is no finality in the development of thought, but here is the vision appropriate to our desperate need. We open our minds to a new vista of forms. Regions that have seemed to be separated by a metaphysical abyss are now rediscovered in their true unity. The complete view of nature revealed by these symbols must wait. First we must understand ourselves and our fall from organic harmony and undivided thought.

Here an old tradition has developed into a new form, more universal and, though unitary, more generous to diversity. The old tradition had control of the reader's mind during the many years of his immaturity; it may have left him with some of the conflicts and confusions that arise from its prejudiced and dualistic approach. If he gives as many hours to the restoring influence of unitary thought, I believe that those difficulties will begin to disappear. None of us can escape the desire for unity; a unitary mode of thought can facilitate its development.

It is for the sake of this emancipation that man's deep preference for the static must be overcome. Heraclitus, Goethe, Hegel, and Marx have shown the way, but the world they saw was not ours. Each age must meet its challenge alone. The old gods are dead, and men like those that created them are no longer to be found. But decay has renewed the soil and we now enter on fresh ground, the world of unitary man.

Outline of Unitary Thought

Change is universal. Permanent elements may appear to challenge it, but they have no lasting substance. Yet change is not arbitrary. The future unfolds continuously out of the present. Earlier and later states do not confront each other as the senseless juxtaposition of one chaos beside another, but are linked by similarities which pervade change. This meaningful order underlying change is realized as a continuity in the sequence of change. In so far as change reveals this continuity and is not arbitrary, it is called *process*.*

Moreover this continuity is universal and constitutes the unifying order, which can be recognized throughout the diversity of all particular changes. This comprehensive unity is called *nature*. Nature is continuity in change, and unity in diversity. But nature can only be recognized in particular processes, and the characteristic of any particular process by which its continuity is recognized is called *form*. Form is the recognizable continuity of any process. In the limiting case when change vanishes, only approached towards the absolute zero of temperature, the form of the process becomes the perfect symmetry of a static pattern. Some forms may appear to be static, but they none the less partake in the processes of the whole. A process is fully identified when its form is recognized. The interpretation of human history, for example, consists in the

---

*Each of the main concepts of unitary thought is printed in italics when the argument reaches it. A sequence of definitions is given in the Appendix.

identification of the continuity, or form, of the process, either in general outline or in detail.

Any process which displays one general form of continuity is called *unitary*, whereas a process which appears to display two incompatible forms is called *dualistic*. "Unitary" means of one general form, and "dualistic" of two mutually exclusive forms.

A unitary system of thought is a universal system based on a single concept of the form of process, and is the form of thought which is now appropriate. Unitary thought is not a completed organization of established fact. It is the continuing activity of recognizing one universal form within the diversity of particular processes.

But a unitary system of thought was not possible during the first phase of the systematization of thought. We shall see that man was then bound to seek continuity in the form not of process but of permanence, and that in doing so he separated himself as subject from the rest of nature as object and so divided the continuity of process into two incompatible forms: conscious purpose and material necessity. The source of this dualism did not lie in any general characteristic of nature, but in the temporary conditions which caused man to seek a static permanence, both in his individual life and in the words used to express his thought. We shall see that these conditions played a special role in the development, dominance, and final disintegration of European man. Moreover it is the passing of these conditions which now makes it possible to recognize the unitary form lying behind the dualism of purpose and necessity.

But man can no longer maintain his separation as subject from the objective nature which is now the field of such intensive study. The recognition of a single form underlying purpose and necessity will make possible the reconciliation of subjective experience and objective knowledge. During the dualistic period which we are about to study, thought tended to display either a subjective or an objective bias. On the one hand, believing that conscious purpose directed his own life, man could discover purpose at work in the rest of nature. This view led to an emphasis on one dominant tendency, and hence to over-simplification and neglect of detail. On the other hand, where man's attention was drawn to the diversity of the detail of natural processes he tended to emphasize the material permanence of the atomic mechanisms by which that diversity could be explained. The first view stresses the unity of process leading, apparently, to a preconceived end, and the second the atoms of permanent substance of which it seemed that the diversity of nature was composed. Both views were mistaken, though appropriate at the time. There is no universal preconceived end, and there are no permanent material parts with constant identity. These conceptions no longer provide an adequate clue to the form of the continuity of process. Static aims and static particles, however subtle their interplay, cannot represent the more general form of process which man can now identify. The need for a comprehensive conception of process has been recognized for two centuries in historical and biological thought. But only now, with the passing of the conditions which created European man, has its formulation become possible in a unitary system of thought capable of providing the basis of a unitary science.

Process consists in the *development* of form by the decrease of asymmetry. Development is decrease of asymmetry. In simple processes development is unmistakable as the separation, persistence, and extension of symmetrical form.

This process of development is universal; it is the form of the order of nature. But it has to be discovered within processes which appear to display conservation, decay, or confusion rather than development. The task of unitary thought is to discover the decrease of asymmetry in nature. Where contrary processes appear to be at work, this illusion is due to the faulty separation of a particular process from the wider processes to which it belongs.

The decrease of asymmetry can already be recognized in four different types of process which may be called molecular development, mechanical development, statistical development and organic development. Two of these do not concern us here: mechanical development, in which separate objects move towards a symmetrical equilibrium state (of minimum potential energy), as in the pendulum; and statistical development, where the individual forms cannot be traced but there is a general process of evening out in which part displays increasing conformity with the whole (increasing entropy), as in the conduction or radiation of heat or electricity. Each of these forms of development may be locally reversed in the development of a wider process. The increasing conformity of statistical processes often overrides the local development of form.

The other two types of development are more relevant to the general characteristics of man. Molecular development, though apparently unrelated to social history, is important because it illustrates certain general characteristics of the unitary process which are essential to the understanding of man. Organic development provides the main subject of this chapter, because it covers the special case of the social development of man, including the history of European and Western man.

Molecular and organic development present a fundamental contrast. Molecular development is the separation, persistence, and extension of symmetrical forms, such as molecules and crystals, which can change no further and are therefore relatively static and, within limits, stable. Organic development, in the individual organism, is a complex process which never reaches complete and static symmetry, but continues as the development of process forms. Within the system of the organism no complete separation of symmetrical form is possible, and the extension of existing structures by the orientation of new molecules always remains subject to the pattern of the whole organism. Inanimate molecular processes lead to static symmetrical patterns, but organic processes never get so far and continue to develop as the processes of the living body, until the life-sustaining conditions fail and the processes lose their organic character and culminate in the static symmetry of inanimate forms.

The source of this contrast lies in the different degree of complexity of the two types of process. Process is always the decrease of asymmetry. Where this comes about by the separating out of a simple static form, the process has the unmistakable character of the development of symmetry. In such molecular development process is in a limited sense teleological, for it leads to a relatively isolated, definite form. But where such separation cannot occur, the process of development consists in the mutual adjustments of the parts of a complex system, as, for example, an organism and its environment. Here no static equilibrium is reached but there is a developing process equilibrium within the system as a whole. The processes of the organism and of the environment are in equilibrium, and life is stable, within limits. But in this process of organic development there is no close approach to complete symmetry. Form is developed, in the symmetry not of static form but of process in equilibrium. Organic development is not teleological, but is a process of continuing adjustment.

In the simpler case of molecular systems, simple static forms separate themselves out, and in doing so tend to perfect their symmetry, to become stable, and to persist. The molecules of the growing crystal separate out from the solution and settle into their stable pattern on the crystal face. If conditions permit, the process is repeated and the form grows. In this case development consists in the separation, persistence, and extension of static forms. This process is seen not only in crystallization and the formation of inorganic molecules, but also in the reproduction of molecular units of organic origin (polymerization; protein synthesis; the multiplication of genes, and possibly of viruses and enzymes; and the growth of the cellulose walls of plants).

These examples of the tendency for asymmetrical forms to become more symmetrical illustrate the universal form of process. Asymmetry tends to decrease and may therefore be regarded as the source of process. *"C'est la dyssymetrie qui cree le phenomene"* (Curie). In simple situations process is persistence, and extension of form. But separation is never complete, form is never perfect, process is universal, and the development of any particular system may be reversed in the course of the development of a larger system.

Unitary thought uses the term *formative* to describe the character of a process of development, "developmental" being reserved for organic formative processes. Whatever displays development, whether in process, arrested, or completed is called a system. The process of the development of a system, which occurs if it is compatible with the processes of the larger systems of which the system is a part, is called its *tendency*. Every system displays a formative tendency, which is realized if it is consistent with the tendencies of all the larger systems of which it is a part. Unitary thought remains speculative until it can determine which tendencies are realized where the tendencies of two or more systems are incompatible.

The method rests on one idea, the conception of a universal process of development in which asymmetry decreases. We have now to see how the basic concepts of a general system of thought can be developed from this one fundamental conception by applying it to special situations.

When any simple molecular system (such as a crystal) separates out from its matrix and approaches complete symmetry, no further change occurs, and the system is stable. Such an internally developed, symmetrical system is called a *structure*. All crystals and stable molecules are structures. But such structures are still part of the system from which they separated out, and if conditions permit the asymmetry between the structure and its matrix will decrease through the further growth of the structure. Thus structures tend to develop externally, i.e., to extend their form, by a repetition of the process by which they were originally formed. A crystal tends to grow by a repetition of the process of crystallization by which it was formed; in doing so, the asymmetry of the larger system is lessened. A structure is thus a system which is internally developed, is stable, and tends to develop externally. But separation is never complete, structure is never static, and the concept of structure is valid only where the process of the whole can be neglected. There are no categories in unitary thought which can challenge the universality of process. There is no sharp division between structure and process, because structure is a limiting case of process.

We have now reached a conception which is of importance for the understanding of all organization, such as is played, for example, in the human body or in human society. Though this conception arises first in the simpler processes of inanimate systems, it finds its ultimate application in the processes of human thought. We have seen that the presence of a crystal nucleus in a solution promotes the process of crystallization, or, more generally, that the presence of a structure furthers the repetition of the process by which it was formed. This phenomenon may be regarded either as the external extension of an existing symmetrical form, or as an internal decrease of asymmetry in the wider system of the structure plus its environment. The external development of a smaller system is here identical with the internal development of a larger system. But the larger and smaller systems are not on a par. The crystal, or structure, is an already stabilized structure of a given pattern, and the presence of this established pattern is often decisive in determining the development of the larger system.

This situation is of great importance and is called *facilitation*. Facilitation is the tendency of structures to extend their form by repetition of the process by which they were formed. A structure is said to facilitate a process if the tendency of the structure to develop externally implies the recurrence of that process. Thus all structures facilitate the processes which develop them, though this tendency will not always be realized. Crystals facilitate their own growth; molecular units, such as genes, facilitate the process of their own multiplication; cellulose plant walls facilitate their own growth; organic tissues and organs (though they are not fully developed static structures) facilitate the repetition of processes which develop them. The records of memory and the verbal symbols of conceptual thought (though not isolable as separate structures) behave as structures in facilitating the repetition of the mental processes by which they were formed. Ideas facilitate the patterns of behavior to which they correspond. In general, the formative process tends to develop structures which facilitate further development. Process has a self-developing tendency; it facilitates its own development.

It is convenient sometimes to emphasize the fact that every structure provides evidence of the form of the process by which it was formed, by calling it a *record*. Every crystal constitutes a record of the fact that sometime in the past a formative process of a given type took place. But the term will be extended to include the organic tissues, organs, memory patterns, and words which, though they are not developed static structures, constitute records of the past processes by which they were formed, and facilitate their repetition. A record is thus a process or structure which preserves the form, and facilitates the repetition, of the process by which it was formed. Crystals, genes, organs, and words are all records which facilitate the recurrence of the past processes which they record.

The fact of facilitation underlies all order in nature and all organization in organic nature. If systems did not facilitate their own development there would be chaos. The concept of facilitation asserts that the universe is a cosmos in which there is the degree of ordered unity which is implied in the existence not only of discrete physical systems with definite characteristics, but of organisms and of thinking organisms. Without the fact of facilitation there would be no reason for anything to happen here rather than there. But as things are, if there is a crystal here, then at its surface there is a tendency for a particular process to occur, and, if conditions are favorable, the process of crystallization will continue, not in a haphazard manner, but just where the structure of the nucleus facilitates it. But the existence of this tendency does not imply the presence of some special cause such as a physical field of force, but merely that this is how things do in fact happen. "Physical causes" in general and "fields of force" in particular, are provisional methods of thought which lose any claim to independent reality once the way things happen can be described in a unitary manner.

Facilitation contains an important asymmetry. The record of the past tends to determine the present; the already formed crystal nucleus influences the present process of crystallization. This asymmetrical relation is called *dominance*. Dominance is the relation of a structure (or a record) to the process which it facilitates. It has no ethical or moral implications. A system of processes connected by relations of dominance is called a *hierarchy*. A complete hierarchy of processes is a hierarchy in which one process is dominant to all others, and this is the simplest form of organization. Biological and social organization is largely hierarchical. The recognition of a hierarchy does not imply a relative valuation of its elements.

In the concept of hierarchy we have reached the point where this outline of unitary thought passes from general situations to those found only in the organic world. The terms: development, formative, system, tendency, structure facilitation, record, and dominance, apply to process in all its forms. A hierarchy is a system of a kind hitherto identified only in organisms and groups of organisms. The following development of unitary thought is concerned mainly with organisms in their environments, the extension of unitary thought to cover the properties of inorganic systems being reserved for consideration elsewhere, as is also the process of the selective evolution of species.

The system *organism-environment* is marked by an oscillating equilibrium between two sets of processes: the processes of a hierarchical system (the organism) and those of the wider system (organism and environment) of which it is part. The result of this oscillating equilibrium is the development of an organic process form characteristic of the organism. The internal tendencies of every organism, if isolated, lead to its disintegration. But the processes of the wider system sustain and modify those internal tendencies, by "nourishing" them and gradually increasing the mutual conformity of organism and environment. This increasing mutual conformity of organism and environment is called "adaptation" to, or "mastery" of, the environment by the organism. "Life" is the formative tendency in the system organism-environment, which maintains the organism and heightens its conformity to the environment through the processes of nourishment and adaptation. But this life maintaining formative tendency is in conflict with the inner tendencies of the organism, which, if isolated, will in a few moments develop some parts of the organic system into the static patterns of the inanimate. To maintain life is to arrest the development of each component process in the organism by sustaining it with the complex hierarchy of the whole, which in turn is sustained by the processes of the environment. Isolation is death; life is the developing conformity of the whole.

Crystals and organisms have this in common: in both the universal formative tendency is unmistakable. But in crystals the tendency is fully realized in the formation of static symmetrical structures, while in organisms the tendency is sustained in a complex system of processes which never attain perfect symmetry, but continue to develop complex process forms. There are thus two ways in which form may persist: by relative isolation from the environment in the stabilization of static form, as in the crystal, and by the development of a characteristic process form in the balance between a complex system and its environment, as in organic processes. Static form persists in crystals, and inside organisms in genes; process form persists in individual organic species. The elasticity of the crystal, which tends to restore a distortion, and the self-regulating and regenerative processes of the organism, which tend to compensate any disturbance of the organic process equilibrium both express the restorative effect of the formative tendency.

The simplicity of the crystal form makes possible complete separation and the establishment of static structures, in certain circumstances; the complexity of the organic hierarchy implies that its characteristic form cannot be separated out in a static symmetry, the organism must remain set in its environment and can never, while still organic, display complete development of its own formative tendencies. This contrast between crystal growth and organic growth reveals an important difference: the crystal is a separate entity which, so long as it persists, can be considered in relative isolation; the term, crystal, begs no questions, so long as we remember its environment. But the organism is not, while it persists, separable from its environment; its life consists in that inseparability. The terms, organism, organic processes, tendencies, beg important questions, and beg them wrongly. Organic tendencies and processes are local and transient components of processes which, if isolated, lead back to inorganic, static forms. Life is not autonomous; it is maintained by the influence of the environment.

Anything which facilitates the development of characteristic organic form is called *proper* to the organism. Organic processes continually acquire forms which are not proper to the organism; organisms develop distortions, fall out of balance and die. In the case of man, it is evident that organisms may even follow an inner isolating tendency and destroy or damage their own lives, either by suicide or by accepting the dominance of some tendency, altruistic, creative maniac, which upsets their own organic balance. In all these cases where the proper developing balance of environment and organism is progressively damaged certain separate processes in the organism develop their own form in a manner prejudicial to the lie of the organism. If any separate process in the organism is developed too far, that is, in accordance with the universal form of process towards the static perfection of its own separate form, then it damages life. Such processes are never proper, but this recognition does not imply a moral valuation. Situations can occur in which the only possibility may be a process which is not proper. Death, suicide, madness, and forms of heroism and genius, are not proper; the revolt of the system from the limitations of life, the fulfillment of inner tendencies of the organism at the expense of the vital balance with the environment. The chief task of unitary thought in the organic world is the study of the failure of proper organic development and its interpretation as the consequence of some other overriding process of development. But this can be approached only when unitary thought has already identified some of the proper forms of organic development.

We have already defined structure as an internally developed, symmetrical, static form. *Organic structure* is partially developed structure, forming part of the hierarchy of an organism and facilitating a process called its function. *Organic function* is the process which an organic structure facilitates, and is often also the process by which the structure was developed. Function develops structure, and structure facilitates function, thus furthering its own development. But the use of these terms and the interpretation of the relation of structure to function, are limited by the fact that they are not sharp or static classifications, but unitary concepts representing local and temporary situations within the whole system of organism and environment. Organic structures are never perfectly symmetrical but are distorted to conform to the system of the organism, just as organic processes are timed to conform to the general process which develops the organic form within its environment.

The partial development of a local organic structure (or process) facilitating a process proper to the organism is called *differentiation*, and the arrangement of such structures (or processes) so that organic form is developed is called *integration*. These terms represent two aspects of the *organization* of organic systems; organization is integrated differentiation. The organization results from the existence in the organism of the ordered system of dominance relations which we have called the hierarchy of the organism.

The organization of every organism is thus largely, if not entirely, hierarchical in form. This hierarchical pattern is most clearly evident in the animal nervous system. The cell nucleus is probably dominant in relation to the processes of the cell, such as cell division, etc., but definitive knowledge may here be lacking. In the nervous system the brain is dominant in relation to the subordinate nerve ganglia, and these in turn are dominant in relation to the efferent, or outgoing, nerves. Each dominant center in the nervous system is a structure which at appropriate moments facilitates the processes of the parts of the system subordinate to it. Within the whole hierarchy there is at any one time a single dominant process (or system of processes), and this is called the *organizing process*. In man, the main controlling organ may be the thalamus which directs attention to the processes either of the cortex or of the hypothalamus. The organizing process is the process in the human system which at any moment actually molds the general pattern of behavior and thought. The term, organizing process, is elastic and may be used to refer to either potentially dominant processes (e.g., of conscious thought in a man walking) or the processes actually dominant in the sense of controlling behavior at a particular moment (e.g., the unconscious neuro-muscular responses).

When the form of any stimulus (either external or internal) is conveyed to and impressed on the dominant organizing processes of an organism, then the *attention* of the organism is said to be directed to that stimulus. Unitary thought uses the term "attention" where it is necessary to avoid the dualistic implications of "consciousness." Attention is not a unique condition or a form of reality, but a particular relation either between the organism and a part of its environment or between the organism and a process internal to itself. Attention is a relation which implies receptivity in the organism.

In the evolution of the higher mammals, one dominant structure has been of special importance, the brain or superficial cortex. The brain is important because it constitutes a record of the forms of past organizing processes which facilitates the formation of delayed responses to the environment. The other parts of the central nervous system may be adequate for the repetition of earlier responses, but the operation of the brain, and hence some delay, is necessary for the co-ordination of present stimulus and past experience into a new response. The development of the brain represents the differentiation of a new center of dominance, i.e., of a new controlling organ, not directly related to motor activity but capable of retaining a record of its own states of polarization (i.e., of the forms of past organizing processes) and of forming new responses to new stimuli. The special features of the human brain, which distinguish it from all other systems, are its highly differentiated unity, its great retentivity, and its extensive facilitation of the development of the forms characteristic of the species. These three features are commonly described as the unity of thought, the faculty of memory, and the formative tendency of thought.

We are now in a position to approach the main dualism of European and Western thought: the antithesis of matter and mind. In unitary thought these are regarded as names given to aspects of process and the relation of the two has to he found through a unitary interpretation, not of these abstracted nouns, but of the adjectives *material and mental.* These terms, as used in unitary thought, do not imply any general dualism, because they are defined in relation to one universal form of process. Unitary thought defines "material" as "related to the permanent aspects of process," and "mental" as "related to the facilitation (by brain) of the formative aspects of process." The essence of "material phenomena" is that they are concerned with conservation or permanence, and of "mental phenomena" that they are concerned with the formative process itself, in those situations where it is facilitated by a brain. Matter is static, self-identical permanence; mind is the formative tendency, highly facilitated by appropriate structures.

But the two terms, material and mental, are not on a par. "Material" refers, in effect, to all the unchanging aspects of process; "mental" does not refer to all the formative aspects, but only to the formative aspects of organic processes in the particular cases where a brain facilitates a delayed response. The instantaneous nervous reaction of a lower ganglion is not a true mental process; the essential marks of a mental process are that it requires time and involves memory. Mental responses are delayed, because the stimulus has to be digested in the brain, i.e., the form of the stimulus has to become part of the record of past organizing processes, and the brain system has to develop the form of the new response. Without this delay and without the operation of the records of the past, no organic process can appropriately be called mental. But mental processes, so defined, include all the processes of emotion, will, and intellect, as well as the unconscious processes which contribute to the general organization of behavior.

We now come to three terms which will be of special importance in our consideration of man, corresponding to animal instinct, animal intelligence, and human intellect. Processes (and behavior) are called *instinctive* when they are formed by organizing processes resulting from stabilized hereditary forms. In each generation certain hereditary structures and processes are matured as the individual develops, and these result in instinctive forms of behavior. In contrast to these forms, behavior will be called *intelligent (in* the sense of animal intelligence) when it involves the facilitation by a brain of non-stabilized, i.e., individually learnt, responses to particular situations. The mammals, for example, are capable of learning new methods as the result of the individual finding himself in a new situation. The human intellect is a further development of this faculty of learning, which finally led to the establishment of a social tradition using language. A *word* is a part of speech, either formal in character or associated with some situation or thing and acting as a symbol for it, and a *concept* is a generalized verbal symbol. *Intellectual* will he used to mean "involving verbal symbols" (either spoken, written, or operating without immediate motor activity).

An organizing process in conceptual form is called an *organizing principle*. When an organizing process in man acquires conceptual form, i.e., is represented in words, it becomes an organizing principle. An organizing principle, being in symbolic conceptual form, can operate either as a silent mental process or as the spoken or written word. The efficacy of organizing principles is determined by their general form, not by their literal content or symbolic meaning. The literal content of a principle may be invalid or meaningless, and yet the principle may be effective if its form corresponds to the form of the organizing processes appropriate in a given situation.

The only other unitary terms necessary for our *argument are time, space and quantity; and static and process* concepts. The time sequence is the continuity of asymmetrical relations (before and after, earlier and later, etc.) derived from process. The space frame is the field of symmetrical relations derived from persisting structures (relations of physical objects). Quantity is what is measured. Static concepts are timeless concepts, i.e., those not including the asymmetrical time sequence in their reference, and process concepts are time-like concepts, which, refer to the time sequence. The poverty of language in process concepts compels unitary thought to use "process" as both noun and adjective. Formation, growth, development, destruction, decay, are process concepts; god, idea, number, matter, energy, are static concepts lacking the asymmetry of the time sequence and implying permanence.

At the first hearing of a work by a new composer the strange idiom may disturb or stimulate our emotions, but neither the unity nor the detail can be clear at once. At most we have the vague sense of a new language seeking to communicate a fresh experience of truth. This brief outline of unitary thought is intended to promote this first stirring of a new order within the brain. If we change the metaphor to present another aspect, the "thirty years' war" of 1914-1945 was the insulin shock applied to the split mind of Western man, the fever is now subsiding, and here is one of the many forms of the regenerative process: the growth of a form of thought adapted to give man mastery of himself, by restoring the unity of thought and nature.

Mental processes are a part of nature, the part in which, above all, nature facilitates her own development. In the processes of thought certain components of the processes of nature work out their own development at lightning speed, far more swiftly than the corresponding, but more complex, processes in the rest of nature. In the symbolic processes of thought, that is, in the changing states of polarization in the brain, nature in man is at work facilitating the development of her own processes in man. But nature is no sovereign or arbitrary power, no goddess created by man to compensate his own ignorance. Nature, in unitary thought, is the comprehensive unity of process. To say that nature is at work in man means only that there is no division between subject and object or between thought and matter. As we have seen, process has a self-developing property; structures are formed which facilitate the further development of process. The human mind is the sensitive, elastic, and formative organ through which the organic processes in man record and facilitate their own development.

But while thought is a part of nature, a system of thought is also like a pattern though which nature is viewed. If the general scheme of the pattern is wrong, we see confusion in place of the general scheme of nature, even though the pattern may reveal some special regularities. But if the pattern is right the general scheme of nature is then unmistakable, though close attention may be necessary to discern the fine detail. Even if the pattern is right only in certain respects, it will to that extent bring out the true form of nature. The unitary method of thought has this natural magic it throws immediate light on certain aspects of the general arrangement of nature. It leads at once to simple universal principles, as relevant to man as to the rest of nature. Three of these refer to economy, waste, and novelty.

Nature is as sparing in the use of general forms as she is wasteful of individual forms: from one universal tendency she produces all the world's variety. From this profound economy arises the conservatism of nature. This is expressed in the conservation of matter and energy, which are thus licensed to masquerade as the basis of the general order; in the unchanging persistence of the tendencies and forms of systems, until circumstance intervenes. Economy, conservation, inertia, and conservatism mark the dominance of the one tendency.

But circumstance is arbitrary in the sense that it bears no necessary relation to the system whose fate it determines. Nature is a unity in its form of process, but it is not a coherent unity. The general order which exists does not ensure the permanence of harmony. Man, in his immaturity, demanded this comforting coherence and called it god. But there is no god. The individual is at the mercy of what he calls chance; a meaningless clash may frustrate the culmination of long-developed tendencies. The fate of every individual is unknown. Nature has no piety towards herself; in the relentless play of circumstance what has been perfect does not remain so. Perpetual wastage marks the dominance of circumstance.

Yet when neither tendency nor circumstance is dominant but the two are in balance, novelty is born from their interplay. Tendency is conservative of past forms, and circumstance may appear to be formless, but their balanced interplay is an inexhaustible source of novel forms. When circumstance modifies a system without destroying it, the result is a new system revealing the same universal tendency in a new pattern. Novelty always has this dual character: as a modification of the old it echoes the tested forms of the past, but as a response to a new situation it is alien to the past. The novelty inherent in the separation of unitary thought out of the earlier tradition is thus like a watershed linking and separating the climates of two worlds.

Unitary thought postulates a unity of the general form of process, but it emphasises the uncertainty of any particular development. It asserts: form develops, when circumstances permit. It is appropriate that a fundamental postulate should consist of two parts, the first claiming knowledge, the second admitting ignorance. When thought passes from universal to particular facts, knowledge becomes conditional. It has to distinguish this system here, whose tendency may be known, from the rest of nature, whose complexity is beyond knowledge. In doing so it creates the cardinal duality of thought which became a virulent dualism distorting knowledge and issuing finally in the destructive dissociation of Western man.

It is necessary to distinguish between the duality which is inherent in the arrangement of things, and the dualism of behavior and thought which so easily results from it. In unitary thought the term "duality" is used for all dual aspects of nature, and "dualism" for a duality whose two aspects are incompatible. Nature everywhere has the same general form, but dual aspects arise as soon as distinctions are made. The primary duality from which all others spring is the separation of this system here and the rest of nature, of this particular process and its whole environment. There is nothing incompatible about this duality, which is inherent in any world which can be conceived. But from it arise all the harsh intellectual dualisms which separate what is not separated in nature. The most important of these are the separation of absolute time and space, of the preservation of forms through time and the extension of forms in space, of organic process forms and static material forms, and of mental and material processes. None of these categories are absolute; each refers merely to an aspect of a unitary process.

One example is of special importance. The cardinal duality expresses itself in a dual development of the central nervous system which, in intellectual man, has broken out as damaging dualism. We have seen that the formative process has the property of forming structures which facilitate the development of the process. Such structures tend to fall into two classes, corresponding to the preservation of forms through time and the extension of forms in space. In the development of the central nervous system the organic structures in question are the retentive nerve masses of the brain and the conducting fibres of the sensorimotor system. The brain retains records of form, while the nerves transmit the forms of stimuli through space. This differentiation of contrasted structures, each facilitating one aspect of development, has far-going consequences. As the nervous system developed in the higher mammals, the nerves conducted more quickly and the brain became more retentive, the organism being thus better linked both to environment and to its own past. This specialization of function was controlled by the formative tendencies of the dominant organizing processes (in the brain and elsewhere) so that the two types of structure co-operated, the interaction of past records and present stimuli producing new responses.

But the divergent tendency of the specialized structures constituted an organic weakness, which sooner or later was bound to
make trouble, as it did finally in intellectual man. Each structure
tended to dominate the system. The higher brain, with its organized record of the past, tended to organize behavior by facilitating the deliberate repetition of processes which had successfully
organized behavior in the past. But the afferent nerves, perpetually
drawing the attention of the individual to present stimuli, tended to
produce swift responses and to challenge the control of the delib-
erating head. A proper differentiation of the nervous system thus
was converted into the conflict of cortex and hypothalamus, of
reason and instinct, of slow deliberate responses based on continuity with the rationally organized experience of the past and immediate instinctive responses to present situations. Yet in man instinct
plays a reduced role. If certain special conditions had not prejudiced integrity of the organizing processes, this duality in the nervous system might never have become the dualism which lies so
deep in the experience of European man. The chapters which follow tell the story of the appearance, persistence, and final disappearance of those conditions, and of the resulting emergence,
dominance, and disintegration of European and Western man.

3

The Characteristics of Man

The aim of unitary thought is not only to aid the discovery of new truth but also to reorganize existing knowledge so as to increase understanding. The unitary view of nature leads at once to a unitary conception of man. From the fact that man is an organic species unitary thought can draw conclusions which go beyond the uncertainties of contemporary thought. Moreover, the fact that man is distinguished from all other species in certain ways permits further conclusions which throw light on the place of man in nature.

The most general features of the unitary conception of man arise from the general nature of unitary thought. As a unitary system, the normal state of man is one of integration marked by the development of one characteristic form, and the breakdown of this integration is to be interpreted as the result of special circumstances. I shall therefore develop the unitary picture of man by considering first the most general characteristics of *homo sapiens,* as a species displaying normal organic integration. The purpose of this general description is to provide a frame within which the various special types of man may find their place. Here there is only occasion to consider one such type. I shall not refer to the different primitive civilizations, or the types that developed in Asia, Africa, and the Americas before Europe became the leader of all. The only type dealt with here is European and Western man. This is not an arbitrary choice; Europe and the West, in spite of all their failures, hold the clue to the further development of man. The structure which marks Western man, though developed furthest in Europe and America owing to special geographical conditions, is the expression of an organic and physiological tendency common to all types of man. More can be gained from a study of the strength and weakness of Western man than from any other sub-species of the race.

This chapter therefore deals with the characteristics of man in two parts: first, the normal or general integration, and second, the special tendency to disintegration or dissociation, which is furthest developed in Western man. A study of the basis and limits of harmony is followed by an analysis of the most common form of disharmony. Organic integration is the dominant fact, disintegration can only be temporary, if a species is to survive. Unitary thought uses the general postulate of integration to draw attention to the special factors which gave rise to the dissociation of European and Western man.

In regarding man as an organic species we imply that the human race is continuous with organic nature and that it is nevertheless distinguished from other organisms. The continuity means that there has been an unbroken chain of descent from earlier and simpler organisms. On the other hand the fact that man is a species distinct from other species means that fertilization with neighboring types of animals has ceased for some time and that the human group has established itself as a separate development entity with its own distinguishing characteristics.

This much is implied in the current conception of man as an organic species, but unitary thought can go further. The continuity of man with organic nature is not merely one of descent. Man shares the special form of the universal formative process, which is common to all organisms, and herein lies the root of his unity with the rest of organic nature. While life is maintained the component processes in man never attain the relative isolation and static perfection of inorganic processes; the human process consists in the continued development of process forms. The individual, may seek, or believe that he seeks, independence, permanence, or perfection, but that is only through his failure to recognize and accept his actual situation. As an organic system man can never achieve more than a continuing development in response to his environment. The factor which stabilizes and harmonizes all the component processes in the individual and in society is not permanence but development.

An organic system is like a fountain balanced upon a pyramid of fountains; if the process of development ceases at any point the stability of the whole is prejudiced. The ideal of perfection is an impostor; to claim it is to deny further growth. Man's yearning for the absolute expresses itself in the approach to perfection of his greatest achievements in thought and art, in which the formative tendency transcends the processes of organic adaptation. In old age the individual may seek to live in a world of eternal truth, but this withdrawn harmony is a transition back to the inanimate. Human personality cannot in general be integrated through the ideal of a static perfection, for organic systems are limited to the development of process forms. We have seen that these process forms are not restricted to the maintenance and development of life. They may result in a development that carries with it the denial or destruction of life. But they can never separate themselves from the environment and so achieve the appearance of a static perfection without forfeiting the organic balance which can be maintained only as the accompaniment of continued development.

These conclusions follow from the unitary conception of the organism. But the human species is distinguished by certain special capacities. We must now examine these and see what additional light is thrown on them by unitary thought.

Homo sapiens is a member of the higher primates in which certain special faculties, such as high manual dexterity combined with gregarious habits, have made possible the use of tools and a unique development of the art of communication by means of speech and script. The gradual separation of the symbolism of language from the organic situations which it represents, and the subsequent refinement of conceptual thought, have enabled the human individual to communicate not only with his contemporaries, but also with subsequent generations. Animals call to one another, and mammals communicate to their young a tradition of forms of behavior which are not instinctive and have to be learnt. From such origins in the intelligence and mimicry of mammals man has developed the technique of speech and the silent symbolisms of script and of thought, which in turn have made possible the progressive accumulation of a conceptually organized social tradition and the ability to reason and to predict. Man dominates nature because he has developed a brain which can not only preserve and organize his experience but also communicate it to his kin.

These faculties arise from a special development of the central nervous system in man. We have referred to the fact that the mammalian nervous system developed in two directions, the nerves and the brain being adapted respectively to the transmission and the recording of forms, though this dual specialization remained subject to dominant processes which co-ordinated behavior as a whole. This specialization is already marked in the other mammals, but in man it is carried further by the greatly increased retentive power of the brain which allows the dominant organizing process more time in which to develop new fusions of past and present experience. The retentivity and the plasticity of the human brain respectively enable it to record stimuli and to mold from them new patterns of response to an extent far surpassing the elementary adaptations of animal intelligence. Moreover, the high sensitiveness of the human system, the slow maturing of the young, and the gregarious habits of the species gave the art of communication a unique status in man.

The key to this development of human faculties lay in the perfecting and stabilizing of the forms of speech and thought by a process of separation and clarification, followed by the spreading of the stabilized forms. Primitive cries were gradually separated from their context and became symbols for particular situations. The spoken word was eventually recorded in script and so developed into a concept whose form guided the unspoken processes of thought. The formative processes in the brain are often slow compared with the transmissive processes of the nerves, and the cerebral cortex developed as a new organ through which the residues left over from immediate responses could be gradually absorbed into the organized record of the brain and so finally lead to a more complete delayed response. The extension of this slow process, in which the forms of experience are assimilated, is a novel development in man. Nerve signals are transmitted in a fraction of a second; mammalian intelligence operates in seconds at most; but in the human system hours or even years may pass before the fusion of some unusual stimulus with the conceptually organized record of the past is completed and prepared for expression in action. The extension of the time component of human mental processes is of great importance. In his immediate reactions to physical stimuli and quick instinctive responses one man may be much like another, and even behave like his close neighbors in the animal world. It is only in the long-delayed deliberate responses that there is scope for the immense elaboration and variety of individual behavior characteristic of man.

The original appearance of man was made possible by gradual evolutionary changes in the hereditary constitution. But the relatively rapid development of man during, say, the last ten thousand years has been due to a cumulative modification of the social environment of each maturing generation rather than to evolutionary changes in the hereditary constitution. Every feature in an adult is the product of a particular heredity matured in a particular environment, and neither heredity nor environment can be treated as the sole cause of a given adult feature. But differences in adult types may be ascribed to differences in heredity, or in environment, or in both. The rapid development of adult man in recent millennia has been due mainly to the influence of a progressively changing social environment on the young of each successive generation, rather than to changes in heredity.

Ten thousand years represent only some four hundred generations, a small fraction of the evolutionary history of most species measured in generations, and the greater part of human history lies within the last half of this period. It is improbable that selective evolution, even under the special conditions of civilized life, has greatly modified the average hereditary constitution in so short a time This means that the environment of the embryo has almost certainly also changed little, the physiology of the womb having remained practically constant during these five thousand years. The climatic or other changes which have occurred in the postnatal physical environment cannot be regarded as responsible for the rapid progressive changes in the speech and thought of adult man. We are therefore left with the changes in the human environment of the developing child as the progressive factor responsible for the intellectual development of man.

There is little doubt that the source of human development in this period has been the steady accumulation of a social tradition of modes of behavior, and of speech, script, and thought. New forms of behavior and new methods of organizing behavior are perpetually arising in individuals; some of them become stabilized and enrich the social tradition. The community thus brings to each successive generation a progressive inheritance expressed in habit, speech, and script. These three elements make up a developing environment which brings out further capacities in successive generations from a relatively constant heredity. Though there have been local reversals and periods of regression, the potentialities of each successive generation have in general been matured by a further-developed social environment; the novelties produced by each generation thus tend to surpass those of the last and the tradition is further enriched. This steady accumulation of new patterns of behavior and thought may at any time be interrupted, but man is what he is today because this process has been maintained through at least the last five thousand years. The cycles of past civilizations have been set within this general trend which has made man supreme and will maintain his supremacy as long as it continues.

There are two aspects, the formative and the conservative, to this process of the self-development of man, and these correspond broadly to the roles of the individual and of the community. The first step in the development of new forms occurs in the individual, for though the inner tendency of the individual man is conservative, novelty arises from his response to fresh circumstances, new forms of thought and behavior being developed to their final expression in single brains. The individual is formative, but his life is short. On the other hand the community tradition is conservative and retains for long periods the records of all that it has absorbed from individuals. Social development thus depends on the interplay of the two. The individual forms the new and enriches the tradition; the tradition molds and matures the individual and enables him to carry the process further. The failure of the individual to maintain and further the tradition, or of the tradition of any community to organize the life of its members, represents an aberration from the proper relation which ultimately spells the collapse of the community.

This social development of man is supported by a special characteristic in which he surpasses all other species, the extreme variability of the individual members of the species. This characteristic lies so deep in the development of man that it cannot be treated as either cause or effect. It is evidenced in the wide range of intermarriage between the different geographical branches of the species; in the considerable lack of uniformity in man's hereditary constitution; in the varying influences of a rapidly changing and cumulative social tradition; in his glandular, neural, and mental plasticity; and finally, in his love of travel. The great diversity of heredity and environment which man enjoys is the source of his rapid development.

Such is the orthodox conception of the human species. Unitary thought accepts this conception and strengthens it by giving precision to the vague idea of development. The long-term evolution of the species by selective modification of the hereditary constitution is separated from the more rapid process of the development of the potentialities of human heredity by a developing social tradition. The former process is set on one side for later consideration, while the latter is treated as an example of the universal formative process. Moreover we saw that all formative processes are self-developing in the sense that within an appropriate environment they tend to form structures which facilitate the further development of the process. This property of self-development (in a suitable environment) finds its fullest expression in man. By recognizing this supreme human characteristic as the furthest development of a property potentially present in all processes, unitary thought establishes man in his correct place in the system of nature. In man the formative property of all process finds its fullest development; therein lies the secret of his dominance.

The dominance of man over the rest of nature is a direct expression of the characteristics of the process of development, as it has been here defined. The human system contains a special organ, the brain, which facilitates the development of organic process forms to a greater degree than any other organ or structure in the whole of organic nature. In the case of man the organic process forms in question are all the forms of human life, the entire system of behavior and communication which make up the social tradition. The human brain facilitates the development of the forms of human life, firstly, by separating them out and clarifying them in the symbolic forms of thought (which, however, being organic can never be wholly isolated from their matrix); secondly, by preserving them more efficiently through an improved faculty of memory; and thirdly, by extending them further, both in more comprehensive delayed responses to the environment and through their symbolic communication to others. Facilitation consists in the furthering of the development and extension of forms, and the facilitation of the proper forms of human life implies the heightening of the dominance of man over his environment. Man dominates nature because his brain is the most powerful facilitating structure yet developed.

Unitary thought thus leads to conclusions concerning man, which follow from its postulate regarding nature as a whole. If the method is now appropriate, then certain truths can be recognized, and mankind cannot any more neglect them without thwarting its own development than it can prematurely go beyond them without loss of continuity with its past. The importance of these conclusions justifies their repetition here.

Man is one with nature as an expression of the universal formative process, and one with organic nature as an expression of a formative process continually developing its own process forms but never attaining static perfection. Man is supreme in nature because his organic structure permits the highest facilitation of the development of form, and therefore gives him the greatest dominance over the environment. Man is unitary as the expression of a form of process which is not subject to any fundamental division which must disrupt organic integration. Man is transient; for the individual nothing is certain but his ultimate death. Man exists and develops as part of a wider system; when the environment is no longer appropriate, the internal processes of his system follow out their own courses and lead back to the static structures of the inanimate world. Man is inseparable from nature, and can only be understood as part of the whole system of nature. Both the behavior of the individual and the trend of history have to be interpreted, not as the consequence of special agencies, but as particular examples of the universal formative process.

Hitherto we have been concerned with the unitary conception of man in general. But this picture must be supplemented by a description of European man, who reveals in a marked form a general tendency latent in all groups of the species. This is the tendency to lose proper organic integration, and its presence in the organism man in a paradox calling for explanation.

In the next chapter I shall deal with the historical process by which this came about. Here we must consider how such loss of

integration is possible. Unitary thought starts with the positive af-
firmation that every system tends to develop its characteristic form.
Within that single form there may be dual aspects, and so long as
these do not disturb the single form they will be called a duality.
But if the characteristic form fails to develop, the duality has become a dualism. In every dualism unitary thought looks for the
original duality. The problem is simple: if there is continuity in
nature, the dualism in contemporary civilized man must be the result of some duality which can be traced back to its ultimate source.

In the previous chapter we saw that the tendency of systems to
preserve their form through time and to extend it through space is
reflected in the dual development of the nervous system to preserve records of form and transmit signals of form. The recording
faculties of the brain tend to emphasise the records of the past,
while the transmissive processes of the nerves link the organism
with the challenges of its present environment. There thus develops a tendency for systems of deliberate behavior, which make
greater use of the organized records of the past, to separate themselves from the immediate responses in which the higher faculties
of the brain are not involved. This dual specialization is useful and
does not damage the integrity of the organism, so long as the operation of these two partial functions is kept in balance by the regulative processes. So long as the self-regulation of the organism
allows the influence of past records and of present stimuli to operate only at the appropriate moments, the organic balance is maintained and the dual specialization assists the development of
characteristic form.

In the early stages of the development of this dual specialization
the contrast between the two modes was not excessive and the
balance was adequately maintained. But the two aspects of the func-
tioning of the nervous system express tendencies which, though
not incompatible, tend to diverge when circumstances lessen the
efficacy of the process which should co-ordinate them. The first
period of the development of the human intellect was marked by
such an adverse circumstance. While the nerves kept man in contact with the changing processes around him, the organized record
in the brain retained clearest impressions of static or recurrent situations, or of the static aspects of changing situations. Though nature is organized as a system of formative processes, systematic

thought had first to be organized as a system of static concepts. Gradually the contrast of the two functions produced an organic lesion; deliberate behavior was organized by the use of static concepts, while spontaneous behavior continued to express a formative process; that special part of nature which we call thought thus became alien in form to the rest of nature; there grew up a disjunction between the organization of thought and the organization of nature. Nature displays everywhere the symmetry of a process in which earlier and later states show characteristic differences, but the earliest systematically organized sets of verbal symbols lacked this asymmetry and referred to static properties which remain unchanged or recur in an unchanged form, as though isolated from the process around them.

This is the curse laid on *homo sapiens:* as intellectual man he could not escape this dualism until it had exhausted itself. The history of Western man is the working out of this fate. The curse has fallen most heavily on the male, for the special functions of woman link her thought more closely to those organic processes which maintain the animal harmony. Woman tends to think in terms of the individual process, man at first in terms of static abstractions. Intellectual man had no choice but to follow the path which facilitated the development of his faculty of thought, and thought could clarify itself only by separating out static concepts which, in becoming static, ceased to conform either to their organic matrix or to the forms of nature. This tendency to develop sharp static concepts was necessary for the recording and organizing intellect at the stage, and yet the separation of static forms corresponds to the development of non-organic forms and is essentially alien to organic development. In life development is primary and permanence secondary, but in the history of thought permanence has to be understood before development. From this paradox arises the metaphysical confusion and the spiritual tragedy of intellectual man. Like a new limb which has to grow through an initial phase of fundamental maladjustment, thought had to develop first along a path in conformity with inorganic rather than with organic processes, a path which it must retrace if organic harmony is to he restored.

In the evolution of thought the conception of persisting things took root long before the conception of a process of development could acquire any clear meaning. As language developed and primitive cries and chants gradually shaped themselves into the grammar of words, the noun, first as the symbol of a situation and later as the name of a persisting thing or class of things, became the sovereign part of speech. Moreover we shall see that as man's attention was increasingly drawn to the processes occurring in his own person, he began in his thought to separate himself, the persisting subject, from the changing world around. These two developments are aspects of a single situation. The separation of the noun from the matrix of sounds which preceded grammatical speech, and of the subject from the changing pattern of relations which make up its life, marked a decisive step along the path which led to dominance over nature at the cost of an inner maladaptation. The separation of the static concept and of the persisting subject facilitated the development of man and therefore was itself facilitated and developed further until that inner lesion could be tolerated no longer.

Unitary thought regards this condition as a dislocation of the dominant organizing processes in the human system, necessarily affecting in some degree all the internal processes and the external behavior of the individual. But until the unitary language is more mature this dislocation can best be discussed in terms of the separate aspects through which it is revealed: thought, emotion, and behavior. Of these three it is in thought that the disintegration is most evident.

The noun is not necessarily static. The terms: process, development, decay, birth, and death, represent forms of change which contain the asymmetry of earlier and later states, and do not, like static concepts, refer to the persistence of an unchanging property. Yet at the beginnings of systematic thought a vague idea could be developed into a precise concept only if a noun could be formed which did not involve this asymmetry. Time-like conceptions remained vague and general, while static or space-like nouns became reliable tools for systematic thought. But the latter could not represent the organization of nature as a system of processes.

Thus when primitive man began to develop rational systematic thought, static nouns formed the primary tools of thought, while the characteristics of process were represented only by vague implications. But any particular group of static nouns could represent only the apparently permanent aspects of a particular process and had to be supplemented by a complementary group referring to the process aspects. For example, at one stage of thought, the group of inert material things had to be supplemented by a group of conscious spirits capable of purposive action. Similarly during the development of scientific thought the permanent spatial frame had to be supplemented by pure duration.

These considerations are essential to the understanding of any type of highly developed civilized man, and in particular of European man. Intellectual dualisms constitute a biological maladaptation, and their roots lie in an organic situation beneath the level of systematic thought and influence every aspect of behavior. This separation of static and process concepts is the source of all intellectual dualisms. On the one hand there are the static concepts, developed first and capable of systematic and precise formulation, on the other hand the process concepts, remaining relatively vague and formless, but accepted as referring to the asymmetry of the time sequence and therefore expressing a fact central to all human experience though relatively neglected by systematic thought.

The object set in *space* and formed of *matter* follows *the necessity of quantitative law.* Here is the world of permanence, precision, and clarity. With these instruments man emancipates himself from his treacherous subjectivity. He hypostatizes, or establishes as real entities, the permanent features which he has abstracted from process, dividing nature in order to master it.

But man cannot think by these alone. The *subject experiences memory in time* and the *freedom* of his *will.* In these conceptions man struggles to express the central fact neglected in the static picture. He fails because a dualistic language cannot express the true form of his unity with the processes of nature.

The first set of concepts is symbolized in the concept of *quantity.* This represents the extreme of conceptual precision, the complete separation of symmetry and permanence from the general process, or the isolation of a closed cycle. The complementary set is epitomized in the concept of *conscious purpose,* in which man's thought — still betraying its secret desire for permanence — seeks to cast a net of preconceived aims and permanent ideals over the elusive process of development. Thus the immature mind, unable to escape its own prejudice in favor of permanence even in approaching the neglected process aspect of experience, fails to recognize the actual form of the process of development and is condemned to struggle in the strait jacket of its dualisms: subject/object, time/space, spirit/matter, freedom/necessity, free will/law. The truth, which must be single, is ridden with contradiction. Man cannot think where he is, for he has created two worlds from one.

Static concepts describe forms which can be exactly defined because they are either unchanging or periodic, while the complementary set attempts to represent aspects of process, but fails to identify their specific form. Each set is degenerate, in the sense that it represents only one aspect of the phenomenon; precise form without the asymmetry of process, or the asymmetry of process without specific form. This division of the proper unity of thought into two incompatible tendencies, neither of which is adequate, runs through European history from the beginnings of systematic thought to the present frustration of the proper development of man. The paradox of a mechanical civilization lacking a co-ordinating tendency, with the sense of a great potential development ahead but without any clear conception of its form, reflects this basic dichotomy of thought.

We must now turn to consider how the inner dislocation which is expressed in this intellectual dualism reveals itself in behavior. If a stimulus calls out from an animal a particular instinctive pattern of behavior, such as that of sex, hunger, or attack, this pattern tends to inhibit attention to other stimuli, so that one instinct dominates at a time and co-ordination is maintained. This general co-ordination is evidenced in the higher animals by intelligent adaptations to novel situations, and by forms of behavior which are learnt by mimicry and form part of an animal tradition handed down from parent to offspring. Such behavior is co-ordinated by the dominance of general tendencies which, by facilitation and inhibition, control all the local processes and functions of the organism.

But in thinking man, as we have already seen, the specialization of the recording brain and the development of long-delayed deliberate responses present a definite challenge to the demands of neutrally transmitted stimuli on the attention of the organism. Two general types of behavior gradually separate out. On the one hand the retention of records in the cerebral cortex permits the slow digestion of experience; the establishment of systems of long-delayed responses; the development of verbal symbols, of deliberate behavior, and of the intellectual life. On the other hand the nervous transmission of stimuli maintains a perpetual call to action, stimulates immediate responses and the patterns of instinctive and spontaneous behavior. The more plastic human behavior becomes and the less absolute the dominance of specialized instincts, the greater the likelihood of clash between the two tendencies leading respectively to deliberate action and to immediate response. Moreover as the intellect extends its scope it tends to dominate the entire system and to force to one side, and in doing so to distort, the forms of spontaneous behavior. Because the immature intellect has a static prejudice and is therefore partially divorced from the processes of the organism it cannot itself provide a general co-ordination capable of uniting deliberate and spontaneous behavior. Conscious and unconscious, reason and instinct, are divorced, with consequent mutual distortion.

It is important to see this process in its true biological proportions. It had little or nothing to do with changes in the hereditary constitution. The process expressed a dual tendency latent in the physiological organization of every individual, a tendency which was likely ultimately to endanger the integrity of the organism, though it was temporarily favorable to physical survival. But it was the influence of an immature and dualistic tradition which developed this divergent tendency into the dislocation which ultimately became the dominant characteristic of European civilization. The conflict between spontaneous and deliberate behavior would never have represented more than a normal difficulty of choice had the influence of the social tradition been favorable to the maintenance of the overriding co-ordination.

But the trouble had penetrated the social tradition in the form of the, fundamental dualism of thought which we have just analyzed, and each maturing generation, instead of being helped by the social tradition to maintain its integrity, had impressed on it the doctrine of an absolute division running through nature and human nature. The accumulated results of this dual tendency of thought had hardened into a metaphysical dualism which reinforced the tendency for conflict to develop between deliberate and spontaneous behavior. In the more superficial aspects of religion and morals the dualistic influence of the social tradition has been obvious in Europe and the West. But more important is the pervasive influence of this double fact: in every young person there are latent the dual tendencies of the deliberate and the spontaneous life, and in a civilization using static concepts this duality, harmless in itself, tends to be aggravated by the corresponding dualism in the tradition into a conflict of incompatibles. This division runs far beyond the field of conscious ethics, since it affects the entire organization of behavior in a civilized society suffering from this condition. In order to emphasise both the organic root of this disharmony and the fact that it is not characteristic of all types of men, or even of all civilizations, I shall call this condition the *European dissociation.*

The term dissociation is here used for a condition in which the organizing processes in an individual fail to develop one characteristic form, and two or more mutually incompatible systems of behavior compete for control. The criterion which distinguishes dissociated from integrated behavior is that the former tends to stabilize two or more incompatible and distorted forms of behavior, while the latter tends to develop a unitary form. A developed dissociation implies disorganization of behavior, emotional conflict, and intellectual dualism. If a dissociation becomes part of the social tradition of a civilization it tends to impress itself on all individuals and thus becomes a characteristic mark of a given type of adult man. In less robust individuals it reveals the main features of a civilization in psychopathic forms such as obsessions and compulsion neuroses. In healthy individuals who are little affected by the tradition it may he scarcely noticeable. But none wholly escape its influence.

It is not possible to consider here the degree to which other civilizations have maintained a proper organic harmony, or the form of their dissociation; we are concerned only with the European dissociation. This is a particular form of disintegration of the organizing processes in the individual which, though arising from a tendency latent in a physiological characteristic common to all races, attained its most marked form in the European and Western peoples during the period from around 500 BC until the present time. During these two and a half millennia this dissociation became a permanent element in the European tradition and the distinguishing mark of European and Western man. Its origin lay deep in the nature of the art of communication through which alone the human stock has realized something of its potentialities. The demands of communication led man first to emphasise permanent elements, but man, like nature, is a system of processes. The inescapable contrast prejudiced organic harmony. The whole-natured behavior of primitive and ancient man broke up into two ultimately incompatible systems, neither of which could employ the entire human being: the system of spontaneous behavior, of immediate responses to present situations, relatively unaffected by the rational organization of past experience; and the system of deliberate behavior, of delayed responses based on the systematized experience of the past to the relative neglect of present stimuli. Both modes are distortions of properly integrated behavior; the one integrates present stimuli but neglects the past, while the other integrates past records but is relatively blind to the present. They respectively express the physiological dominance of the instinctive centers connected with the hypothalamus and of the organizing records of the cerebral cortex. In the European dissociation reason and instinct are at war.

The existence of this conflict, not the dominance of either tendency, is the mark of the European dissociation. From a limited point of view the Western tradition expresses the claim of reason to supremacy over man's instinctive tendencies. But the claim was only partially realized, and the determining factor in the tradition, beneath its apparent content, is the form of the conscious conflict, and beneath the conscious conflict, the form of the underlying dualism in the organizing processes. Different communities worked this out in different manners: by the temporary dominance of religious, moral, or ethical disciplines over the instinctive tendencies, interrupted often by reversals into the opposite state; by a relatively balanced dualistic mode distorted by the repressed conflict; or by a continual oscillation from religious, rational, or merely industrious asceticism to the extreme of an equally distorted sensuality. These different modes are all evidence of the same underlying dissociation.

It is not possible here to contrast Western man and other types, though this description would acquire more significance as part of a comparative anthropology. The characteristics just described may not be evident in the lives of the majority of Westerners unless a standard has been set by the examination of the startlingly different characteristics displayed by other societies. The concept "human nature" is a trap set by the unconscious in its attempt to resist change, and only a study of the contrasted patterns of culture of different past and present communities can reveal the varied potentialities of the human stock. Against such a background European and Western man stands out as a highly developed but bizarre distortion of the human animal. But it is not necessary even to go beyond Europe to learn what Europe is. Genius is a blend of poverty and riches; lacking the satisfying adaptation of the common man, genius explores to the limit some aspect of the tradition in order to compensate his need. Often genius is the tradition-obsessed man, and his emotions, his thought, and his behavior sometimes present — in Europe at least — an exaggeration of the general dissociation to the point of parody. European genius, religious, intellectual, artistic, or practical, provides ample evidence of the dissociation. The exceptions are not representative Europeans; they stand for some more permanent or universal kind of man.

But the dissociation is held in check by the far-reaching regenerative capacity of the human system. The regulative processes in every organism tend to restore damaged organic forms, and the capacity for healing extends also to distortions of the specifically human faculties. The tendency to dissociation is resisted by a tendency for the organizing processes to recover proper control; circumstances determine which tendency dominates. But the damage done to an individual by a distorted tradition can only be repaired by the influence of others; the individual cannot cure himself of a distortion which is of social origin. Mutual aid is indispensable and one kind of person may complement or repair the deficiencies of another kind.

It is here that the relations of the sexes played a special role in European and Western society. We are concerned now, as throughout this study, with European and Western man as influenced by the tradition, and the following remarks refer to the dominant types which gave Europe its stamp. The European dissociation is primarily a male distortion, and man has the opportunity of recovery, or at least of compensation, through woman. This regenerative opportunity lies deeper than the innocent sentimentalism of early romantic love, and even than the deeper awareness of later attachments. It operates on every level of the human being from the glandular stimulation of the thalamus to the formative power of the comprehensive Eros and the interplay of family life. Under the influence of Eros man becomes malleable and offers the regenerative processes their supreme opportunity. But these processes failed to save the tradition and in late European man we find the dissociation breaking out in a sick romanticism which can no longer hide the cruelty of the spirit towards the flesh.

The characteristic variability of the human species refutes every sharp classification, yet in organically normal individuals there is a tendency for the two sexes to diverge into complementary types. Man is primarily concerned with specialization to master circumstance, woman with the inner continuity of process. Her organic course is marked by a finite rhythm of a few hundred opportunities. If she misses them all, some organs will never mature, and she must turn her energies elsewhere. She therefore knows the value of time, and can only at her peril neglect the present stimulus for the long deliberation. Her thought is therefore normally in concrete process forms, her experience of antagonistic tendencies in her own nature less than that of man, her system closer to the permanent organic rhythms.

This brief outline of the unitary conception of man will be developed further as regards Western man and unitary man in the chapters that follow. But one difference between the traditional and the unitary view has still to be made clear. The traditional view of man ascribed human behavior to various causes, material or mental, conscious or unconscious, self-seeking or altruistic. But in the unitary view the processes of the human system are all of one general form and cannot be isolated and ascribed to such separate causes. These processes, including the general behavior of the individual, develop as one system and cannot be split into parts attributable to the agency of separate causes. Understanding of the human system is not to be reached by the search for causes, but by tracing the complex hierarchy of formative processes of which it is constituted. These processes require no cause. It may be convenient sometimes to suggest that the universal formative process expresses itself in a particular type of behavior, but this only implies that such behavior displays the characteristic of a formative process. Since development is the general form of process, development can have no cause. That is just how nature and man are. It therefore becomes of importance to understand the relation of the various traditional causes of human action to the unitary process which is to be substituted for them.

The new attitude implies a far-reaching change in the interpretation of man. European languages in general begin with a subject-noun whose action is expressed in an active verb. Some apparently permanent element is separated from the general process, treated as an entity, and endowed with active responsibility for a given occurrence. This procedure is so paradoxical that only long acquaintance with it conceals its absurdity. For example, "consciousness" is separated from natural processes, it would seem for the very object of serving as an agent to influence them. Similarly the concept of matter or substance is abstracted from process, and "material agencies" are then made responsible for the processes of nature and of history, though by its definition matter lacks any formative property. These difficulties arise because since the beginning of systematic thought it has been customary to think, and to build sentences, in terms of permanent entities which are imagined as engaged in some action, often directed towards some other entity.

But such isolation of entities cannot aid in the interpretation of any process which, like development, displays an asymmetry in time; what is static cannot account for process. Since nature, and human nature, are systems of processes, all that we can do, and all that we need to do, is to trace their form. We shall find special correlations, for example in the development of an incompatible dualism from some earlier duality, and the earlier form may be treated as the cause of the later form. But if process is of one general form, it is meaningless to assert that human behavior has any special cause, such as either consciousness or material agencies. Distortions of form may be traced back to earlier distortions, which may be regarded as causing them, but the general form of process has no cause. It is the morphology, or sequence of developing forms, of social history and of individual behavior which must be identified if human behavior is to be understood.

As we have seen, unitary thought rejects the dualistic implications of the conception of consciousness, and suggests that the valuable element in it is the reference to a relation of attention between the organism and a particular external or internal stimulus. Though a given stimulus may leave a permanent impress on the processes of the human system attention to it is always transient. Nothing ever remains continuously "in consciousness." It is therefore wrong to isolate those transient moments of attention to particular forms, to endow them with a special metaphysical status as a "state of consciousness," and then to ascribe to consciousness the supreme directing role in behavior. The dominant organizing processes control the general form of behavior (that is what is meant by "dominant"), and attention is an essential prior condition to adaptation to any novel stimulus. But these isolated moments of attention are merely points at which the processes at lower levels momentarily influence the dominant processes of the hierarchy. Attention is only a transitory focusing of the extended system of processes which guide behavior. It is an inherent weakness of subjective thought that it must misconceive and exaggerate the role of attention. When man became self-conscious he was bound at first to make this mistake, and therefore also, two thousand years later when he became aware of the historical process, to ascribe to consciousness an excessive role in the processes of history.

A complementary error which arose from the same dualistic prejudice was the materialistic interpretation of individual behavior and of social history. Strictly there can be no materialistic interpretation of history since matter, or substance, is a name for what is permanent, or static, or conserved, and history is an asymmetrical process in which later and earlier states differ intrinsically. Permanence cannot account for novelty or development; material science can embrace only what is static or cyclic, and history must remain beyond its scope. For example, the attempt to transpose the Hegelian dialectic of the mind, that is, the formative processes of the mind, into a dialectical materialism is not merely logically absurd but philosophically disastrous. Such "materialism" has little or nothing to do with the concept of matter, or with the processes already understood by physical science. To assert dialectic of matter is to land thought in complete confusion. The attempt to do so was for that none the less grandly prophetic, because the forward impetus of its process thought repeatedly led it to repudiate its own materialism and so to anticipate a radical unitary interpretation of process.

The clue to the bizarre situation of dialectical materialism as a philosophy is that there is no parallel between the material and mental components of process; by their common usage these terms refer to aspects of process which have different and indeed anti-thetical forms. There can be no psychophysical parallelism, if the psyche is the formative aspect and matter the permanent aspect of process. In seeking to transpose the Hegelian dialectic from mental to material processes the Marxist doctrine assumes a parallelism which cannot exist. There can be no consistent interpretation of the historical process which is not based on a unitary concept of process.

Similar difficulties are met in the dualistic approach to the human individual. For example, the division of the human system into physiological and psychological processes frustrates the advance of a comprehensive science of man. What are called psychological processes are the mental components of the whole system of processes, the components in which the brain organizes past and present experience into new responses. The mental components are essentially formative, they extend old forms into new situations and so develop novelty. On the other hand the subject matter of quantitative physiology is the material aspect of process, i.e., the conservation of energy, materials, and local structures. For certain purposes one of these methods of approach may be applied independently with considerable success. Some forms of illness are clearly psycho-genic or mental in origin, while others are as clearly somato-genic, or physiological in origin. But even illnesses of these extreme types rapidly create a general state of disequilibrium which cannot be described by either method alone. Emotional shock disturbs the glandular balance, and a sharp localized pain may depress the emotional tone. Moreover most types of illness cannot be ascribed to a cause of either type alone, but are due to a lowered general metabolism bringing into evidence the Achilles' heel of the system in the form of a local symptom. Thus local rheumatism may be psycho-genic. Fear or frustration lowers the general vitality and a special symptom appears. Similarly a local disturbance may be the cause of a general depression.

In the absence of a single language it is not surprising that physiology cannot even describe the facts that appear to lie in its own field such as the glandular balance, or psychology successfully analyze mental processes such as the relationship of instinctive and deliberate behavior. Neither of these part-sciences can cover even its own aspect of the human system, restricted as each is by a language that deals only with limiting cases. Every distortion of the organic balance is a disturbance both of the general organizing processes and of local organic structure. The proper form of the organizing processes implies proper local structures and vice versa, but it is only in unitary thought, which makes this fact axiomatic, that the dualism disappears. Attention, on the one side, and physiological quantities, on the other, refer to special aspects only of the organic system of formative processes. The system is single and requires a single language.

A similar confusion arises in the attempt to define the roles of intellect and emotion in determining behavior. So long as these two are regarded as independent entities operating as active agents in forming behavior, no clarification is possible. The intellectual processes arise by the specialization of symbols first of speech, then of script, and finally of silent conceptual thought. This process was guided by the progressive sensorimotor refinements involved in the use of tools, writing, and other human arts. The intellect is therefore mainly related to special local stimuli and specialized responses. The emotions on the other hand are related to the sustained co-ordination of behavior, and express states of polarization of the system as a whole, which maintain the integration of activity along one general course by facilitating some modes of behavior and inhibiting others.

Intellect and emotion are related respectively to specialization and co-ordination. But this does not imply that they are separable. Co-ordination means the organization of specialized processes, and the development of such specialized processes is possible only within a co-ordinated system. Every concept has some emotional tone, but to assert the fact is equivalent to an admission that the terms "concept" and emotion" are misleading unless they can be reinterpreted as aspects of a single process.

Yet the development of the intellect has so far depended on a gradual process of separation of language from emotion. Baby language, battle songs, and sacred names are symbols for communicating patterns of behavior in which this separation has scarcely begun. As it continues the intellectual processes become more specialized and abstract until the intellect seems to rid itself of all emotional emphasis. In special situations where the formative aspect of the mental processes nearly disappears, they assume the disguise of an abstract reason whose operation consists in the logical manipulation of tautologies, an exercise like the play of children. At the contrary pole in other special situations all sense discrimination and memory recording may cease for a moment, and the mental processes lose all specific form and dissolve into a formless passion like the fury of a beast. Each of these forms of behavior is a degenerate limiting case. The abstract analytical intellect denying the formative tendency and manipulating static forms, and the passion which is blind to specific form, both lack an essential component of complete human behavior. Human personality means the expression of the formative tendency in a specific form. If the individual seeks to deny either the formative tendency or the limitation to a specific form, he loses a part of his humanity.

Word and emotion are both essential to man, but as aspects of development, and in the process of unitary development the two lose their separation. The European oscillations from rationalism to activism, and from the practical to the emotional life, display the instability of the dissociated system. Neither reason, nor the emotional consciousness, is man's proper criterion. The doctrines that proclaim the extension of human consciousness as the supreme good, share the same error. Consciousness, or attention, is merely one aspect of the formative system of man. To see in it the aim of human life can lead nowhere.

But if unitary thought is valid this confusion is only temporary. In the beginning was the deed, but within it was the universal formative process. In the process of developing the community, each individual will necessarily share in some degree in the general development. The unitary emotion which inspired both religion and science will accompany and guide the further development of man. But in this process the word has a crucial role. The intellect is man's unique asset. Words are necessary for communication from man to man. The uttered word operates by calling the attention of others to the existence of a particular situation. Until a situation is jointly recognized by verbal communication no fully effective human co-operation is possible. The couple whose love remains in suspense until the first word is spoken, and the group whose emotion is impotent until the word is passed around which releases co-ordinated action, are evidence of the role of the uttered word. "Unitary" is such a word, communicating a message. Its implications are inexhaustible.

4

European Man

The ground is prepared. We can now apply this method of thought to the development of European man and the diagnosis of the present condition of Western civilization. Our task is to trace the changing organization of man, that is, the degree of differentiation and the form of integration which resulted in different periods from the influence of a developing social tradition. We are not directly concerned with the subtlety or variety of the individual, but with the stamp of the social tradition on each maturing generation and the dominant types thus produced. Moreover in emphasizing the impress of the tradition and relatively neglecting the more balanced and persistent characteristics on which it is imposed, the analysis deliberately presents a parody of the general condition in each period. Only at special moments such as the present does this method perhaps cease to exaggerate the actual condition of society.

Throughout history there runs one main trend: a progressive differentiation, or passage from simple to more complex forms in behavior, thought, and social organization. Over sufficiently long periods this tendency is unmistakable, and in the recent acceleration of technical development it has been so intensified as to dominate all other social processes. We shall therefore disregard, both in our glance at the more distant periods and in our closer study of recent centuries, the cycles of vitality, maturity, and decadence which mark earlier local civilizations. We shall also ignore individual historical events except in so far as they symbolize important stages in the continuous sequence of transformations which has led to the present state of man. We shall be unable to refer to the history of art, though this would perhaps offer the most direct approach to the unitary process of the changing condition of man.

Moreover the story will be further simplified by omitting all reference to those cultures in Asia and elsewhere that do not form part of the sequence which leads from primitive to European and Western man. The continuity of this sequence is clear. In spite of local cycles the developing social tradition which has led to Western man followed one dominant path: the ancient civilizations of the Near East provided the stimulus to the establishment of European civilization, which in turn decisively influenced the communities of the West.

Though this story covers a period, which we are accustomed to regard as one of considerable length, it is necessary to view it in its correct proportions. The biological and social process with which we are concerned is formed of a series of steps represented by the influence of the tradition on each successive generation of, say, twenty-five years. The evolution of the human species from its simian ancestry occupied a period of the order of a million years, or 40,000 generations, but this period covers the slow process of selective evolution which lies outside the present study. The gradual appearance of *homo sapiens* amidst the earlier manlike hominoids may have taken place some 2,000 generations back, but the story of community life does not begin until the development of agriculture, stock-breeding, and urban settlements a mere 400-300 generations ago. On this scale the history of European culture is a short experiment in human adaptation: Socrates is separated from us by less than 100 generations, and Kepler and Galileo at their prime by only 14. These figures fix the measure of this study; three hundred generations cover the history of civilization, ten may suffice for fundamental changes, and a single generation represent a critical moment of transition.

This perspective draws attention to the acceleration which seems to have marked the recent development of society and now to threaten the stability of the process. While the biological unit, the generation, has scarcely changed, the rate of social development, particularly in technique, has grown continually more rapid during the last three hundred years. The biologically paradoxical position has thus been reached where the lessons of childhood have to be unlearned by the adult, for by the time he has attained maturity they are already out of date. It is improbable that any species could remain healthy under such conditions, and a diagnosis of contemporary man must take account of this situation. Yet it must be remembered that the general rate of human processes is not changing. The main physiological and developmental processes in the individual still require the same span of time measured against the sun and stars; the acceleration of the differentiation of new techniques and of their social consequences represents an anomaly which cannot persist indefinitely. If we desire to understand the processes which have shaped European and Western man we must forget the present instability and go far back to their origins. The present rate of technical development bears no direct relation to the main rhythm covered by our story.

It will be convenient to divide prehistory and history into four main periods which mark definite stages in the development of the species through its leading types to Western man, though they do not imply any uniformity in the different communities of each period. The first is the period of primitive or savage man, from the emergence of the species until about 8000 BC. The second is the period of ancient man, from the discovery of agriculture and stock-breeding until the first centuries of the millennium before Christ. This period extends from barbarian Neolithic communities to the civilizations of the Bronze Age. The third may, for the purpose of this work, be called the period of European man, extending up to the foundation of exact science at about AD 1600. The fourth period, up to the present day, is that of Western man. We shall now consider each of these in turn.

During the first period men were savage, living from hand to mouth in small communities, either nomadic or sheltering in caves, and hunting or collecting their food. This period covers part of the Palaeolithic Age and closes about the time of the first Neolithic arrowheads and pottery. The differentiation of individual behavior and of social organization had not then proceeded far. Racially inherited instinctive tendencies dominated behavior and verbal symbolisms played only a small role. Even at the end of the period the most advanced communities had only a limited faculty of speech and few general conceptions, while the memory of the individual may have extended no further back than a few years. The social tradition was communicated to the next generation almost wholly by example and mimicry, aided by only primitive verbal suggestion. Behavior was still integrated, as in the higher mammals, by

the balance of the instinctive tendencies, though the forms of social behavior characteristic of primitive man were being built up as
the accumulated result of the intelligent adaptations of individuals,
which were mimicked by others and so stabilized as a continuing
tradition.

Though development was slow, the formative tendency was
operating continually, both towards greater dominance over the
environment and towards the adaptation of man to the environment. This formative process is displayed in the tendency of primitive man to improve his tools and to establish more general and
effective methods of communicating his slowly developing
thoughts. Normally these changes occurred very slowly. But when
favorable circumstances made it possible for the community not
only to protect itself from day to day but in addition to establish a
margin of security and collect a surplus of food, the attention of
some of its members was liberated from preoccupation with immediate needs, and they began to exercise their developing faculties
in ritual, play, and experiment. The formative tendency is here seen
at work in the instinctive struggle for survival, in the improved
adaptations of animal intelligence as developed in man, and in the
constructive activities that led towards culture.

Viewed biologically this period is marked by the unchallenged
instinctive control of behavior. The general co-ordination of behavior is still determined by the balance of instinctive tendencies,
for though the developing of social tradition is gradually extending its influence over the pattern of individual behavior, the tradition itself is as yet primarily directed towards the satisfaction of
instinctive needs. Man is a tool-using animal, slowly developing
the use of language.

In the course of any process of development, long periods of
slow change may be followed by a sudden transformation revealing potentialities of which previously there has been little indication. Such transitions can only occur when favorable internal and
external conditions coincide. It may be that the human system had
for long been ready to develop new faculties, and that climatic and
other external conditions in the Near East about 8-4000 BC suddenly provided the opportunity for them to mature. The slow development of nomadic or cave communities, primarily instinctive
but exploiting their animal intelligence in the human use of tools,

had been proceeding with fluctuations for perhaps fifty thousand years, or two thousand generations, and suddenly in less than 200 generations there appeared the various techniques which provided the basis for civilization. The expression of conceptual thought in script as well as speech, the practice of agriculture and stock-breeding, the discovery of bronze, and the establishment of urban societies capable of supporting an extensive specialization of individual function, all occurred for the first time within this relatively brief span. Favorable circumstances gave man the opportunity to increase his material security by improved methods of obtaining food and shelter, and to use the leisure so won for the development of new and more complex techniques no longer limited to the satisfaction of immediate material needs.

By 3000 BC this surplus formative vitality had produced the splendour of the earliest civilizations of the Near East. The basis of this unprecedented expansion of human life was provided by the farmer and stockbreeder whose produce made possible the establishment of urban societies capable of supporting a greatly increased specialization of function amongst the members of each community. Before 6000 BC there is no evidence of urban life; by 2500 BC civilization had reached an advanced stage in many parts of Asia, Africa, and Europe. For reasons which we shall consider in a moment this period may be regarded as ending soon after 1000 BC and it therefore covers the early civilizations of the Near East, Egypt, China, India, Crete, and Greece, and perhaps others of which the record has been lost or not yet been found. This period of ancient man opens in prehistory, but from about 3100 BC, when the first events can he dated with some accuracy in Sumer and Egypt, it enters the historical age. Until about 2000 BC the records tell mainly of mythical figures of great kings and founders of empires, but during the following centuries the individual definitely enters history, and traits of personality begin to be recorded, some of which may be assumed to correspond to those of a historical person.

The millennia from 8000 to 1000 BC include so many different forms of society from the Neolithic communities to the ancient civilizations that no single generalization can cover them all. Nevertheless, if these societies are considered from a biological point of view one tendency is evident throughout this period. Compared with the relatively static and simple forms of life of primitive man, a quicker development is now in process towards a more complex differentiation of behavior, both within the life of each individual and in the different functions of the individuals within the community. The responses of primitive man to his environment were relatively swift, that is, they followed the stimulus either immediately or after only a short delay. His memory was too short and his attention too uncertain to permit him to plan far ahead, and his power to dominate the environment was correspondingly restricted. In the language of unitary thought the characteristic forms of primitive man persisted (in memory) only for short periods, and were extended (in molding the environment to suit his needs) only to a moderate degree. But with the advantages of urban life ancient man was able to exercise faculties that had previously had little opportunity; he developed new tools for action and new words for thought, found that a better organized brain could remember longer, and so gradually evolved the complex and extended patterns of deliberate behavior characteristic of civilized society.

Certain features are common to all the more highly developed communities of this period, the chief of these being a social hierarchy (more complex than that of primitive communities) of individuals with specialized functions usually dominated by a priest-king, and the use of written records, including codes of law, to supplement oral tradition. In contrast to the relatively quick responses of primitive man, a considerable part of the whole of human activity is now composed of the systems of deliberate behavior connected with the various occupations: the priests, officials, merchants, soldiers, craftsmen, and serfs. These systems of behavior, which include deliberate planning and rituals extending over months or even years (compared with the days or weeks covered by the plans of primitive man), are controlled and communicated from one generation to another not only by mimicry but increasingly by the use of words. Speech, script, and conceptual thought are now of rapidly growing importance in the organization of society. The concept, or idea, has become one of the main instruments of social co-ordination, and ideas begin to be linked in sequences which permit reasoned attention to be given to novel situations, and so lead to the long-delayed deliberate responses which result from sustained thought.

Nevertheless, though the social tradition was already complex and far-reaching in its modelling of the earlier instinctive and traditional forms of life, it did not yet include any general verbally organized mode of integration which might rival the dominance of the instinctive control. The hereditary instinctive tendencies still provided the ultimate control which kept the complex traditional life in balance. The ancient civilizations did not challenge the instinctive life, but developed and differentiated it into a rich social pattern of special activities communicated and organized by a verbal tradition. Until the closing centuries of this period, from 1400 to 1000 BC, the dominant components of this verbal tradition did not recognize any separation of idea from fact, or of man from the world around him, or any general antithesis between man as he is and man as he should be. Prior to 1000 BC ethical formulations are the exception, and by contrast serve to throw light on the pagan background of the ancient world.

Nature and man were accepted without critical or systematic attention. Words were mainly symbols for naming particular situations or objects and for organizing specialized modes of behavior. Thought was concrete. The general control of the individual's behavior and the factors determining choice in situations of difficulty or conflict were not yet the subject of general attention, and hence also not yet the subject of verbal formulation as an accepted part of the tradition. There was still no need for a general conception of man as an independent person with the faculty of choice in accordance with his individual character. The fact that individual behavior was co-ordinated by certain general tendencies had not yet come sufficiently to man's attention to form part of the tradition. The civilizations of the antique world and the modes of life recorded in the earliest Egyptian scripts, the *Iliad,* or the first Vedic hymns, represent, compared with Neolithic man, an advanced stage in the differentiation of deliberate behavior. But these systems of deliberate behavior still retained the character of a rich flowering of primitive life; they were sufficiently stable to operate without any single conceptually organized integration of the whole pattern; with certain striking exceptions the developing social tradition had not yet asserted the possibility of organizing the whole of life in terms of one central idea.

The period of ancient man is a transitional stage of development between the period of the instinctive control characterizing primitive man and the deliberate control which has been carried furthest by European and Western man. The power of the word and the general concept to organize behavior is growing but has not yet challenged the dominance of the earlier system. Man is pagan; he has not yet been dominated by one idea and is therefore still free of the inner conflict and external intolerance which result from the ascription of universality to ideas of limited scope. Man is still a part of nature, though already thoughtful; thoughtful, but not yet about himself; an individual, but still displaying normal organic integration. Though they are supplemented by a rich social tradition, the dominant organizing processes retain the integration characteristic of the higher mammals in that no fundamental dualism or dissociation in the individual or in the community has yet challenged the biologic normal degree of harmony.

A momentous change opens the third period; the passing of the ancient world and the development of rational self-consciousness. This transformation coincides with the collapse of the Bronze Age civilization and the expansion of life which resulted from the use of iron. During the centuries from 1600 to 400 BC the processes of history acquire a wholly novel shape, and perhaps temporarily lose their proper form, for now, if ever, is the fall of man. But the new type of man has unprecedented vitality and swiftly assumes the leadership of the species. Starting from various centers on the shores of the Mediterranean he spreads his influence rapidly throughout Europe and finally dominates the world. This achievement is the result not of any specially favored hereditary constitution but of the steadily developing European tradition which grew from the traditions of the ancient civilizations transplanted into European soil. The third period covers the story of this new tradition from its origins in the ancient world up to the opening of the next period at AD 1600. This is the age of states and empires, of monotheism, and of universal ideas. In applying to this more recent historical period the same method of approach as we have used hitherto we shall discover that like its predecessors it is marked by a characteristic form of integration. But we shall also identify the inner weakness in the European tradition which rendered its collapse inevitable, even though at one stage it seemed to stand for a universal and permanent form of society.

What was the nature of the change that produced this new type of man? Between 3000 BC and the opening of the Christian era three great processes occurred, each of them of sufficient importance to rank as an event in the biological story of man and all maturing within a few hundred years of 1000 BC. The first is the appearance of great empires claiming to extend to the limits of the known world. This process began from the supremacy of one city state over others at about 3000 BC, and found its first mature expressions in the Egyptian empire near 1600 BC, in the early Chinese empire from 1400 to 1200 BC, and finally in the Persian empire in 500 BC. The second is the development of the idea of one universal god and the spread of monotheism in the place of the earlier polytheistic religions. This process is represented by Akhenaton and Moses, both in the fourteenth century BC, and later by Zoroaster, Jesus and Paul. The third is the emergence of universal ideas and of the doctrine of rationalism. Plato, at 400 BC, represents its first maturity.

The close succession of these three tendencies and their wide geographical extension suggests that they had a common origin in some profound transformation of human nature at that time, or, more accurately, in the adult human being as matured by the contemporary social tradition and its new techniques. This interpretation is supported by the fact that the feature of universalism is common to all three, and extends even to Lao Tse and the Buddha. It seems that adult human nature, as molded by the developing tradition in the leading areas of Eurasia, was ripe for the universal empire, the universal god, and the universal idea. Stimulated perhaps by the consequences of the discovery of iron, skill, emotion, and thought now claimed the right to extend their scope without limit. But these processes were accomplished by another, more subtle but no less definite. This was the attraction of man's attention to a novel field, the mental processes occurring in himself. The outward-looking pagan became introspective; man became aware of moral conflict, aware of himself, and aware of his own separation from nature. Knowledge of conflict led to self-consciousness and to the sense of guilt. Man fell from innocence. For reasons which we shall analyze, universalism was achieved at the cost of inner dissociation. The struggle of the spirit against nature had begun.

Everyone who pauses to consider the significance of this moment in the story of man must be held in awe by the grandeur of the transformation that was consummated in so short a time. The processes which organized human behavior had, it seems, been ready for a swift reorganization; the human pattern had become unstable and now settled rapidly into a new shape. This great readjustment, expressing the continuity of the formative process in man, found its historic agents within the communities concerned: a few young men scattered here and there knew some aspect of this process at work in themselves, recognized their mission, and became Socrates, Plato, Alexander, Caesar, Jesus, Paul. These names represent the culmination of the process as far as Europe is concerned; there had been other equally remarkable individuals before them. It has no meaning to separate the parts played by the individual and by the community in so comprehensive a process. Individuals like these appear to have contributed much to Europe because each of them was molded by the general necessity of the time. Had they not themselves been consumed in the process, they might be regarded as catalysts of the transformation that was shaping European man. They were in fact the nuclei from which the reorganization spread with the speed which showed how timely it was. These men were great because they were in a profound sense the willing agents of a general need. Each willingly became its agent, his own will expressing the continuity of history as well as of his own personality.

The significance of the three parallel tendencies and of their common universalism is not far to seek, if we apply the unitary conception of man. In the ancient civilizations thought and social organization had attained a degree of differentiation which had not yet been compensated by the development of correspondingly extensive co-ordinating ideas. Thus wherever the traditions of these civilizations were called in question there arose the opportunity and the need for a co-ordination of the new complexity of life and thought within a single comprehensive system. Improvements in all the technical arts of production, war, and communication, made it possible for small states to be united until empires were established claiming to control all the peoples within their borders. This process cannot be ascribed solely to personal or national ambitions, to military or economic necessity, or to the spread of ideas or principles, since all these tendencies are special cases of one general process: the tendency for patterns to extend their form. Material and economic conditions determine little unless mental processes conform, and mental processes are ineffective unless they can extend their patterns in the external world. But neither of these aspects is in general prior to the other; both are expressions of the unitary process.

It is therefore natural that, parallel with the development of universal empires, we should find the same unifying process at work in the world of thought leading to the establishment of universal ideas in terms of which man sought to explain the whole of experience. At the same time, in the field of religion the local tribal gods and the polytheistic hierarchies gradually gave place to the universal god whose realm often extended to the boundaries of the new empires. Each of these movements displays the establishment of one organizing principle claiming universality within its own sphere. Thus the external aspects of the transformation which occurred at the opening of the third period expressed the tendency for the forms which organized human behavior to spread without restriction, i.e., for social systems and systems of thought to be organized around principles of universal application.

But this interpretation covers only one aspect of the transformation and in order to understand the significance of the self-consciousness which developed side by side with the new universalism we must consider in more detail the biology of the human situation at that time. During the period of ancient man the ultimate control of behavior had been instinctive, and the complex systems of behavior which were stabilized in the traditions of the ancient civilizations had not challenged the instinctive background of life. So long as these traditions were adequate there was no clash between the spontaneous instinctive life and the deliberate patterns of behavior expressed in the ancient traditions.

In the pagan age man could think out practical problems without finding himself involved in any general or persisting conflict. Thought and action were never far from immediate instinctive needs, no dualism of incompatibles had yet become dominant in human nature or in man's thought about himself, and though decision on a particular course of action might sometimes be difficult, such difficulty seemed to lie in the nature of things rather than in his own nature.

Yet this primitive condition was bound sooner or later to be disrupted, either by the increasing differentiation of thought and of deliberate behavior, or by the clash between different modes of life brought into contact by the improved methods of communication. When this occurred the old assurance collapsed, instinctive and traditional systems ceased to be adequate to organize behavior, man became uncertain what to do, and so unsure of himself. This hesitancy meant that instinct and tradition having proved inadequate the individual was being compelled to rely for guidance on his own mental processes. Instead of being aided primarily by instinctive responses to external stimuli and by mimicry of the form of a stable social tradition, the individual was now increasingly dominated and controlled at moments of decision by the special forms of his own thought processes. This dominance of the individual's own mental processes means, in unitary thought, that his attention was drawn to these processes. Instinctive and traditional responses to the outer world no longer sufficed to organize the whole of behavior, decisions had now increasingly to be made in accordance with forms internal to himself. Thus man became self-conscious. The individual became aware of his own thought.

This development was partly the result of the increasing plasticity of human behavior. The rigid and undiscriminating organization of behavior by the instinctive tendencies and the social tradition had become inadequate, and had to be supplemented by a subtler and more variable control expressing the dominant tendencies in each individual person. The pagan, even with his highly developed animal intelligence, could no longer cope with the complex variety of situations in which he was finding himself; to do this his attention had to be drawn to the characteristic continuity of his personal life, he had to become aware of himself as a person.

This, I suggest, is the biological significance of the human situation at the opening of the third period. Let us now examine the historical facts supporting this interpretation. The Bronze Age civilizations of the Near East, and of Egypt, Crete, and Greece were usually dominated by one figure: the king, lawgiver, or priest. The traditions of these societies were relatively stable since they rested mainly on elements that had been developed locally over an extended period, and were focused in one person whose unquestioned authority tended to assure the stability of the community.

But as these different civilizations grew and with improving means of communications spread their influence beyond their original borders they came into contact and mutually influenced one another. This situation was continually occurring, but in the Near East from 1500 to 500 BC such fertilizing exchange acquired an importance it had never had previously. After 1200 BC the development of iron upset the old civilizations and created a ferment in which the continuous exchange of materials and ideas extended over vastly greater areas than ever before. Sea-borne traders and adventurers could acquire experience of different cultures and carry home their influence. The experience of the Mediterranean traveller in these centuries epitomized the characteristic situation of the time in that part of the world: men found themselves comparing different forms of society and different systems of thought. Choice, doubt, and conflict began to appear to a degree far beyond that which had hem possible within the relatively static societies of the antique world. The organization of society came under attention and ethical and political problems began to be discussed. For the first time the individual began to pay consistent attention to the fact that he was alone in a world where things could not be taken for granted. Amidst this new uncertainty he consciously yearned for security, for the recovery of his lost assurance and innocence, in a word, for salvation. In place of the habits and traditions symbolized in one priest-king the individual began to develop general ideas which could help him to find his own way through the new complexity. The only method by which this uncertainty could be overcome was by the establishment of universal ideas including a conception of man himself as a personality with freedom of choice, and a conception of the pattern of behavior to which he should conform.

Thought has for so long been distorted by the verbal dualism of mind and body that the development of self-consciousness is commonly regarded as a peculiarly mysterious process. But it is no more than the development of the dominant mental processes to include not only the impress of the forms of external stimuli on instinctive and traditional patterns (as in the extrovert pagan), but a persisting form characteristic of the individual personality. The circumstances of human life demanded that individual choice, based on personal consideration of the problems of behavior, should to an increasing degree dominate behavior. The attention of the individual was drawn more and more to his own thought as well as to external stimuli, and he became aware of himself as a thinking and feeling person endowed with the faculty of choice.

The operative factor in this situation was the uncertainty which often prevented action from following the stabilized patterns of instinct and tradition and compelled the mental processes of the individual to dominate behavior, i.e., drew the attention of the individual to his own thoughts and feelings. In the instinctive or traditional life of ancient man response followed stimulus along established paths, and the dominant factor holding the attention of the individual was the world of sense around. But now that the old traditions were inadequate, situations continually arose in which this flow of stimulus into response was arrested, and no adequate action was possible until the extended processes of thought had worked out the appropriate solution. The organizing processes instead of following, as previously, a universal pattern adapted both to the individual and the community tradition, had now to form a special response for each individual in accordance with the tendencies that happened to be dominant in each. Each person had increasingly to shape for himself his own dominant form, to develop his own personality in his own actions.

The part played in the production of self-consciousness by uncertainty arising from the inadequacy of habitual patterns of behavior is evident in the process of Western adolescence which mirrors certain features of the historical process which we are considering. At adolescence a boy becomes aware of tendencies in himself which he does not understand breaking through the harmonious mode of life which his family environment has developed in him. He becomes uncertain and distrusts his own spontaneous tendencies, since they now lead him along strange paths. His hesitation between these new disturbing inclinations and his earlier socially accepted habits draws his attention towards himself. Though the analogy is not complete, we see here the same factor of delay in response, the consequent dominance of a new inner process of thought requiring a finite amount of time, the deflection at special moments of the individual's attention from the environment to himself, and his discovery of himself as a unique person separate from everything around him.

The process which we are considering may be regarded as the development of individual personality. Under the new circumstances which we have described the opportunity arose for the frequent appearance of responses to the environment expressing the past experience of the individual. The organizing processes which had previously been either instinctive or traditional now began to develop forms characteristic of the individual, and these individual forms began to dominate behavior repeatedly and continuously. His behavior expressed his own personality. Moreover the personal continuity of form which dominated his behavior was therefore the subject of his attention, and he became aware of himself as a person with special desires, sometimes different from those of the individuals around him. But the individual's awareness of himself as a person could not arise generally until the circumstances of the time had rendered traditional forms of behavior inadequate and provided a stimulus to individual thought. Though there is evidence that isolated individuals had become aware of their difference from others up to 2,000 years earlier, it was only during the first millennium BC that this degree of self-consciousness became sufficiently widespread to affect the social order.

This interpretation explains the origin of a widespread increase in the individual's awareness of himself at the opening of the third period, but we have still to consider the quality of that state of awareness, or more accurately, what man's attitude was to the self which he had discovered. We have to account for the change from the pagan man of the antique civilizations around 1500 BC to the self-critical ethical type which developed rapidly in Egypt, Palestine, and elsewhere, and culminated, as far as Europe is concerned, in the spread of Christianity. Early Egyptian and Greek records reveal no concern with the inner relation of the soul to god; the moral conscience is absent, and the sense of sin is only recognized as an expression of the external consequences of action. Egyptian religion was concerned with man's practical needs in the next world, while Greek religion existed to make man feel at home in this world. In contrast the Hebrew books and the Christian epistles are essentially subjective, the sense of sin has become an internal experience.

In the pagan period language and ideas were mainly concerned with particular situations and special responses to them. But the field of behavior covered by verbally formulated ideas steadily broadened, and when instinct and tradition failed to provide a sufficiently discriminative response to the more complex situations in which ancient man found himself, there arrived both the opportunity and the need for universal ideas which could be applied by each individual in deciding general issues for himself.

In order to appreciate the significance of the unitary process by which universal ideas, at once religious, ethical, and intellectual, were developed, it is necessary to consider various aspects of this process in succession. Complementary to the uncertainty in face of a new and more complex social situation for which traditional methods were no longer adequate, there was another factor, no less important, which displayed the same unitary process at work. Instinctive modes of behavior had been woven by primitive tradition into a system of life which, during the ancient civilizations, was relatively stable. The instinctive tendencies were, as I have already indicated, held in balance by a physiological control, similar in character to the organic control in less developed mammals. But as the ancient civilizations acquired more powerful technical methods and the community, or at least some of its members, were assured of immediate survival, a new and unsettling factor entered. Since instinctive fulfilment gave satisfaction, favorably placed individuals could devote their surplus in material security and technical instruments to the deliberate pursuit of instinctive pleasures. The organic balance of the instincts, which had been adequate to maintain a proper co-ordination of behavior while social conditions were still primitive, doubly failed in this new and more complex situation. It not only failed to establish adequate responses to new and pressing situations, but it could not even maintain a proper balance of the instinctive life, now that the individual was aware of what gave him satisfaction and possessed the instruments with which he could deliberately exploit and intensify this satisfaction.

The change in material conditions transformed the innocence and integrity of primitive and pagan man into the sensuality and bestiality of the decadent periods prior to the rise of monotheism. Primitive man had also sought instinctive pleasure, but ancient man as he became decadent exploited the satisfaction of his instincts to the point at which it disturbed the organic balance and upset the proper co-ordination of his life. But parallel with this new deliberate sensuality, upsetting proper co-ordination and therefore accompanied by sadism and masochism, there developed also the new deliberate idealism which expressed itself in all forms of spiritual endeavour. Both the sensuality and the spirituality were new, and represented the dualistic and therefore distorted substitutes for the prior organic integrity.

Thus the new uncertainty and the revolt from the degenerate life of the ancient world both stimulated the development of universal religious and ethical ideas.

In becoming aware of himself, man simultaneously formed a conception of a single authority, or god, and a conception of what that god expected of man. Man did not become aware of himself naively, but, with a judgement prejudiced by the growing dualism of his thought, considered his own nature and found in it not one harmonious organization, but two principles which he called good and evil. The divided state and the prejudiced approach to it both came about, as we have seen, because a potential separation of spontaneous and deliberate behavior (due to the dual structure of the nervous system) was aggravated and made effective by a corresponding dualism in the verbal tradition. The tradition was in course of developing a system of ideals for organizing deliberate behavior which had no direct relation to man's instinctive and spontaneous activities. Man considered himself in terms of these ideals and felt ashamed, for he knew that a part of his own nature could not conform to them. His self-consciousness had therefore the quality of conflict, shame, and guilt. Man fell from innocence to sensuality and monotheism.

It may at first sight appear strange that an animal species endowed with the faculty of animal intelligence, such as pagan man, could conceive the dualism of good and evil, come to regard the more recently developed deliberate behavior as "good" and the undisciplined satisfaction of his instincts as "evil," and then establish, in some degree at least, the dominance of this "good" over this "evil." If man is animal, continuous with animal nature, how can spirit suddenly arise and discipline the flesh? How did the spiritual element master the sensual in this transformation from the ancient pagan to the ethical idealist?

Thus formulated the problem appears baffling, but the difficulty is the result of the deep prejudice which lies in the form in which it is expressed. Ancient man was neither spiritual nor sensual, but simply whole. The complementary distortions, spirituality and sensuality, were the result of the dissociation, and there is no cause for surprise that one of these two elements, both of which represented distorted components of his primitive human nature, should in certain respects dominate the other. The spiritual dominated the sensual—in the sense that the community preached the one as against the other—and not vice versa, because the spiritual represented the further development of the formative process. The complex forms of deliberate activity organized by the new religious tradition helped to maintain and develop the species, even though at times they came into conflict with instinct. It was a victory of spirit, not over a properly co-ordinated instinctive life, but over an exploitation of instinctive pleasures which had already become damaging. Ideas were effective in facilitating the further development of man, and so the development of ideas was itself facilitated. Ideas, and in particular the new religious ideals, offered a means of integrating life even though only partially and so were accepted and developed. What we call "religion" is the operation of a partial substitute for complete organic integration.

The organizing process in any animal tends to suppress the activities of any one instinct when these threaten to damage the organic balance. Nothing is more common than for men to resist their instinctive tendencies for the sake of an integrating principle, patriotic, religious, or idealistic. Because the bias of thought towards static concepts prevented the development of a rational principle which could facilitate the co-ordination of the whole of human nature, man accepted what was available, the new standards of monotheism, even though they carried with them a lasting sense of guilt. But since the community tended to support the new spirituality and condemn the new sensuality the Bible story is at fault. The fall of man represented the victory not of instinct, but of deliberate thought. But the community taught the individual that his fall from grace was due to his instincts, whereas we can now see that his tragedy was that he could not avoid accepting as inescapable an inner conflict which had been aggravated by a temporary dualism in the tradition and was not due to any permanent dichotomy in his own nature. The fact that some civilizations do not suffer from this dichotomy shows that the fault lies in the tradition, and not in the hereditary constitution of the species.

The new man was able in some degree to conquer his instinctive nature because he had fallen in love with the patterns of his own thought. Without realizing the fact he was from now on fascinated by the images formed by his own mental processes. The god of his own thought was henceforward man's chief source of inspiration. If man's view of himself had been complete and his self-love had been whole natured, history would have been different. But the religious narcissism which was the basis of monotheism unfortunately extended to one aspect only of contemporary human nature. In its immature state the new faculty of thought could not reflect in one pattern the whole of man. Man's image of himself was therefore faulty; neither Platonic nor Christian man saw himself whole. Beneath the formulated ideal, adapted to organize the deliberate life, there remained the complementary spontaneous life dissociated from the former and therefore distorted. Reverence for the spiritual was inevitably accompanied by hate and distrust of the sensual. Socrates and Jesus loved the soul of man, but even they could do no better than forgive the flesh.

By the opening of the Christian era the transformation from ancient to European man was complete. We cannot trace this process in its historical detail, but certain points must be emphasized which concern its relation to the general development of man. This transformation was not merely a local phenomenon which might repeat itself in the cycle of each transient civilization. Though processes similar to this awakening of self-consciousness may have occurred previously in the history of other civilizations, they only prepared the way for this final transformation which affected the whole of mankind about the opening of the third period. All sections of the race did not simultaneously undergo it in the same degree. Yet as the result of the leadership of European man the whole species was ultimately led through this transformation.

Moreover the two main centers of civilization did undergo this transformation simultaneously, though it took somewhat different forms in the two areas. In the eastern Mediterranean the final transition on the intellectual side occurred about 450-400 BC, when Greek thought ceased to view man unself-consciously as the innocent bearer of either a fortunate or a tragic fate, and adopted the subjective, rationalistic, analytical attitude which resulted from increased self-consciousness. The Homeric poems are clearly in the ancient world; so are Heraclitus (540-475 BC) and Aeschylus. Socrates (470-399), Plato (427-347), and Aristotle (384-322) represent the transformed man, from whom the European intellectual develops without further radical change. The representative character of the Greek philosophers thus enables the intellectual aspect of the change to be dated closely. If the other aspects are considered, and other areas around the Mediterranean, we find that the entire process took place between 1600 and 400 BC.

Meantime in China we find an ancient imperial authority in gradual decay from 900 to 400 BC and a social transformation in process leading to a similar development of intellectual enquiry. Lao Tse (b. 604, not a historical person?) recommends the innocent spontaneity of an earlier and simpler state; his ideal is an unselfconscious unity with the natural course of things. He corresponds broadly to Heraclitus; these two are the last great thinkers whose view of process is scarcely touched by the analytical consciousness. On the other hand Confucius (551-478) corresponds to Plato; both sought to use the power of conscious reason to create or recreate a social order; both are transformed types. The significance of such parallels is limited. Yet the simultaneity of similar processes in different areas indicates a universal situation to which different sections of mankind responded in their own ways. It was only in Europe that the transformation took so radical a form as to make a permanent effect on the subsequent history of the entire species.

So far we have been concerned with the general features of this transformation, and we must now examine certain aspects of it more closely, since these resulted in the establishment of the institutions characteristic of Europe. For this purpose we shall appear to split the process into three independent components, though in fact these are no more than special expressions of the general transformation. In primitive communities there was little individual specialization of function, and it is impossible to separate what we now recognize as the economic, religious, political, and intellectual aspects of social organization. In the ancient civilizations characteristic of the second period a complex hierarchical society with a considerable degree of professional specialization had already been established. Nevertheless the hierarchy was normally dominated by one person or dynasty, in which all forms of authority and power were vested. In most of the communities of this period authority and power were single; the different forms of authority to which we are accustomed today had not yet been differentiated from the single relation of dominance between the ruler and the rest of the community. This total monopoly of power is not identical with tyranny. It only becomes tyranny when the many have become aware of it owing to its failure to facilitate their further development.

In the ancient world there was no fundamental contrast between East and West. The division occurred when Europe discarded the single organization of authority, while Asia retained it. This divergence was the consequence of geographical factors which had become of decisive importance under the technical conditions of the time. Now those conditions have changed again, the geographical differences have lost their importance, and the paths of East and West are converging. Only during some three thousand years or less has the scale of social organization been such as to render the geographical contrast of Europe and Asia a dominant factor in their development. In earlier times communities were too small, and today they are too large for the relative diversity of Europe and uniformity of Asia to lead them apart. Technical conditions separated the hemispheres for three millennia; now they bring them together.

During the time when East and West followed different paths it was Europe, and later the West, that led the main trend of differentiation and development. The first stage in this process consisted in the disappearance of the simple unity of the ancient societies and the development of a new tradition by communities in Greece, Palestine, Italy, and elsewhere. This new European tradition was marked by definite characteristics, some of which we have already considered. It developed from three main components which may be summarized as Greek thought, Christian religion, and Roman law. This radical simplification of a complex but unitary process offers a convenient starting point. These components may not have been specially emphasized in the life of the three communities, but they represent broadly what Europe has absorbed from each. The possibility of their combination in one tradition is partly due to the fact that they correspond to three complementary aspects of the mind: thought, emotion, and will. Europe absorbed from Greece the tradition of the free contemplative intellect seeking harmony in nature, from early Christianity the tradition of an independent community of individuals seeking personal harmony in an experience relation to a universal god, and from Rome the conception of an ordered society in which the wills of individuals are co-ordinated by tradition and law. As these three elements represented complementary aspects of the mind they could combine to form a balanced tradition. Though Europe was also affected by Jewish, Moslem, barbarian, and other influences, these three were its fundamental components. They were the necessary and sufficient materials for a Europe.

In the ancient civilizations these aspects had been inseparable; in the new period they are expressed in independent institutions. "Render unto Caesar that which is Caesar's, and unto God that which is God's" is the manifesto of the new type of community in which secular and religious power are divided. Academies are also founded, devoted to the furtherance of learning as an independent activity not necessarily subservient either to religion or to politics. The growing complexity of the social tradition invited this differentiation which continued through the history of Europe while thought, religion, and politics still possessed a basis stable enough to permit them to develop independently. Only recently has this basis been prejudiced and the total unification of authority reappeared in Europe.

But if different components are to blend and form a stable tradition, it is not enough that they represent complementary aspects of the mind; they cannot fuse into one system unless they represent aspects of the same general kind of man; their forms of organization, or the state of differentiation and integration which they represent, must be similar. Alien components may co-exist, and even be a source of vitality or of originality in an individual, but a community can absorb into its tradition only elements whose structure is appropriate to its own state of organization.

It was no coincidence that the three main European components had similar structures, since they had developed simultaneously as expressions of the unitary transformation which had affected most of the societies around the eastern Mediterranean. Greece, Rome, and the Christian centers each emphasized and developed different aspects of the new social order resulting from that transformation. It lies beyond the scope of this study to consider why the first mature forms of the new society appeared in certain areas. But we may note the westward and expansive tendency which links the sequence of the leading communities in history: the small farmer colonies of the first urban communities of the Near East; the city states of the Eastern Mediterranean; the group of peoples and nations in Europe; and now the world group of major centers of power.

The process of social development, as of evolutionary selection, is favored in communities which combine unity with variety, and the leading communities of each historical epoch are marked by this combination. As the technique of travel, trade, and communication improved, larger areas acquired the degree of cultural unity within which local variety could provide the stimulus of fertile exchange. It is probable that in the Bronze Age, about 2000 BC, Europe had already achieved a moderately uniform type of culture, subject nevertheless to a wide range of local variation. If this is true, and the geographical conditions of Europe certainly provided the opportunity for it, then Europe constituted the most favorable field for the development of the new kind of man. While in the East civilization was spread through the expansion of military empires, in Europe it was carried by the trader and colonizer. In China or India where conditions were more uniform, the forms of the ancient world would develop more slowly. These areas avoided some of the maladaptations of Europe, but sooner or later they were bound to fall under the spell of the European mind. Europe was the first testing ground of what seems to be the only path of continuing development; the fate of the species turns on the outcome of the European experiment.

It has not always been evident that this was an experiment of uncertain result; during many periods European or Western civilization has seemed, at least to some of its own more fortunate inheritors, to offer the clear line of a progressive development. European civilization has displayed a unique capacity for stable development as a system capable of undergoing great changes and of producing a vast variety of forms without loss of continuity. For two thousand years Europe has continued to develop its own characteristic institutions: colonial empires, churches, political institutions, professional societies, schools of art, and systems of thought. Wars, revolutions, migrations, and plagues have not affected the core of this tradition. Until recently the Bible, the Platonic dialogues, and Roman history still provided the basis for Europe's highest education. Even today when this inheritance is doubly challenged by the attack of its enemies and by the doubts of its heirs, there remains in many the sense that Europe stood for more than an ephemeral civilization, was more than yet another experiment which failed. Beneath all that was transient in Europe there may have been some positive human principle which can be identified, reformulated as a universal truth, and realized in the coming world system.

Europe has stood for freedom, truth, equality, personality. Even if the European attempt to express these aspects of the maturing of human life was faulty, the attempt proves the existence of a tendency which being brought to light may provide a general human principle. If this is so, then we have to ask, what was this permanent truth within the European tradition and why did Europe fail to express it in a form whose continuing influence might have saved the continent and the world from continued disaster? Our analysis of the biological organization of man during the first three periods has already provided the background for the answer. But the clue to the strength and the weakness of Europe can be found only in a more detailed examination of the components of the tradition.

5

The European Tradition

Whether monotheism spread from one source or sprang up independently in several areas, its rapid extension proves that the soil must have been ready. We have seen that there prevailed about the opening of the third period a degree of differentiation in thought and behavior which invited a compensating development of methods of integration. The formative tendency had always been at work leading man to develop new modes of behavior, and with them ideas of increasing generality; the novel feature was that the next step led to the establishment of methods and ideas of universal scope. The immediate stimulus came from the collapse of an ancient traditional society or from the wider vision brought by the expansion of an empire. The polytheism of family and tribal images faded under the ascendancy of the one god of a larger community. The first example was the most splendid of all: the Pharaoh Akhenaton, in a dazzling prophecy of all subsequent monotheisms, proclaimed the universal god Aton. Soon after him Moses led his people away from pagan images to recognize theirs as the one true God. Zeus gradually dominated the rivalries of the Olympian family. The time had come when the further development of mental processes was bound to produce universal principles, and since these could best be conceived as a person there appeared: Aton, Yahveh, Zeus, Jupiter.

Whatever is truly universal is unique, and whatever pretends universality cannot admit challenge. But a universal god must be an impostor, for a god is a principle of perfection which compensates the imperfection of each individual man, and there are countless varieties of men, each with their own imperfections and their corresponding gods. So long as gods are needed, there will be not one, but many. This plurality can be overcome only when the individual forgets his personal limitations in a more comprehensive unity. Then gods are no longer necessary and an impersonal and universal principle can take their place. Europe, true to its own past, gave its god a special personal form which could not be universal. But this fact could not be admitted; the one God was a jealous God. With the ideal of universality appeared intolerance.

For a moment we will ignore the religious significance of the conception of God, and treat these divine names as examples of the many verbal symbols that were being used in the organization of experience and behavior. Such symbols are not abstract ghosts of a transcendental world, but the very organs of human power, developing within, facilitating, and dominating the organizing processes in man. Viewed from this point of view the idea of the one god has a unique status: it was the first concept which was conceived as standing in a direct relation to everything. Within the frightening indifference and complexity of nature God appeared as the guarantee of fertility; the universal father and mother; the supreme innocence, wisdom, and power; and beneath these conscious factors as the key to all relationships, the universal correlator. God was not merely a protective rationalization of human fears; he was equally an expression of the need to organize thought, to find order in fact and harmony in the self. Fear is the sign of a situation in which the attention of the individual leads to no adequate response; where action is adequate there is no fear. Fear can therefore be overcome only by a principle which determines the proper response to every situation. God provided an acceptable answer to every question; that was his function. But it is a positive act to expect or demand a universal answer, to establish an idea of this scope. To develop the need to give a name to one universal relationship uniting everything great and small—this was an achievement beyond parallel.

Without the formative tendency which expressed itself in the conception of God, scepticism has no opportunity. Doubt has no meaning, except as an aspect of the search for a uniting truth. The establishment of the idea of the one god and the development of monotheism set human thought its standard and put scepticism to work. This was the essential fact. The narrower aspects of which man was aware: the specifically religious significance of God; the selection of a person-God; the differences between Aton, Yahveh, and Zeus—these things were of lesser consequence. The symbol of the monotheistic God was of unlimited potentiality; like the dominant center of a new and dominant organ it was at once the point of most rapid growth and the most vulnerable and easily misused component of the new man. Monotheism is neither good nor bad; so long as it aided the development of man, he remained loyal to it and benefited from it. As a mode of co-ordinating the passions and will, it became easily a means of subduing man. But it was not only opium, it was also bread and wine.

We have already examined the conflict which was developing between the deliberate and the spontaneous life, and the tendency of the organizing processes to develop universal integrating ideas. This tendency was experienced as the appeal of simple, general ideas, and the conceptions to dominate the organization of life was experienced as the need for faith in a personal God, since at that stage the authority which man could most easily conceive was a father or person. The increasing control over behavior of the integrating principle was experienced as the need to act in conformity with God's wishes, and the process whereby instinctive or traditional tendencies came under this new central control was known as the surrender of the person to God.

In certain circumstances this process of surrender might be innocuous. There is no *a priori* reason why the symbol of an ideal person might not provide the most effective dominant form for the organization of behavior and thought. If the idea of a "person" were at once simple and universal in application, monotheism might have offered a permanent organizing principle. But the idea of a personal God lacks any universal standard of validity, and surrender to such a god left the way open for religious and temporal interests to misuse divine authority for their own ends. This has been and will remain the failing of every theistic church; there is no guarantee against the abuse of faith by those who have either a different faith, or none at all, and in its place the ambition for power.

But monotheism, in its characteristic European form, displayed another more serious defect. As we have seen, the religious life, being an integration of deliberate, long-delayed responses, conflicted with the instinctive tendencies, and the development of the religious consciousness was accompanied by the appearance of a state of uneasy tension which is called the sense of guilt. The appearance of the sense of guilt in the monotheistic religions, though it was absent in primitive and ancient man, is evidence of a state of conflict between the spontaneous tendencies and the deliberate behavior expected of the individual in accordance with the prevalent social ideals. The transformation from innocence to guilt is the result of the exploitation of instinctive satisfactions in a materially rich community, which is then condemned by the new social conscience since it conflicts with the proper balance of individual and social life. In extreme cases this conflict and tension may lead to a state of exhaustion in which the instinctive tendencies which seem to be the cause of so much pain cease to dominate behavior, never appear openly in the field of attention, and leave the person apparently dominated by the new devotion to God. This transition from guilt to faith is known as conversion, and it can happen only to a previously unintegrated individual. Conversion, in this form, changes a morbid state of conflict on which the attention of the individual is focused, into a superficially harmonious condition which nevertheless conceals a dissociation so painful as to be permanently withdrawn from attention.

"Religion," in the European sense, is the operation of an incomplete substitute for complete organic integration. The individual exchanges a conflict of which he is partly aware for a dissociation of which he is unaware. This at least is the nature of complete conversion to an absolute Christian faith; in most persons the change is incomplete, and the, struggle to overcome the spontaneous desires may continue without respite or success. There is also the possibility of the conversion of conflict into wholehearted harmony, but that is not a religious process and here we are concerned only with the influence of the European tradition which did not facilitate any such complete integration. The load of guilt may have been conscious in some and unconscious in others but it has sometimes lain so heavily on European man that he believed it to be inherent in his manhood, though an elementary knowledge of other human types is sufficient to disprove this.

There are two main aspects to the new self-awareness which appeared at the opening of the third period, both of which are reflected in the structure of monotheism. The individual became aware of himself as a thinking person with freedom of choice, and also aware of his own separation from the rest of nature. Monotheism met this situation by personalizing God and by treating the personal God as a mediator between man and nature. In the age of magic, man, not being self-aware or separated from nature in his own thought, believed that through magic he could control nature directly. But in the self-conscious age of theism man places God between himself and nature, and seeks to influence nature through the mediation of God. At the same time he seeks to use God as a protection against his own instinctive nature. Thus on both sides of the double separation of the conscious subject, from external nature and from his own instinctive nature, God is introduced as a controlling link. The idea of God helped to maintain this double separation which was the origin of man's need of God. Muscles atrophy where a splint takes the strain. The power of God the Father compensated for the weakness of his children and tended to maintain that weakness. The European religious consciousness cast a veil between man and the unprejudiced recognition of the forms both of external nature and of internal human nature.

But this self-awareness led also to a more vivid sense of the precariousness of the individual life. To become self-aware is to become conscious of the perpetual threat of nature to the security of the self and of the inescapable fact of death. So long as man is fully part of the whole no demand for permanence can arise, but once alone and afraid man fears to return within the action of the whole, and instead desires eternal life. God denies him escape from the sense of separation, but as recompense promises immortality.

To be made content with so spurious a substitute was the inevitable price of man's misunderstanding of his own nature and of his part in the whole of nature. But it is interesting to note that not all great religions have made this frivolous promise of personal immortality. The Jewish people, for example, emphasized the spiritual value of the community tradition rather than of the individual person and demanded from their God a guarantee of their survival not as individuals but as a people. In place of the Christian hope of joining God in heaven, he was to descend and live within their tradition on this earth. This was a more reasonable expectation, because capable of partial fulfilment, but also a more dangerous one, for the same reason. The illusion of personal survival is relatively harmless, because meaningless in a unitary world, but the permanent distinction from all other peoples which was an essential element in the Jewish faith has been granted to them as a curse which will continue until the Jewish and Christian attempts to monopolize the truth have dissolved within a broader vision.

The relation of Jewry to Christendom is of special importance in the interpretation of the European tradition. Here we reach a point so sore, and so subject to misinterpretation, that if safety were the aim, silence would be proper. But the Jews have never been safe. Let those who are too proud of their past to wish to learn condemn themselves. Unitary thought cannot hesitate to subject the Jewish tradition, where it is relevant, to the same radical scrutiny as it applies here to the European. Indeed the two are inseparable. In its structure the Jewish tradition is an exaggeration of the European; the orthodox Jew is a more intense European, different only in so far as he has deliberately separated himself from other influences. We are concerned here only with the impress of a given tradition on the individual, and generalization is therefore legitimate. The unitary world can learn not only from the failure of Europe but also from the fate of Jewry.

The debt of Europe and the world to the Jewish people needs no emphasis. Jewry achieved the first stable monotheism, at a time when that represented a unique advance. Indeed the Jew can only be understood as a premature monotheist: all his characteristics follow from that. Akhenaton had shown the world the possibility of faith in one universal God shared by man and nature. In a moment of splendour he revealed that the future may anticipate itself in the vision and will of a single individual. In originality he surpassed Jesus. But his god Aton, being socially premature, fell with him, and when the Hebrews entered Palestine and absorbed the Egyptian and Babylonian culture they set out to create a monotheism which would last, because they would defend it with their whole being against the alien world. Measured by their own absolute standards that was a mistake; universality cannot be defended, for it can admit no enemies and must transcend all divisions. Akhenaton had known this and refused to fight for his God. The time was not ripe for a stable monotheism, but the Jewish people prepared the way. In a decadent world grown brutal they had no choice but to defend their faith by methods which must lead to disaster. There is no monopoly of the spirit. An exclusive God must be a false God.

Early Jewry, seeking what Europe sought later in more favorable circumstances, was bound to develop in more intense form the same characteristics as subsequently marked the European. Revolting from the instinctive excesses of decadent ancient man, the orthodox Jew became the man of deliberation, ever under the eye of God; rejecting the senses and their flattering images, he proclaimed the prior truth of the word; denouncing all other gods, he announced "the Lord is One"; repudiating the ancient hierarchies, since men of the faith are equal before God; converting all his reactions from the alien world around into a stubborn defence of his privileged truth: "Hear, O Israel, the Lord is our God." The unlimited radiance of Akhenaton, transient as all intense beauty, has become the stable defensive discipline of Moses and the prophets.

Fear of God, and of other religions and peoples, fear of the loss of his own religion, and fear of spontaneous vitality, are expressed in the unique institution of a ban on intermarriage fusing continuity of descent with the claim to a unique religious privilege. In the dread isolation of a people separating itself from cross-fertilization, in the intransigent suppression of spontaneity, the orthodox faith repudiated the unity of process and so determined its own doom. In the species as a whole the intellect was developing as part of the organic processes; within the European tradition it grew in the formal separation of static concepts abstracted from process forms; but in the Jewish tradition the separation was aggravated and projected as a social division from the rest of the race.

The Jew has been the conscience of the European, and conscience is negative. His sense of moral superiority was necessary to conceal a division that lay even deeper than the European, just as his aspiration is more intense. From this conflict there was no redemption, not even the illusion of conversion, and he must await the Messiah. Tribulation led him to divorce fact and idea earlier than Plato; since he could have no worldly dominion, he would at least be supreme in the world of the spirit.

The European, as I have described him, is a particular distortion of the universal form of man, which displays certain distinguishing characteristics. The Jew carries these further, as a polarization of European man. Thus the Jew stands beside the European Christian as a sister type, rather than beside any individual European nation or people. This is the historical anomaly: the Jew, having separated himself as a polarized European type, has no home and must fit in somewhere beside Europe. Having achieved continuity in time by an extreme device, he has forfeited stability in space, and is driven from place to place. Only outside Europe and beyond the dominance of its tradition, that is in Asia, can he escape his separation, for there he no longer needs to defend his faith. The Jewish tradition began in the centuries after 1400 BC as a response to the situation which also created the European, and the two must collapse together. When the European idea is exhausted, the Jewish books will also lose their inspiration. The common features and mutual polarity of European and Jew will disappear when they transform their traditions and accept new roles within a unitary world. When the European develops a hatred of the Jew he is releasing his dislike of his own tradition against an exaggerated form of it. Widespread anti-Semitism is thus an inevitable accomplishment of either a temporary or a permanent decline of the European tradition. When the Jew finally renounces his tradition it will be a sign that a unitary society is already is sight, for then he need no longer defend his spiritual mission. Integrity supersedes conscience.

To observe what is incomplete in the achievements of the past implies no lack of appreciation. Development means that broader aspects of experience become evident, and failure to take them into account would be a poor tribute to those who, by their own development, created the past which we have inherited. The tendency in man which enabled him to create monotheism now gives him the sanction to recognize that all particular forms of religion are conditioned by their time. We have to overcome two thousand years of European monotheism by the same love of unity as enabled Akhenaton to transcend the two thousand years of Egyptian pagan civilization. The personal god of the European dissociation fades before the unitary principle of an even more splendid emancipation.

The demand for the unitary principle of life and thought is now inescapable. But during the period under consideration it was monotheistic religion, and Christianity above all, which expressed the supreme aspiration in its richest form and allowed Europe to develop. The quality of European endeavour was nourished by the religious component in the make-up of European man. We shall identify the source of that quality in a moment, when we have considered the intellectual and political components of the tradition. But the religious component was primary, being not only the ultimate sanction of the social order but also at once original inspiration and the expression of the search for harmony. This is true of the past, though in the wider vista which is today opening before man, and which he cannot deny, monotheism has nothing further to offer.

We now turn to the second component of the tradition, the development of universal ideas. It is convenient to treat these components separately, though they are responses to a single situation which differ only in emphasis. As a result of his new self-awareness man had begun to project into nature different aspects of the processes which he discovered in himself. So far we have considered mainly the ethical monotheism, of which the Jewish tradition provides the clearest example, in which man seeks to overcome an emotional conflict by projecting his need for an integrating emotion in the form of a personal or father-god. God is here the righteous ruler; mankind are his sinful people. In India, the emphasis was not on conflict and sin, but on the unreality of the world. Man here projected his failure to cope with nature in a mystical faith in the higher reality of another world.

But in favored Greece, in an environment where man was relatively well adapted and inherited the fruits of two thousand years of Egyptian and Near Eastern, civilization, he was more concerned with the contemplation of the variety of nature, and with the attempt to find order in this variety. The Greek mind sought neither the discipline of a universal father, nor blind escape in a mystical intuition of another world, but the Logos, or universal reason, which inspired the order of nature. The formative tendency in the mental processes of the Greeks led them to seek universal ideas, and these they projected into a transcendental world, more real because conceived to be more permanent than the world of process and appearance.

The Hindu denied the reality of this world in a vague emotional pantheism which was anti-intellectual in tendency; Plato, and his followers, respected the concrete detail of this world, and sought only the higher reality of an intellectual clarity which would interpret and master it. This Platonic doctrine expressed the tendency of thought to establish clear, static ideas even at the cost of their separation from and neglect of the universality of process. This tendency is seen both in Greek philosophic speculation and in Greek mathematics. The Pythagorean numbers and the Platonic Ideas together constituted an important factor facilitating the development of the European tradition together with its accompanying dissociation.

But we are mainly concerned with a broader tendency which emphasized the importance of conscious thought, and isolated it as an order of reality *sui generis.* I shall call this doctrine rationalism. By this term I mean the view that experience is to be interpreted and behavior organized by the deliberate use of the conscious and autonomous faculty of reason. Rationalism seeks the clarity of static ideas as the basis both of knowledge, and of the deliberate control of behavior. It assumes that reasoned analysis of fact is the true basis of knowledge, and that an adequate critique of reason can be supplied by the subjective or introspective application of reason itself. Rational, conscious thought necessarily leads to truth—so it is assumed. Rationalism has a subjective bias; it is interested in the mastery of nature by conscious thought. This subjectivism is common to Christianity and rationalism and expresses an important feature of the situation at the time of their development: the social tradition was ready for an integrating principle, but man could then only conceive an organizing power in the two forms known to him in his own experience, a supreme person or a supreme idea. Rationalism also has a static bias, for in seeking clarity it abstracts permanent elements from the general process.

During the period when monotheism and rationalism represented the two main methods whereby consciousness supplemented the traditional organization of thought and life, it was natural that the differences between them were emphasized rather than their underlying similarity. We are accustomed to thinking of rationalism as meaning the explanation in terms of reason of what has previously been regarded as supernatural. But this interpretation is inadequate.

Now that both methods are being outgrown we are in a position to look back to identify the common features which were less evident in earlier times. Faced by the increasing differentiation of thought and the conflict between spontaneity and deliberation, the rationalist and the monotheist both tended to distrust instinctive impulses and sought to rely on repressive moral ideals to guide and control behavior. Both attitudes moreover express a dislike of the implications of process, and a fear of the transience of the individual life. The Christian seeks the solace of ultimate harmony in a life after death; the rationalist tends to neglect the real world and takes refuge in a harmonious and permanent system of thought. Again, both attitudes reflect the dualism of the self-awareness in which spirit is separated from nature: ideas exist in a world of their own, independent both of the external world and of the organic processes in the thinker, and the soul is distinguished from nature and from the transient physical frame of man both by its permanence and by its partaking in the harmony of the divine nature. This isomorphism, or identity of structure, is inevitable, since both methods developed in response to the same human situation. Indeed it is misleading to regard the two methods as distinct; some communities gave thought a religious, and others a rational emphasis, and sometimes, as in the scholasticism of the Middle Ages, the distinction is lost in a complex system of religious rationalism.

The development of monotheism and of rationalism is thus an expression and reinforcement of the divorce in thought, and therefore also in the organization of behavior between the background of instinct, impulse, and universal process, and the ideal forms of religion and intellect, between Dionysian vitality and Apollonian measure. This divorce and the resulting conflict was the source of tragedy not only in Greek drama, but also in the life of the European. We have already seen that its ultimate origin lay in a duality of the central nervous system, which had served animal species well until in man the achievement of a symbolic or rational control of behavior had at first to be paid for by a dualism that passed out of the control of the organic balance. The conceptual organization of behavior implies that standards of behavior must be established, and at that stage a standard had to be clear and definite, and therefore universal and unchanging. The ideals of monotheistic religion and of rationalism were therefore necessarily static and antagonistic to the developing forms of all processes, and in particular of human vitality.

This fundamental antithesis of form is of great importance; it pervades the thought and behavior of every European and every Western man, in so far as he has been influenced by the European tradition. In unitary thought a formal difference is neither abstract nor unimportant; formal correspondences and antitheses are the significant factors through which alone the processes of nature and of man can be understood. The only truth is to be found in form; the apparent content and spurious substance that constitute the body of language are merely late types of magical incantation.

For example, we shall not be misled by the Christian who seeks to conceal his own lack of faith and to follow contemporary trends by asserting that Christianity can transcend the division of spirit and matter. Christianity can be re-interpreted without limit, and names may not matter, but so long as emphasis is placed on a personal god as the guarantor of the survival of individual personality, a static idea, in the formal sense of a timeless one, is made dominant, and everything else is secondary. Even those forms of Christianity which recognize the tragic character of life still pay their due to the general cry for comfort and rob experience of its validity by promising consolation elsewhere. If death is robbed of its sting, life is patched up with a silver lining. Illusion may still be necessary to make life tolerable, but this particular superstition loses its appeal for those who have recognized that spirit and flesh have no meaning except as aspects of the process here and now which makes each of us what we are. Indeed if this analysis is right the enthusiasm which is indispensable to every great adventure can now be created only by the objective discovery and personal recovery of unity in process, and this is prevented where static ideals are given a dominant status.

This antithesis between the static conceptions of monotheism and rationalism and the process character of nature as a whole must be interpreted not merely as a dualism in man's thought, but as a contrast of two alien types of form which lies deeper than conscious thought. There is a close correlation between rationalism and self-consciousness, which reveals their common root deep in the structure of mental processes. Rationalism implies that man is aware of his ideas as separate from the external world, and to be aware of this separateness man must also be aware of himself. Self-awareness is thus implied by rationalism. In establishing general ideas man uses a part of his own thought for the interpretation of the world. The processes which drew man's attention inward thus produced two simultaneous results: first, the integration of the continuity of personal experience in the conception of the self; and second, the integration of the verbal symbols of language in the conception of universal ideas. Self-awareness, rationalism, and monotheism were thus intimately related expressions of the state of the social tradition during the early development of European man.

The antithesis between the static conceptions of self-conscious rationalism and the process forms of nature had further consequences. The images of the imagination were separated from those of the senses, the tendencies and desires of the conscious subject were regarded as independent of the tendencies of other natural processes, and the subjective will appeared to stand in sharp contrast to the general course of nature. This division led to the conception of the autonomous and responsible moral will as "free" of the "necessity" which appeared to govern natural processes. In what follows I shall use the term "morality" to express the attempt of the conscious will to control behavior to conform with social standards in ignorance of the conditions of proper organic integration. During the metamorphosis from ancient to European man, self-awareness, rationalism, monotheists and morality all developed in parallel as expressions of the influence of a new form of social tradition on the organization of the individual. In less marked forms these features were also present in previous societies, and elsewhere in the world, but in Europe they acquired a peculiar emphasis. Europe forced the new mode of life till it produced a definite dissociation, for self-awareness did not then bring with it an adequate understanding of the self; religion could not offer a complete integration; the rational intellect knew nothing of its own origins, limitations, or mode of operation; and morality necessarily failed to realize its aim.

This was the general tendency of the new tradition. If we select any particular period in European history, or any individual whose life we may believe we can reconstruct, we may find that the impress of the European tradition was less important than the influence of special tendencies and local situations. Moreover the underlying instinctive and habitual patterns of primitive and ancient life continued to determine the general forms of life upon which this European organization was gradually imposed. The institutions of marriage and the family, the rituals of religion and craft, the alternation of peace and war, and the preoccupation with the struggle for survival—all tended to preserve a balance and to protect the individual from taking the European tradition too seriously.

Nevertheless the dissociation eventually affected all to some degree, and some to a disastrous degree. Individuals and communities that were deeply affected by the European ideals showed the result in instability, oscillation between asceticism and excess, conflict, neurosis, or insanity. European genius and insanity have been often associated; the temperament which gave a whole-natured response to the implications of the tradition often paid the full price. Some latent organic weakness, not being protected by whole-natured function, was aggravated by the dualistic tradition until the organic self-regulation was frustrated and the dualism achieved its logical fulfilment in schizophrenia. The supreme exception checks the rule: Goethe rejected the European dualism in all its forms and escaped its distortions. This is not a moral or aesthetic valuation, but a statement and interpretation of fact. On the other hand those who attempted to give the most radical expression to the religious, educational, and intellectual idealism of the European tradition announced not only their own impending breakdown, but also the ultimate collapse of Europe.

We have so far been able to neglect the political component in the tradition. The political and social organization of any community tends to display its special characteristics less sharply than do its religion or its ideas. The polity of a community is at any moment a compromise between habits inherited from the past and new methods which have still to develop their full influence. For this reason we find the European dissociation and its various aspects much less clearly expressed in its political than in its religious and intellectual forms. Nevertheless the same essential features are present. Europe absorbed from Rome the conception of society as the conscious integration of individual wills within a social order. It is as if in Rome the new subjectivity had emphasized the subject's awareness, not of his emotion or his thoughts, but of his will to action. Therefore in place of the one god or the universal idea, Rome was chiefly concerned with the co-ordination of individual action within a consciously developed political system. The Roman mind, becoming aware of tradition, transformed it into law and established the conception of a political community in which every full citizen shared in law-making and enjoyed equal justice.

Since Roman political methods, blended with the Christian-rationalist system to form a single tradition we must expect to find that they have a similar structure. But Rome met each aspect of the new situation in its own characteristic manner: the increasing differentiation of society by a conscious organization of its activities; the growing conflict between spontaneity and deliberation by a realistic adaptation to the requirements of the social order rather than by a moral decision; the sense of the separation of man from nature by the recognition of the power of the human will to mold nature; and the realization of the transience of the individual by emphasizing the continuity of the family and of the political community. In common with Greece and, Palestine and in contrast to the ancient civilizations, Rome stressed the deliberate control of aspects of social life previously dominated by habits and traditions which had not been the subject of conscious attention. But unlike the other two components the Roman polity, being based on a practical compromise between the instinctive tendencies of the individual and the social circumstances of the time, tended to lessen the conflict between spontaneity and deliberation.

Roman traditions, law, and ethics lacked the absolute character of Christianity and rationalism, and drew their sanction not from any strictly religious source, but from a principle of continuity. Like the British people much later, the Romans lacked every fanaticism except the passion for continuing; for them a slowly developing tradition expressed natural human law. Neither the Greek nor the Christian communities had this practical quality which enabled Rome and the societies developing from it to preserve much of their traditions through the disintegration of the ancient world. Rome provided the realistic continuity which, though in some respects antagonistic to the contemporary intellectual, artistic, and religious movements, nevertheless provided the soil in which they could be preserved as part of a cumulative tradition. In the same way the temperament of the English-speaking peoples may enable them to provide the link between the dissipated European culture and a re-organized world community. Just because the Romans and the English-speaking peoples do not take thought seriously, they are able to act as its carrier without themselves succumbing to its weaknesses.

We have now completed the analysis of the transformation which produced European man. Emphasis has been laid on those elements which formed the distinguishing characteristics of Europe up to 1600. It has not been necessary to consider the peoples who inhabited Europe in earlier times, nor shall we discuss the movements which during this period determined the main pattern of European history: the barbarian invasions, the growth of feudalism, the medieval church, the communes, the Crusades, the gradual appearance of the government and the people, the Renaissance, the Reformation. Important as these developments were, their consequences remained within the general form of the European tradition as I have described it. The fundamental conception of a Christian church, the standards to be aimed at in thought, and the general idea of a political society remained essentially unchanged. The history of Europe consists in the interplay of these principles within the changing historical and technical conditions of the different centuries.

The possibility of this interplay arises from the fact that in European, in contrast to ancient civilization, the unity of society was differentiated into a number of specialized institutions and groups: the monarchy, the aristocracy, the church, the government, the people, the academies and professions. This differentiation was the main source of the rich variety of Europe and the guarantee of some degree of liberty and continued development. The ancient civilizations had a more simple and relatively static unity; European civilization displayed a differentiated unity which, as we shall see, contained the stimulus and opportunity for the progressive maturing of the potentialities of the stock. It has long been realized that the co-existence in Europe of theocracy, monarchy, autocracy, democracy, and of varied creeds and outlooks prevented the tyranny of any one system and promoted fertile interchange. European civilization owes its supremacy to the fact that it was diversified rather than exclusive. This feature was present at the start, and has dominated its history until the twentieth century.

We have here come close to the permanent truth latent in the European tradition which it has been our aim to discover: the combination of unity with sufficient diversity to ensure the possibility of continued development. Yet this principle is indefinite. What is sufficient diversity? What conditions determine whether the possibility of further development is in fact realized? We have still to discover the essential condition which Europe satisfied during the period of its ascendancy. The criterion for the continued development of the species must be that the community tradition facilitates the development of the individual. This implies that the only permanent social principle must be one facilitating this balanced relation between individual and community. In animal communities the proper relation of the members to the group is of less importance and is adequately maintained by the conservative tendencies of heredity, instinct, and mimicry. But in man a new relation has developed between the individual and the cumulative social tradition, and society has today reached the stage when the proper form of that relation must be explicitly recognized and incorporated as part of the tradition. The proper relation of the individual to the community tradition cannot any longer be maintained without an explicit formulation which is generally accepted and becomes itself an element in the tradition.

At the commencement of the third period the increasing complexity of life destroyed the ancient unified communities and resulted, on the one hand, in a differentiation of authority between church, state, and academy, and, on the other hand, in the organization of empire, religion, and thought on a potentially universal basis. The species was insufficiently developed, and its knowledge inadequate, for a single universal synthesis of thought and authority. Thus while universalism was realized in certain respects, this was limited by the partial separation of religion, politics, and thought. Europe was favorably placed to take advantage of this situation, and we can now identify the clue to its success.

The social principle which made possible the unique achievement of Europe was this: in the European tradition the individual is conceived to be in direct relation to the universals in terms of which individual and social life are organized; every man stands in direct relation to God, to the world of ideas, and to the law and justice of the community. In the centralized ancient societies the formative tendencies of the individual were stifled under the rigid system which dominated him; the new communities which laid the foundations of Europe threw aside that tyrannical bondage. It was the

individual alone with his emotions in the desert, the isolated traveller perplexed by the contrasts of different ways of life, the philosopher contemplating nature and human life, the artist giving
permanent expression to his personal experience, who established
the new universals, and from their origin these universals retained,
at least potentially, their direct significance for every individual
brought up within the European tradition. Vested interest builds up
its hierarchies to confuse and dominate the many; the great systems of economic, political, religious, and social privilege develop
their jargon and rituals to fortify themselves and intimidate the out-
sider. But the European never wholly forgets that the great symbols of European life are not the monopoly of a privileged group,
but were created by individuals like him from their own experience. He only needs to laugh at the vast system of incantations,
and he has conquered it, for it has failed to intimidate him. He is
free to think, to pray, to interpret justice, for himself. Europe is the
name of this priceless inheritance.

The European tradition is unique in the status which is granted
to the individual through the assumption that all men are potentially equal, each and all having direct access to God, being endowed with the faculty of thought, and entitled to the appropriate
forms of justice. This was an ideal, and was not realized. But that is
not the point. The declaration of this equality of opportunity encouraged the individual. This declaration is unmistakable in Greek
thought, in Roman law, and most of all in Pauline Christianity:
"Glory, honour, and peace to every man that worketh good, to the
Jew first, and also to the Gentile: for there is no respect of persons
with God." This assurance Europe gave to all its members.

The most important consequence of this element in the tradition
was not the raising of the social status of the individual, since it
could not prejudice the hierarchy of power which exists in every
ordered society, but in its effect on the subjective confidence of the
individual in his own abilities. Nothing is more certain than that the
human individual cannot stand alone; without example the individual can never learn to stand on his own feet, either literally as
child or morally as adult; separated from the community his humanity perishes within him. But the new tradition gave the individual an assurance that was far-reaching in its effects. In earlier
communities only the fortunate could view their lives with any

feeling of security. The European system gave the individual the hope that he might discover a secure basis for his own life and so escape misery and frustration. The security in question was not primarily economic; scholar and saint did not hesitate to set out on lonely paths, since they were sure of their own way. With the illusion of a loving god, a free mind, and the promise of justice, the individual dared more than he ever could before.

This may appear a strange feat of auto-suggestion! The subjectivity of the tradition had been exploited with powerful effect. It was natural for man to believe that he had direct relation to universals which were projections of aspects of his own experience. He could scarcely help having a personal confidence in those universal ideals which had come into being precisely to satisfy his own need. Yet strangely enough he was able to derive encouragement from these projections of himself. He took courage from them as might a lonely man in a hall of mirrors gain comfort from the company around him, believing that the big battalions were with him. It was as well that the European did not know that the supporting company were mere echoes of himself, or he might mistakenly have concluded that the universals were as frail and transient as he felt himself to be.

But here the analogy fails, and we observe that a mistaken interpretation may provide the basis for a modification which can correct it. The growing sense of security had this justification: the universals were not merely expressions of the characteristics of one individual; they were more reliable than the character of any one person could be without them, because they represented part of the accumulated and tested content of the social tradition. The efficacy of the European assurance to the individual arose from the fact that the new universals, though arising from the contributions of individuals to the tradition, had become stabilized as symbols which had proved to be effective in the organization of European life. These universals were the inspiration of European character. Here is the criterion we are seeking. The permanent truth which inspired the European tradition was the principle that every individual has direct access to the dominant elements of the social tradition. (Or shall we say every man, since woman was largely excluded.) The organization of power in any community has the form of a hierarchy which tends to confine the individual to relationships with those who are his neighbors in the social pattern. But if he is to be able to make his personal contribution to the enrichment of the tradition he must also have direct knowledge of universals which can assist him to escape the tyranny of local power and habit and to develop his own characteristic form of life. Here is the ultimate truth which enables Platonism, Christianity, and democracy to aid the development of man.

The fact that Europeans were often unaware that this was the underlying principle of the civilization which they were creating tendered it no less effective. The religious inspiration of the one God and the idealist aspiration towards simple eternal truth could be shared by all in varying manner and degree. The individual sometimes dared to stand alone against tradition and tyranny because of this sense of power within him. This is the permanent gift of Europe to mankind, which no other civilization or continent has equated. It is this which justifies the respect which all the world has paid to the Europe now past. It is this too which justifies the inclusion, within this study of the development of European man, of an anticipation of the reorganized society which may inherit this principle from Europe.

Here we again reach the central theme of this study: Europe held the clue to so extensive a development, and yet it collapsed. Europe incorporated and made real this permanent truth, and yet in failing to maintain it has itself disappeared. In the West the individual has lost his foundation because there are today no universals, recognized within the tradition, of which he has direct unquestioning knowledge. The earlier convictions have disappeared, because the dissociation on which they rested has itself collapsed. The convictions were necessary and stable because they expressed and compensated the dissociation which lay deeper. This means that the history of European man can only be understood as the development and disappearance of his characteristic dissociation. This is a typical procedure in unitary thought; the universal formative process is postulated in order to emphasize and invite explanation of its distortion in particular circumstances.

We have already analyzed the origin and underlying features of the European dissociation, and in the next chapters we shall examine its intensification and final collapse. But before tracing this further historical development it will be useful to examine some of its

consequences. The fundamental division is between deliberate activity organized by static concepts and the instinctive and spontaneous life. The dissociation of two components of an organic system
results in a common distortion of both. The instinctive life lost its
innocence, its proper rhythm being replaced by obsessive desire.
On the other hand rationally controlled deliberate behavior was
partly deflected towards ideals which also obsessed the individual
with their allure of perfection and disturbed the rhythm of tension
and release. This similarity is not accidental. In splitting the organic system in a given manner, the same form of distortion appears in both dissociated components. In this case the periodicity
of whole-natured process is transformed into a dual obsession; it
matters little whether the aim is union with god or woman, the
ecstasy of the pursuit of unity or truth, of power or pleasure—the
sustained intensity and lack of satisfaction proves the European
stamp.

The European soul never truly loses itself in God; the mind never
finds ultimate truth; power is never secure; pleasure never satisfies.
Bewitched by these illusory aims which appear to promise the absolute, man is led away from the proper rhythm of the organic
processes to chase an elusive ecstasy. Morbid religiosity,
hyperintellectualism, delicate sensuality, and cold ambition are some
of the variants of the dissociated personality's attempt to escape its
own division. The oscillations from emotional mysticism to rationalism, and from rationalism to a materialism of power, which mark
the history of Europe, do not represent any essential change. They
only express the successive oscillations of the search for novel
stimulation within the limits set by the basic dissociation. Superficially they may appear as reversals of pole, but the structure of the
tradition has not changed, the strenuousness, the absence of natural rhythm, and the sense of inner conflict remain.

In those whose constructive tendencies are thwarted, the disease
may turn outward in the intolerance of the repressive moral will.
We may call this the projection of the cruelty principle, self-hate
turning itself outward upon others. But such terms leave the dualisms unresolved. The actual form of the situation is that a partial
tendency (rationally controlled deliberate behavior) has achieved
dominance, another component (spontaneous behavior) being
thereby simultaneously distorted; this act of self-distortion involves

the tendency to strain oneself, which is masochism; and this form, like every other, tends to extend itself, which implies sadism, though it may disguise itself as morality desired for others.

But beneath all these special forms lay the fundamental division between two ways of organizing behavior. Europe experienced this division more intensely than any other continent because it went further in differentiation. Though the roots of this dichotomy lay almost hidden in the organic and mental processes of the individual, Europeans could speak of little else. Their language tells the persisting story of two distorted and incompatible tendencies: heaven and earth, spirit and flesh, Apollonian and Dionysian, super-ego and ego, deliberate and spontaneous. With rare exceptions the procession of European genius maintains the dualistic chant. The best proof that the day of that Europe is over is that we can look back dispassionately at the structure of the turbulent story. The biologist and ethnologist know that there is no one "human nature," and that other civilizations have displaced other types of structure. The dissociation of the typical adult European is a consequence not of any universal human nature, a term that has no meaning, but of the influence of an inadequately organized tradition.

The condition which we have analyzed characterises the whole of the third period, in the sense that during it the tradition retained this dominant structure. For two thousand years this mode of organization was stable and effective; its influence on the lives of individuals tended to increase as the centuries passed. The results of the transformation which took place around 1000 BC matured in European society from AD 200 to 600 as the ancient world disappeared and the medieval world took its place. During the subsequent centuries until AD 1200 medieval society was relatively stationary and displayed many features of the dualistic state which has been described. But its stability was only temporary. The formative tendency, already evident in the adaptive vitality which had developed the European mind from that of ancient man, remained at work, forming new patterns of behavior and new symmetries in thought. Indeed the European dissociation, though appearing to provide a basis for stability, actually intensified the urge to further development. This paradox is characteristic of a biological adaptation which is incomplete, and while meeting certain requirements leaves others unsatisfied as sources of further modifications which must ultimately upset the apparent stability.

Until about AD 1200 the prevalent conception of man was of a passive personality guided by universal authority. The individual had to play his role as a passive component in a stable and static natural order. Change was regarded as irrational, the early Greek philosophies of process being forgotten in favor of the fixed categories of Platonism, Christianity, and the feudal order. Even the individual will which had been vigorously displayed in the Roman polity was a will normally reverent towards tradition and operating within its forms. The barbarian invasions brought in a fresh element of vigour, independence, and variety, but did not modify the dominant doctrines of the tradition. The late Middle Ages were more rational, in the sense used here, than the Age of Enlightenment, for the medieval church believed it was in possession of an adequate intellectual system enabling all important questions to be answered by pure reason.

The collapse of the medieval world cannot be ascribed to any one factor. The adaptive vitality of the species inevitably produced new differentiations to supplement its dissociated and underdeveloped state. This is seen in the gradual development of improved practical techniques of production and construction, in the interaction of cultures, the speculations of philosophers, and all the arts of peace and war. An uncertain current of thought and experiment persisted through the centuries of the Roman Empire, of the spread of Christianity and Islam, and of the Crusades. The tendency towards the greater differentiation of thought and action was in evidence throughout this period but produced little cumulative result compared with what followed later.

Yet the process was at work and about 1300 the veil which religion and scholasticism had imposed between the mind and nature began to fade. Dissociated man had put God as a bridge between himself and nature; but neither scholasticism nor his own knowledge of God could answer the new questions which occurred to him as he observed nature. Religion could not prevent him using his own eyes, though its tendency was to obstruct unprejudiced interpretation. Now, slowly, as he looked around, man's awareness of himself began to change. No longer satisfied to regard himself as a passive recipient of divine favor and doctrine, he began to discover that he could experience things in a manner personal to himself. This transformation, which was most marked in specially placed individuals but rapidly spread to others, was in some respects similar to the previous development of self-awareness of the opening of the third period, and thus was appropriately followed by the renaissance of classical culture. But in other ways it was sharply distinguished from the earlier transformation whose background was poverty and fear. At the end of the twelfth century the individual was becoming aware of his own positive faculties, and the background was now pride rather than fear. What had for many centuries been the experience only of rare individuals now became representative in the sense that it was shared by all the leading figures of the time. The urgent desire to explore, to investigate, to allow new forms of awareness and of thought to develop in oneself, was expressed in a novel form of personal initiative. Marco Polo, Roger Bacon, Petrarch, Columbus, Michelangelo, and Leonardo da Vinci express the new type of active personality. The European genius found itself.

These names introduce a new stage in the history of Europe, which for convenience we shall call the humanistic phase. Humanism, in the sense in which it dominates the development of Europe from AD 1300 to 1800, is a special form of rationalism based on the view that man, as conscious subject, is supreme; his will free, his reason autonomous, his allegiance due only to his own ideals. This attitude is a natural expression of the subjective European tradition. If the humanist view had been valid it might have provided the basis of a stable society; if the subject had in fact had direct knowledge of a personal god, humanism would not have come into conflict with Christianity. But it was based less on the Christian component of the tradition than on rationalism, and so rational humanism became the expression of the new pride of the individual, and for five centuries gained increasing influence.

The pageant of European humanism is the richest and most complex spectacle of history. It lacks the grand simplicity of the antique world, but for variety and scope of new development it is unique. Yet it was not, as many thought, a steady path of human progress. Just as the ancient world, in spite of its relatively static character, generated a movement which gave the leadership of the species to a new kind of man, so the European system with its inner dissociation intensified the process which later exposed its own inadequacy. But this exposure came about by a long deviation. The tension in the European drove him out from the medieval world on a voyage of discovery. In this adventure he was guided and intoxicated by the discovery of a method of discovery. This frenzy led him to neglect himself as subject, but the new method enabled him to explore the mechanism of nature and so to rediscover himself as object. A deep consistency marks the centuries from 1600 until today. We cannot say that all that has happened has been necessary, because that word, except in special contexts, has no meaning in unitary thought. But we can see that the main tendencies of this period are consistent with the assumption of a progressive transformation of the European tradition into a reorganized unitary form.

The obscurity of the present situation and the difficulty of identifying the continuity which underlies these centuries is due to the fact that the principle which dominated this last period, the new method of discovery, is of a form alien to that of the ultimate reorganization. Not only the positive achievements of this final period, but also its limitations and apparent confusion derive from the characteristics of this method. Yet the deeper continuity of development through which this period must be interpreted is in sharp contrast to its dominant science. The general tendency of the period is towards the recognition of the unitary process, but its science is quantitative.

6

Europe after 1600

We now enter the fourth period, the period of Western man. This covers the last three and a half centuries and represents a transitional stage between the European tradition and a reorganized tradition whose appearance will bring it to a close. It is the age of quantitative technique. The continued differentiation of knowledge and of social organization renders the universal ideals ineffective and leaves man without adequate organizing convictions. The individual enjoys neither pagan innocence nor naive religious faith. Religion no longer suffices to stabilize the inner dissociation and the individual develops intense personal ambitions. The old order is no longer accepted, personality becomes active, and the individual sets out to explore and dominate nature. In the age of magic man sought to control nature through ritual; in the age of monotheism he could dispense with this control by relying on the mediation of a personal god; in the age of quantity man exerts his own will and seeks to control nature himself.

During these centuries Europe still led the race, from its surplus vitality scattering pioneers to the new lands of the West. The inheritors of the tradition, confident of the future, multiplied more rapidly than any human sub-species ever had before, until in the old and the new lands they formed one third of mankind. But their influence far surpassed their numbers. The active personality of Western man, expressing itself through the new techniques, ensured his dominance over all other peoples, and every major development during this period sprang from the European tradition. This is particularly evident towards its close. Washington and Lincoln were Europeans in this sense; Japan set out to copy Western technique; Lenin followed Marx, and Stalin is the expression of

Western purposefulness in an Asiatic setting; Gandhi, though repudiating Western force, calls his life an experiment with truth; Chiang Kai-shek, in seeking to preserve his country from the methods of its neighbors, relies on the guidance of a Wesleyan conscience. The world is united in its struggle to assimilate what it has inherited from Europe.

This period has not yet been molded into a clear pattern by the perspective of time. Yet the task of interpretation is easier today than it was even thirty years ago. Since 1914 Europe has become increasingly aware of the processes of change. The crisis which was foreseen during the last century by a few lonely thinkers has now scarred every continent. A double world war has spent its passion upon the old traditions. Throughout the main land-bloc of the European continent there has been a break with the past which cannot be reversed, and continuity is only preserved in a few outposts. If many still regret the old order, that is because they lack ideas appropriate to the time. But the special prejudices which marked this period have been lost, and for that reason we can now look back with greater comprehension on its achievements and its failures.

The life of Europe during these centuries was so rich that no one mind can embrace its detailed variety. The recorded story of the lives of individual Europeans is the inexhaustible monument to the period. But the records offer only sample case-histories from the whole. No one can ever know the scope and intensity of all the individual lives that made up the pattern of this late Europe. Never before had so many individuals developed to such a degree a personal quality in their lives; never had society owed so much to so many.

This flowering of European humanism was superb, and it was entirely new. The magnificence of humanism is not lessened because these centuries failed to realize its ideals. As man develops, his capacity to experience joy and suffering both increase; the sense of frustration and of aspiration are responses to one situation, and must therefore grow in parallel. The waste of individual endeavour in this Europe was beyond measure; the normal lot was poverty, disease, and distortion, Yet though the tyranny of circumstance thwarted most individual lives, greater numbers of men and women than ever before received and accepted the assurance of the tradition that there was more to life than frustration. It was a time, in the main, of economic advance, of expansion, and hope. Until late in the nineteenth century most found encouragement in their expectation of material and moral progress, and rejoiced in large families. They accepted this encouragement because it assisted them to develop, even when these hopes remained unfilled. So within the varied political systems of Europe and the West there developed a vast community of individuals, each seeking to be himself, and also, in so far as he himself was not distorted, to assist others to be themselves. In the final balance of development and frustration the result was a biological and human credit: Europe was in fact developing along the course set by its inheritance and its environment.

This inheritance lacked an adequate principle of integration, yet the course taken by Europe was proper to it and was leading towards a transformation that would ultimately repair the temporary maladjustment. It was not surprising, therefore, that there grew up in this late Europe, headed though it was for disasters that would undermine its own ideals, the sense that behind the sordid frustration of man by man, behind the misery of poverty and disease, there was not far away the opportunity of a rich and free life. Hope was indeed justified, but, since the forms of the future can never be known until they have been formed in individual minds, not the hope that most experienced. Continuing moral progress is a European illusion, doubly irrelevant to the transformation whose approach was beginning to be felt. The processes of history are rhythmic, not steady, and their transformations express the formative vitality of the species and cannot be ascribed to moral ideals any more than to animal instinct.

This misinterpretation of the trend of European and Western civilization expressed a human and not merely a humanist failing. If an individual wants anything badly enough, life usually brings it, but in an unexpected form. The aim may be achieved, but the setting will be different, the subject himself has changed, and the intensity of yearning have given place to the austerity of action. The emotion was a promise of the possibility of a process of development, and this process itself, not its apparent aim, is its justification, for achievement brings with it new tensions and new opportunities. The situation of European and Western civilization was similar. The dissociation produced the intensity of idealist faith and of individual endeavor. This faith and this endeavour promised the further development of man, but it could not then be realized that this development would eliminate the sources of such idealism. It was not surprising that liberal Europe, enchanted by its new ideals, expected too much of political democracy, nor that Europe later rejected this treacherous enchantment for what seemed to be the greater realism of class and racial doctrines.

Human communities are too complex for their condition at any moment to be described in terms of a single spirit of the time. At each stage the social system contains elements characteristic of the dominant forms of past, present, and future. Effete remnants coexist beside dominant forms and forms still in process of development. No interpretation can be adequate which neglects this telescoping of history in each moment of time. Yet the dominant elements, though often far from obvious, are the most important in the sense that they determine the normal processes of the social system. These dominant elements are the elements involved in the organization of power. Though the health of a community, i.e., the existence of an effective social order, depends on the tempering of compulsion within widely accepted traditions and aims, yet the right to interpret and apply these traditions is always distributed in a hierarchy of individuals within the community. This hierarchy is normally determined according to a particular group of functions: family, religious, political, economic, or technical. In the religious age, the religious hierarchy wields power; in the political age, the ruler, nobles, and commoners; in the economic the hierarchy of wealth. The development of Europe during the last six centuries has consisted in the progressive shifting of the hierarchy of power from one set of functions to another.

The existence of the hierarchy of power has been largely neglected by humanistic thinkers because it does not conform to their ideal of man. But an ordered society can admit the equality of all men only in fields other than those which determine the hierarchy of power at any particular time. The establishment of religious equality was only possible at the Reformation because political power had displaced religious power and the various sections of the community had accepted their places in the new political hierarchy. Similarly political equality could be realized during the nineteenth century in communities where financial and economic elements already effectively determined the hierarchy of power. The over-throwing of an old social system from within is possible only by those who can call to their aid a new principle for the organization of power. Humanitarian socialism failed to achieve power because it offered no alternative to the economic hierarchy, and totalitarian national socialism succeeded, temporarily, because it transferred power to the hierarchy of technicians of total war.

This interpretation of the development of society follows directly from the methods of unitary thought, and is more comprehensive than either the idealistic or the materialistic methods of approach. In unitary thought the unity of every complex system resides in a system of relations of dominance whereby each element facilitates, and to that extent controls, the operations of the elements subordinate to it. This is as true for a group of organisms such as a human community, as it is for any particular organism. The unity of society depends on the existence of a hierarchical order which gives each section its special status and function within the whole, and this order may be effective even when it is not recognized. But now, after two centuries of individualism, it is necessary to recognize it, and those who today deny the existence of this hierarchy in every ordered society reveal their ignorance or prejudice. The asymmetrical relation of dominant to subordinate elements is the source of all order in nature and in society. Only snobs can regard so universal a fact as damaging to the dignity of man, just as only the stupid can fail to recognize that at certain moments in the history of a community an old system of dominance must be replaced by a new, if the development of society is to continue.

This hierarchical pattern of dominance relations pervades the whole of society and is the source of what is called power. The history of Europe provides no evidence of religious, moral, or political progress, in any absolute sense. But it does reveal the successive shifting of the hierarchy of power so that the individual can exercise, in accordance with his own nature, more and more of his capacities. The sixteenth century saw the hierarchy of power shift from religious to political elements, and in the early nineteenth this was followed by a shift from political to economic elements. A similar sequence may be found in the history of other civilizations, but these earlier rhythms found their full expression only in the development of Europe.

After each of these steps the European individual enjoyed a new realm of liberty in which he could choose his own way of life without threatening the established social order. In this sense the growth of liberty in the history of Europe is an objective fact. But the idealist who interprets this as the progressive realization of subjective freedom goes as far astray, through his neglect both of the organic background of the personal life and of the persisting hierarchy of power, as the materialist who considers that personal incentive and social power are always economic. These two errors arise from the same source, the original European idealism which seeks to compensate an inner dissociation by clinging to an absolute idea, whether it is the economic process leading to the classless society in which conflict is resolved, or the human spirit realizing its freedom. The paradox of freedom, that men will appear to die willingly for what few can endure, does not arise from some perversity in human nature, but expresses the inadequacy of a dualistic language which separates subjective desires from the history and circumstances of the individual. Men desire the opportunity to develop, but they are also gregarious and require to be guided at all but rare moments. Mimicry must predominate for development to be possible. But the positive aspect of one period of the development of Europe lay in the progressive achievement of a certain degree of religious, political and economic equality, and in the consequent maturing of human faculties.

This preliminary analysis provides the outline within which we can now trace the main social tendencies which marked this period. Our aim is a unitary image of a continuous transformation which, though complex, reveals one dominant form. But this picture must be built up by stages through the consideration in turn of the various component processes which can be identified in the history of these centuries. These component tendencies have no ultimate independence; they are merely aspects of one coherent process. Yet they can be identified for independent study and their different phasing can be noted. One aspect may be already mature at a time when another is only beginning to develop, and the sequence of these overlapping processes corresponds to the pattern of past, present, and future elements which coexist in the community at every stage.

The earliest of these components is the further development and maturing of the humanistic component of the tradition. The

next, and the most important, is the development of the quantitative method in scientific theory and practice, in technology and
industry, in individual and state capitalism, and in warfare. This
process dominates the explicit features of the period but does not
alone provide an adequate basis for its interpretation. A later component is the decline of the tradition and the reaction from humanism which, appearing first about 1850, expressed the despair of the
subject in the power of the human mind. This may be regarded as
the continuation of the first component, but it is not possible to
treat the development and the decline of humanism as one complete
process in isolation from the other factors which influenced its later
stages. Finally, towards the end of the period, we find the development of a new objectivity, in which the subjective emphasis of European humanism gives place to an approach guided by observation
and scientific method. We shall find that these component processes
can only be fully understood as aspects of a general transformation
of the tradition, in which the breakdown of the traditional subjective
integration is complemented by the progressive loosening and ultimate disappearance of the European dissociation.

Many of the special features of our time arise from the fact that
the dissociation of European man has exhausted its efficacy, and
that the earlier unity of primitive and ancient man is in process of
restoration in a form which can, in principle, retain and organize
all the differentiated development of Europe and the West. The last
three and a half centuries display all the complementary processes
which must play a part in any such radical reorganization of the
tradition. The trend of these centuries has been obscure because
contemporary events could not be interpreted as evidences of a
progressive re-integration until the European dissociation had broken down sufficiently to permit it to be identified. In this process
the anarchic exploitation of the quantitative method played the role
of Mephistopheles in loosening traditional structures and so facilitating the growth of the new. The quantitative method was the final
and most uncompromising product of dissociated thought; it symbolizes to the point of parody the specializing tendency of the European mind and its lack of integration.

When any organism, in the course of adaptation to new conditions, after a series of random responses to its environment finally
develops the first elements of a new tissue or organ that is well

adapted to produce an effective response, then the exercise of that new organ steadily reinforces it and its further development proceeds steadily, trial and error being replaced by cumulative improvement. The new tissue or organ grows by use. This process is an example of the self-development of formative processes which was discussed in a previous chapter. The development of a structure which facilitates the dominant tendency of any system is itself facilitated, and the structure grows in parallel with its successful use. The essence of this situation is that the development of useful structures is regularly facilitated, while structures which distort the organism are themselves distorted and tend not to develop further, but to disappear. This self-developing property of the formative process means that ineffective responses are less likely to be repeated, while the repetition of effective responses is facilitated, so that further development becomes systematic, in the sense of continuing the operation of a method which has proved its efficacy.

This property is exemplified in the discovery of the quantitative method. The main trend of human development is in the direction of the increasing differentiation of thought and behavior and of the resulting heightened dominance of man over his environment. This tendency towards further differentiation in thought had been at work for countless centuries before the opening of the fourth period, and had been intensified by the inner dissociation and active personality of the European. Yet no special kind of thought had achieved particularly effective results, except in so far as static concepts had, by a process of trial and error, gradually become clearer and more specialized. The development of thought is a process of adaptation to the environment, in which the structure of thought is developed so as to conform better to the structure of the environment, thus giving man control over it. This process of adaptation had proceeded more or less at random until 1600. Prior to the time of Kepler and Galileo the only developed systems of thought had been religious or philosophic organizations of subjective experience, while such objective observations of nature as had been collected had remained relatively unorganized. Medieval rationalism was subjective; there was as yet no rational philosophy of nature of comparable complexity or precision. For two thousand years man had been observing, comparing, and seeking to classify his observations, but as yet there was no system of thought concerning nature which provided any method which might be systematically used for facilitating the process of discovery and for the further improvement of thought. Discovery was still a matter of sudden *apercu;* the process of research guided by a continuingly successful method had not yet begun.

We have here reached a moment of great significance. About 1600 Kepler and Galileo simultaneously and independently formulated the principle that the laws of nature are to be discovered by measurement, and applied this principle in their own work. Where Aristotle had classified, Kepler and Galileo sought to measure. This bald statement defines an event, but conceals its significance. There is no better way to bring out its implications than to describe it from the several points of view. The discovery of the quantitative method is an important moment in the history of the species because it involved a new adjustment at many different levels in the hierarchy of the human system. We will start at the most general and pass to the more specific descriptions of this event.

The unitary thinker recognizes in this discovery the establishment by the formative process in man of a new class of symbolic structures (quantitative concepts) capable of progressively facilitating the conforming of thought to the rest of nature. The biologist interprets the discovery in his somewhat narrower terms: the adaptive vitality of the species established a method of facilitating the progressive improvement of specialized responses and hence the extension of man's dominance over his environment. When we pass from objective to subjective descriptions the all-important characteristic which we have hitherto described as progressive (in the sense of cumulative) is more easily recognized under the term systematic—but it remains the same characteristic. The social historian notes that the truth-seeking tendency in man led him about 1600 to the discovery of the first systematic method for improving the collection and organization of facts.

Kepler's biographer might accept all these interpretations, but his own formulation is the richest of all, for in unitary thought the most specific has the greatest content. Kepler exemplified all these general processes in the special pattern of his individual temperament. Though Galileo may have made a greater contribution to scientific method, Kepler provides the better example for our present purpose. Kepler's desire to reveal a single divine harmony within the processes of nature led his Pythgorean temperament to the discovery of the numerical laws of planetary motion; these were to him one example of the universal expression of the divine in the quantitative order of nature.

All the facets of this unique moment have a peculiar fascination for the twentieth-century mind. It might be thought that this is due to the fact that we can now appreciate the moment when the principle which has created our age first received explicit formulation. But the importance of 1600 for contemporary man lies deeper than that. If the unitary interpretation is valid that moment will soon be repeated, but in a new manner. We are fascinated with the significance of that first discovery because we already suspect that a second such discovery, complementary to but transcending the first, is now due. What the species has achieved once it can repeat in a more comprehensive form. We look back on Galileo and Kepler and see that the failure of the modem world arises from the limitations of their thought, as its hopes lie in the fact that such positive discovery is possible.

Discovery is the essence of social development and a method of discovery its only possible guarantee. This fact is so far-reaching that it requires a distinguishing epithet. The word "heuristic," from the Greek "heurisko," to find, will be used to mean "promoting discovery." 1600 is the date of the first general heuristic principle, the principle that quantity is the clue to the structure of nature; in the next chapter I shall bring evidence that its scope is nearly exhausted. The special importance of Galileo and Kepler for this study is that the second heuristic method must salute and challenge the first.

Kepler's personality and thought will be considered later in greater detail; here I only give the discovery its historical setting. Certain conditions were necessary before the quantitative method could be established. The main external condition was the availability of a sufficient body of appropriate facts. This was satisfied; the development of technology had made possible observations such as Tycho Brahe's of the planetary motions. The main personal condition was the combination of a sufficiently active independent personality with the special personal tendencies which would facilitate the discovery of general laws. By the sixteenth century the medieval veil between man and nature had fallen: the individual was setting out to express himself through all his faculties. Thus both these conditions were satisfied towards the end of that century and awaiting the appearance of a suitably placed individual with the tendencies which might lead to general discoveries. These are the tendency to retain a true record of environmental stimuli and the tendency to form one comprehensive pattern from this record. These two tendencies express components of the biological constitution of man; they are better known as the love of truth and of unity. Kepler displayed these two passions in high degree. All the conditions were satisfied—and the first heuristic method was discovered. The same process took place simultaneously in Galileo, though in him it received a different emphasis.

Kepler and Galileo not only successfully applied in their own researches the principle that the laws of nature are to be discovered by measurement, but also gave clear expression to it. The process of measurement was the one objectively reliable approach to the structure of nature and the numbers so obtained were the key to the order of nature. After 1600 mankind was thus in possession of a systematic method of research into those aspects of nature which were accessible to measurement. By measuring with steadily increasing accuracy and sifting out the quantitative laws which covered the measurements, man could progressively improve not only the scope of his knowledge of detailed facts but also its organization under simple rules. The new heuristic method guaranteed the progressive adaptation of mental processes, i.e., their increasing conformity to the structure of nature, so long as measurements could be made more accurate or new fields still remained where the method could be applied. What had happened was not the discovery of a law, or of a set of laws, but of a method for progressive discovery, an assurance of man's increasing dominance over the quantitative aspects of his environment.

The centuries since 1600 may well be regarded as the age of quantity. Never before had such a technique been available; it was not surprising that European man was fascinated by it and that his thought and behavior were increasingly dominated by quantity. Number and quantity had been used ever since the ancient civilizations; the balance had been the Egyptian symbol of justice and a feather the symbol of truth but now it appeared certain that quantity provided the sole clue to the understanding and control of nature. The result may he described equally in objective and subjective language: the further development of this successful adaptation was facilitated and accelerated, and increasingly monopolized the adaptive vitality of the community; man was fascinated by the exercise of this new tool, and the obsession blinded him to other aspects of his situation.

The story of the exploitation of the new method is well known. In exact science Galileo's first principles of mechanics have led to twentieth century quantum mechanics, which permits the inclusion within one moderately well-ordered system of all the aspects of nature which can be covered by current quantitative methods. In applied science the mechanical revolution has led to the present phase of total technology, in which the practical application of number is exploited to its limits. The mechanical led to the industrial revolution, and so to the extension of private and state capitalism, the raising of the standards and the length of life, the rapid increase in European population, the extended influence of the masses, and to totalitarian methods in peace and war.

All these developments, and many others of the period, mirror the characteristics of the quantitative method in its primitive, radical form. The symbols of number and quantity are appropriate to the enumeration, analysis, standardization, and accumulation of magnitude, and they tend to neglect, order, development, structure, and quality. The centimetre, the second, the gram, the horsepower, the vote, the £, the Limited Company—these quantity or number symbols were effective instruments precisely because they encouraged man to go ahead without considering the methods by which they were obtained or the results they would produce. This is the main characteristic of the fourth period: increasing obsession with number, and repudiation of those who pointed out that such numbers were symbols representing particular human operations from which alone they derived their meaning.

Today we can look back dispassionately at both the constructive and the anarchic aspects of the quantitative principle. On the one hand we have to record a vast body of achievement: differentiation of knowledge, increase in security and health, the approach of plenty, the continued development of society. Moreover, beneath these well-known achievements lies the establishment of a new type of socially recognized authority. Hitherto all forms of social authority had been static, in that each represented a stabilization of accepted doctrines, and new forms of authority could only become effective after an open struggle with orthodoxy. But the discovery of the first heuristic principle resulted in the development of a corresponding social institution: an authority, the orthodoxy of quantitative science, which was not only capable of steadily developing its doctrines, but was formed for this express purpose. This was novel: an orthodoxy which could modify its pronouncements not merely without loss but with increase of its prestige.

This differentiation within the system of social authority of a self-developing orthodoxy of science was a characteristically European institution. Yet any cultural institution which was intrinsically progressive challenged the static forms of authority. Two types of authority presenting so fundamental a contrast to one another could not permanently co-exist. The result was that static or passive governments tended to disappear; only active governments could understand and use the new techniques to the full. The application of quantitative science thus reached its climax in totalitarian state action, whether occupied in developing and defending the collective community, as in Russia, or in aggression, as in Germany.

Beside the positive results of quantitative technique we can trace in these centuries the consequences of its limitations: its neglect of other aspects of nature, and its anarchic tendency. Because it was the only known heuristic method, the quantity principle was believed to be the only possible method. Because nature had given her sanction to the method, the structure of nature was thought to be wholly quantitative. Aspects which were inaccessible to measurement were treated as beyond the scope of positive science. The consequent damage went far beyond the academies and workshops. All thought and action suffered from the general belief that the quantitative aspect was the determining factor in every phenomenon. The quantity principle was not an isolated thought-form in professional brains; it was the instrument through which social power was actually developed.

There is here a paradox. The first great systematic method for achieving the progressive differentiation of thought was essentially anarchic. Thought and society disintegrated under its influence. Quantity, for all its efficacy as an instrument of research, contains no general principle of form, of order, or of organization. All magnitudes have equal status before the laws of elementary arithmetic, whose operators recognize no distinction between one value and another. Similarly in its social application the quantity concept sets no limit to the pursuit of wealth, the manipulation of the symbols of the markets, or the desire for expansion in any field. Elementary quantity symbols fail to relate magnitudes to the actual or potential order in any system. The explanation of the paradox that a method could be at once so constructive and destructive is that it was a method for the differentiation of thought, i.e., for specialization and analysis, not for integration or organization. It could thus only be effective temporarily, within the general order of the earlier tradition. The further it invaded the tradition, the less effective became the organizing principles of the previous period. The quantitative method set in motion countless anarchic processes of expansion which, like the processes of a virulent cancer, bore no relation to the general order.

For a moment let us forget the historical structure of these centuries and view the period in its biological perspective. The period opened with the development of a new organ, or more accurately of a new method of developing thought and behavior, the principle of quantity. This set in motion an accelerating process of the differentiation of quantitative concepts and of specialized modes of behavior, which were found effective in dominating the environment. The attention of the community was increasingly drawn to this new technique of developing characteristic human forms, but as this continued the technique used in this process of differentiation began itself to dominate the process. Thus gradually the method escaped the control of the human organizing process and became autonomous. The method ceased to be a technique for developing biologically effective forms of differentiation and became the instrument of every anarchic or perverted human tendency. The general tendency for civilizations to pass through a phase which over-emphasized the economic and technical aspects of social life had often been displayed before; this time the emphasis on quantity was of a different order because the method was now being systematically exploited as a method of progressive discovery.

It may appear strange that a community of organisms can pass into an unstable state of accelerating change leading towards disaster without some regulating or compensating process being brought into play. In the animal body fever is the sign of the operation of the regulating processes set in motion to overcome certain forms of unbalance. But society lacks any such normal condition of balance to which it always tends to return; it is, for the time being at any rate, launched on a path of continuing development. Social fever must lead to a new balance, if any, since the old equilibrium cannot be restored. The accelerating rush might have been fatal and the new organ permanently incapable of adaptation to the human system as a component of a general human order. The mad pursuit of quantity might have remained autocatalytic, hypnotic, and lethal.

Some voices were raised in protest. A few thinkers asserted that quantity was not the only avenue to reliable truth; here and there a religious or philosophic thinker warned Europe of the dangers of the road from mechanical science through mechanical industry to the mechanization of human life. But their voices lacked authority, because they lacked certainty of their own rightness. It was not possible to assert with conviction that the achievements of science must be repudiated; only perverted minds could reject the possibility of overcoming poverty and disease. The time had not yet come to subdue the new method, for man was not yet biologically ripe for the readjustment which would then be necessary.

But what was the effect in the meantime of the quantitative method on the basis of the European tradition, and in particular on the development of the humanistic phase? The first influence of the new method on the structure of European thought was to intensify its dualisms, and in his thought to separate man even further from nature. To a divinely drunk spirit such as Kepler, number and the human soul were twin manifestations of the perfection of the Creator. But Europe could not sustain his ecstasy. God was the personification of man's need for a principle of order or organization, number an instrument of analysis, and this contrast led to the separation of the two forms of search: for subjective harmony in God, and for objective harmony in measured number. Kepler's rare synthesis fell apart, and European thought split into two independent realms. In the one there were all the vague, but emotionally powerful, subjective conceptions that expressed man's dissociated being: good and evil, heaven and hell, love and hate, God and man; in the other, across a metaphysical abyss, there grew up the equally

powerful world of quantity: energy and inertia, gravitation and electricity, physical forces and statistical laws—all concepts of number
or quantity, tending to become increasingly precise and ever further distant from the subjective realm. After Kepler no direct connection could exist between these worlds; physical quantity and
the divine soul of man cannot simultaneously be regarded as absolute.

The effect of the discovery of the principle of quantity, through
its influence on thought and practice, was thus at first to reinforce
the European tradition in its separation of the subject from external
nature. Nature became a closed system under quantitative law, the
human mind or soul an independent principle known without the
aid of the senses. Descartes left no doubt about it: matter was extended substance; mind, thinking substance; and this dualism represented the unfathomable act of God. If the human realm of instinct,
will, and thought was ever to become one with the realm of extension and quantity it could only be after another discovery transcending that of 1600. The divorce of mechanical power and
emotional power can only be overcome by a new overriding principle which reveals that they both derive from a single source.

The intensification of the European dualism of subject and nature by the quantitative method was no arbitrary influence coming
from outside the tradition. It was merely one step, though an important one, in the working out of the tendencies inherent in the
tradition. As we have already seen, the search for precise static
ideas reached its final and most radical expression in the concept
of physical quantity. Here at last the analytical intellect, demand-
ing static precision at any cost, even at the price of its own blind-
ness to the cost, gloried in its triumph over nature. There is in this
respect no break from Pythagoras and Plato to Descartes, Newton,
and the nineteenth century. The tradition is working out the consequences of its original impetus.

What is less obvious is that the tradition also set in motion contrary processes which ultimately lead to its own decay. In unitary
thought the modes appropriate to one stage of development always lead to their own suppression, since when they have played
their part and one period is mature, another period opens in which
other modes become appropriate. Thus in any developmental process temporary forms always work so as to bring about their own

decay, though it is not always possible to distinguish in advance what is passing and what permanent in any contemporary process.

We have seen that the conception of God stimulated the changes which led to its being challenged. Similarly humanism facilitated the realization that the individual is not self-sufficient. This does not mean that centuries of humanism sapped the strength of the individual, though it may seem so, but that they developed the individual to the point of recognizing limitations of personality which had always existed but had previously been neglected. This dialectic of transformation has many subtle aspects. Man was fascinated by quantity, but quantity was not directly related to the organizing factors in the individual. Hence the mechanical age, though it demonstrated the power of the human mind as never before, nevertheless brought about a decline of belief in human nature. The exploitation of quantity did not destroy the earlier tradition by direct attack, but it altered the social environment and the balance in the activities of the individual so as to render the tradition effete.

But this only became evident late in the period. The discovery of the first heuristic principle was followed in the seventeenth century by the flowering of humanism in a great array of individual genius. Galileo, Kepler, Rembrandt, Spinoza, Newton, and Voltaire symbolize the advancing maturity of humanism: the individual as active subject rejoicing in the new vision. The individual challenges authority, and empiricism challenges medieval rationalism. If we compare these names with some of those at the opening of the humanistic phase, Marco Polo, Roger Bacon, Petrarch, Columbus, Michelangelo, Leonardo da Vinci, we see that there has been a change in the dominant quality: richness has become precision, and adventure has become less whole-natured and more intellectual, Rembrandt presenting a contrast to the main tendency. By the eighteenth century this movement has passed from the phase of individual inspiration to the theory of intellectual idealism and the mass philosophies of liberalism and nationalism. But during these centuries technique was still primitive, and it was not until the opening of the nineteenth century that it began to prejudice the effectiveness of the European tradition as the basis of community life.

The development of industrialism introduced a new element into the processes of society. All the aspects of industrialism were direct expressions of the quantitative method. As a research technique the method stimulated mechanical discovery; as a method for facilitating man's dominance over nature the method made possible the raising of the standard of life; as the channel of a multiplying and expansive tendency out of the control of the organizing processes of the human personality the method offered an unrestricted opportunity for personal greed, ambition, and aggression. In earlier civilizations the desire for profit and power had never been inflamed by the connivance of a systematic method of expansion.

By the middle of the century this process was gaining momentum, and steadily sapping the vitality of Europe's traditional institutions. Hitherto the instinctive tendencies had been molded into the pattern of European social life by a great system of traditions and ideals, religious, rational, and patriotic, but now society was being transformed by an incentive that bore no relation to the social order. The fierce lust to multiply and expand, whether in power, wealth, territory, or family, knew no restraint. The European dissociation of spontaneity and deliberation remained, but the new technical principles which were beginning to dominate behavior, unlike the great ideals of Europe's past, played no part in maintaining the organization of society. Europe had silently deserted the ideals which had maintained its dissociated state. During the nineteenth century only a few isolated thinkers realized that this must eventually result in an outbreak of the dissociated, and therefore distorted, instinctive tendencies. Europe and the West were on the way to an unholy marriage of distorted instinct and mechanical technique.

It is no figure of speech to regard the quantity method as having got out of control. The organizing processes of a healthy organism, ensure that its behavior is such as to facilitate its own development. The fact that man has been able to civilize himself shows that some such self-regulating development has in the main dominated the history of the species. Local civilizations have displayed cycles imposed on this general trend, but so far neither the species as a whole, nor any important sub-group, has ever shown any persisting tendency to develop along a path which threatened its health as gravely as the world is threatened today through the spread of Western techniques. There has been no cumulative masochistic tendency leading to failure to survive, no universal suicide, no mad development of behavior patterns unrelated to organic needs.

The main forms of human behavior can be regarded as expressing developments of tendencies which form part of man's instinc-

tive and animal nature, and bear some relation to the primitive animal harmony and balance. The European dissociation was a radical departure from the animal harmony, but it provided a system of
partial control. Even war has been limited by unwritten conven-
tions which saved the fabric of community life. The discovery of a
heuristic method set going for the first time in history a cumulative
process which absorbed the vital energies of man and yet was not
subject to any central co-ordinating control. It was as though in the
hierarchy of the human system tendencies and energies flowed
into the development of the new technique and in doing so escaped the dominance of the central organizing processes, just as at
a lower level the proliferating cells of cancerous tissue may escape
the dominance of the formative processes which mold and maintain the individual organs.

During the nineteenth century the new technique was definitely
out of control; it was producing results which no one had desired
or planned and yet were not expressions of instinctive or traditional tendencies. No one willed the social consequences of the
industrial revolution. They were as far-reaching as some vast climatic or planetary disaster, yet they were the consequence not of
arbitrary circumstance but of human action. The activities of countless individuals were producing results which apparently could not
be controlled by any individual or group. A relentless transformation was proceeding of its own accord far beyond the range of
deliberate intention, for man was not aware that he was intoxicated
by quantity. The essential feature of *laissez faire* was the assumption that the automatic operation of the quantity symbols, through
the actions of individuals organizing their behavior by means of
them, would lead to the satisfaction of human needs. Thus, in a
time of general expansion, the new resources of manpower, horsepower, and money power were dominated by private manipulation
of the quantity symbols.

This is no allegory but a situation characteristic of the organization of behavior in organic communities using verbal and alge-
braic symbols, that is, in every human community at the appropriate
stage. A man could sit at a desk in a perverted condition of sustained ecstasy, dream of numerical manipulations, and finally write
a check or a cable. Driven by his lust for expansion, by the relentless passion for quantity which is more general than power, or
wealth, or sex, and gives man the illusion of possessing all of these;

without the catharsis of rhythmic relaxation or satisfying achievement, and therefore perpetually lusting for more; haunted by his
own frustrated life and blind to the lives distorted by his money
apparatus, he commanded the lives of countless men and women.
Another nought on an order, and the world wide machinery of credit
operated without scrutiny of purpose or result, and thousands more
were able to live or compelled to die, to work more or less, to
experience once again the instability of their employment. Every
check written in this blind passion was a forgery of right, every
company registered a conspiracy of theft, every dividend declared
the further reproduction of greed.

The world has had opportunity of late to learn that strange allies
collect when great issues are at stake. When ignorance and privilege struggle against vision and development, then all the vested
interests are found together, however incompatible may seem their
overt aims. That is obvious enough in the political field. But when
the issue is that of abstract thought, systematic, static, and divorced
from life, against the unitary organization of thought as one of the
processes that make up the human community, the alliances are
stranger still and largely unaware of their mutual co-operation.

The great capitalists and industrialists of the nineteenth century,
in so far as they pursued the technique of expansion without
scruple, were supported by the mathematical physicists who neglected the asymmetry of process and acclaimed elementary numbers as the sole key to the structure of nature. While science
maintained the separation of abstract number from real process, it
was scarcely surprising that vested interest would also succeed in
maintaining the bluff that the esoteric truths of finance must operate without consideration of the concrete processes of social life.
These deeper correlations are unmistakable if approached at their
own level, and in the next chapter we shall see that the two partners
of this particular alliance gave up the game at the same moment, as
is appropriate, since their activities expressed a common prejudice. Yet it is misleading to ascribe any degree of conscious intent
to such innocent instruments of the historical process; the capitalist
and the quantitative scientist were working out the final consequences of tendencies that had begun with Plato and Archimedes,
borne fruit in Kepler and Galileo, and were reaching their culmination in Carnegie, Ford, and Zaharoff, and—as we shall see—in

Heisenberg. Yes, it would be unfair, and perhaps libellous, to accuse recent leaders of the West of a mature consciousness of their own historical significance.

The reckless development of industrialism did not go without challenge. The decay of humanism and the nihilism of the new outlook were evident to many throughout the nineteenth century. Behind the trumpeting of progress, which became more strident as the doom of European civilization approached and reassurance was needed, many warning voices were raised. Some were even listened to with tolerance as a pleasantly astringent contrast to the general optimism.

For each of the few who can be cited here, there must have been many other contemporaries who were losing the humanistic faith in the efficacy of rational idealism and in the power of the enlightened mind to control human fate. Schopenhauer, Marx, Dostoevsky, Nietzsche, and many others understood much of what was in store for Europe and the West. Uncontrolled industrialism and an excess of analytical thought were leading man to disaster; redemption might come from the renunciation of the will to power, from the inevitable pressure of the economic needs of the people, from a universal religious vision, or from aristocratic leadership, but not, according to these, through the free operation of the individual mind. Rational thought was a mere iridescence on the surging of the will to power, the historical-economic process, the divine purpose, or the vital impulse of man. These thinkers were at one in their repudiation of the assumptions of subjective humanism; the aims of humanism might be harmless enough, though that was itself doubtful, but man was clearly impotent to realize them. More comprehensive processes than those of the conscious mind control human destiny.

Such was the development of the quantity technique and its effect on the progress and decline of humanism. Throughout these aspects of the general transformation there can be traced one main positive component: the continuing achievements of theoretical and applied science in extending knowledge and gradually liberating man from poverty and disease. But this process of the differentiation of knowledge and behavior was uncontrolled and unstable, and if it had been the only constructive tendency, which marked these centuries, the disorganization and despair would have been greater than they were.

Through the whole of this period another tendency was at work which, because later in development than these others, is of even greater importance for the interpretation of the twentieth century. We saw that as medievalism faded and humanism took root the inhibitions which obscured man's view of nature began to fade. Man, as subject, looked out on nature with less prejudiced vision. To Kepler it was enough that God linked man and nature; to Bruno, his contemporary, it was not. For him, as for many thinkers, from Aristotle and Lucretius to Darwin, Marx, and Freud, the integrity of thought required that man must be understood as a part of nature.

This demand had little influence on the general tradition of European thought until the active personality of the humanist period began to draw the obvious conclusions from the many similarities between men and animals. The discovery of "universal laws of nature" gave prestige to the conception of one all-embracing natural order, the religious inhibitions grew still weaker, and an objective conception of man as part of the animal kingdom began to develop, and even his thought to be regarded as a process in conformity with the general order of nature. In Bruno, Spinoza, and Goethe we see this attitude developing through the forms appropriate to the sixteenth, seventeenth, and eighteenth centuries, or rather, to the genius of those centuries, which in this respect was many generations ahead of its time. Each of these men repudiated the European dualism: Bruno in a confused search for unity, Spinoza in a systematic demonstration of a kind more appropriate to static geometry than to his theme of God, nature, and man, and Goethe in an attitude to life expressed in poetry and philosophic *aperçu*. In Goethe the dualism of the thinking and feeling subject confronted by objective nature is finally rejected and a conscious attempt is made to fuse subjective experience with objective knowledge of man in intuitive formulations which are at once personal and biological.

One of the most profound, and for us certainly one of the most important consequences of quantitative science, because not yet exhausted, was the stimulus which it gave to this tendency to view man and society objectively. In the long run this stimulus outweighed the intensification of the European dualism. The fact that the science of quantity could not provide symbols or concepts appropriate to biological and human organization did not lessen this stimulus to objectivity, but it had the result that the objective picture of man which could be developed at the time lacked any principle of integration or form. Man was therefore regarded as a "machine," a term which begged all the crucial questions. A machine was a thing constructed of component parts, each part being a static independent entity, and the relations between the parts being those of changing spatial arrangement rather than the record of a common history. This conception of man as a machine drew attention away from the organizing aspects of personality which are known subjectively, and this encouraged the decline of confidence in the powers of the subjective mind. The trend towards objectivity thus reinforced the decline of subjective humanism, and the state of science at the time was such that it could provide no adequate substitute.

Language is too restricted in its degrees of freedom to describe at one stroke this many-faceted transformation, for it must proceed in one dimension from word to word and from sentence to sentence, and thus cannot present simultaneously all the aspects of such a process. The historical process is a unitary transformation, a complex form steadily transforming itself, and is too rich for the thread of language to portray in a single sequence. Hence the need to retrace the centuries and follow through in turn the development of each component of the story. Orchestral music might portray the process in one movement: the bass instruments maintaining the slowly modulating rhythm of the genesis, development, and final disappearance of the dissociation, while the others trace the varied discords and harmonies of the changing human habits in which this fundamental rhythm is displayed. Even the musical image would involve too great a condensation, but it is relevant, since music is concerned with the non-verbal expression of this very architecture of the soul.

A better presentation of the transformation of Europe is given by the record of its art, through which the representatives of past times can speak directly to the receptive mind. But here we are reduced to words, and the attempt to express the changing structure of European man in conceptual form would imply a failure to recognize the diversity and complexity of the process, if it were attempted by any other method than unitary thought. Unitary concepts carry with them the implication that they can never achieve more than a partial conformity to the historical process of which they are themselves part. Late European or Western man can understand something of his own history, precisely because that history has made him what he is and brought him to the verge of unitary thought.

Beneath the lovely cadences and threatening discords of humanism in decay there persists this major theme: through the discovery of the objective order of nature the subject is losing his conviction of the autonomy of his own mind. This surrender of the conscious essence of all that had made Europe great is at the same time the prelude to the reintegration of the dissociated Western soul. The separation of subject and object conditioned both the achievements and the limitations of the European tradition. The blended triumph and misery of the last century arise from the fact that those achievements and limitations must come to an end together. Subject and object can only be transcended in a single approach after the decay of the subjective ideals that inspired the old tradition. The objective order is more extensive than the individual subject; to achieve their fusion the subject must first accept the fact that his method of thought has rested on an illusion, the separation and autonomy of his own mental processes.

This step requires the courage that can discard what appears as beautiful and good, trusting that some truth will arise to give new conviction to the anxious soul. Has all the dreaming of Europe ended in this nightmare of recurrent total war? Failure and despair are the commonplaces of the individual life; as individuals we are all always in the grip of circumstance. But the despair of a tradition is graver than personal despair when it seems to herald the collapse of the only conviction that men can accept.

Yet thought, which has led us to this point, can also lead us on—on one condition. To overcome a conflict which derives from the very origins of Europe, thought must be uncompromising in its demand for a single comprehensive method. This implies humility in the subject. If the facts have not already demonstrated the invalidity of the assumptions of humanism, then the need for a unitary method must now displace those assumptions. Once this is accepted the scene is transformed, and a new world is at our feet. In renouncing a dream-illusion, man's imagined feet of clay are rediscovered as the tissues, organs, and tendencies which make him all that he is. We find that what we have surrendered is not the source of human dignity, but only what Europe mistook for its source.

The humiliation suffered by European man in the first half of the twentieth century—which we shall consider in the next chapter—expresses the final loss of the sense of the autonomy of the subject. Through all the fluctuations of European thought the emphasis had been on man as subject, with the objective world as his field of operation. In the subject-object antithesis, the subject had been dominant and the object subordinate. Therefore in the continuous transformation which is leading towards the replacement of this antithesis by a unitary form, the first step was the transfer of emphasis from subject to object, the objective approach being the more comprehensive and reliable. The objective study of nature developed the mind further than could introspective idealism, and in the process of this development the emphasis inevitably swung over. Instead of subject being dominant to object, the object now dominated the subject, though in the new picture of objective nature there was no element corresponding to the constructive mental processes of the subject.

The formative mind was humiliated by the frustration which resulted from this loss of status. Though this was only a temporary phase of a process leading to a unitary form in which the dualism would be overcome, that fact was not recognized at the time and the individual was paralysed by despair.

This glimpse ahead is necessary to allow us now to look back and see how the main processes of the nineteenth century contributed to the preparation of this final collapse of subjective confidence. I am not suggesting that the events of the last century are to be explained as contributing to a given end. In unitary thought the teleological method is as superfluous as that of material causality. Purpose and mechanical necessity are question-begging conceptions, necessary only so long as the mind has failed to identify the continuity which underlies this dualistic appearance. The continuity of the development of process is all that is necessary to organize thought. The requirements of an interpretation of history are satisfied in the case under consideration, if it is shown that processes which were generated at the origin of Europe in the millennium before Christ, and acquired a special form after 1600, display a continuity of development through the challenges of the nineteenth century, the despair of the early twentieth, to the unitary form which we have still to examine. The role of the nineteenth century in this continuity was the challenge to subjective idealism resulting from the anarchic exploitation of the quantitative method and the ascendancy of an objective picture of man which held no place for the formative tendencies of the individual mind. If one looks deep into society, or more accurately, concentrates attention on the most general tendencies of social thought and behavior through this fourth period, then it becomes evident that the "reaction from reason" which began in the nineteenth century was not a reaction back towards a primitive lack of differentiation but the first stage of a healthy readjustment.

Bruno, Spinoza, and Goethe had anticipated the main task of the hundred years after 1850: the replacement of the subjective conception of man by a balanced view in which man and his mind are regarded as elements in single order of nature. Since losing his naive pagan innocence man had developed a distorted picture of himself; the opportunity had now come to restore the innocence not of ignorance, but of an integrity supported by objective knowledge concerning man.

This implies a form of self-knowledge far surpassing the treacherous introspective intuitions of dissociated European man. The power which such scientific self-knowledge can bring to man in his molding of his own destiny transcends that of every element in human culture prior to it. To unitary man in possession of this power the struggles of the frustrated and dissociated European will seem as blind as the animistic superstitions of the pagan primitive did to the European. This does not imply the discovery of a new magic open to arbitrary use by distorted individuals, nor the domination of man by an alien science, but a historical development, sane and stable and realistic: the further self development of the organic processes in man by the discovery of a new instrument of facilitation. This instrument is the second heuristic principle, which enables man to reintegrate and develop what analytical thought has separated.

The power of such scientific self-knowledge is so great that even limited and distorted components of such knowledge have been sufficient to destroy old civilizations and create new ones, and to inspire comparable revolutions in the human mind. Karl Marx saw to the very roots of the dialectical situation in which man was placed in the nineteenth century. His thought was narrow, his theories limited and of temporary validity, and his conclusions often wrong. But the form which he gave his thought, his method of thinking about man, went to the heart of the human situation at the time. The vigour of Marxism sprang from the fact that it tapped this new source of power. From one point of view Marx and Engels were fully conscious of this fact. They knew that if men could recognize the nature of the historical process and accept their own role in it, they could escape the futile struggles of subjective idealism, and recover conviction, integrity, and courage, in the process of transforming the world. This is the universal truth which they recognized nearly a century back, but has still to be fully absorbed into the general tradition. The historical process was to them an economic class struggle and it was for the workers to serve as the willing agents of history, and to redouble their power by becoming aware of their historical role. Here the interpretation given to the situation was too narrow. A new integrity of action replaced the frustration of subjective idealism, but at the cost of a loss of individual judgement. The individual, in identifying his will with the economic interests of a particular class, had forfeited his own right to think.

Much of the history of the last hundred years arises from this dual situation: Marxism obtained its inspiration and power from the new source, scientific self-knowledge, but its achievements were conditioned by the restricted degree of self-knowledge which it brought to man. Just as the Jewish religion had been established as a premature and therefore narrow monotheism, so Marxism was a premature and limited form of unitary process thought. The tradition was not then ripe for a comprehensive unitary reorganization. By emphasizing the economic interest of the masses, Marxism heightened the frustration of those individuals who could not lose themselves in collective action on a partisan issue. By over-emphasizing the role of the economic productive factors in the historical process, it tended to impoverish the personal life already established in Europe. The same restrictions led to the rapid obsolescence of its interpretation of society and the consequent failure of revolutionary socialism throughout the world. The single exception was in Russia where the individual had for long been ready to lose himself without reserve in the collective, and economic forces were still in the ascendant.

It will be useful to consider certain features of dialectical materialism in more detail. Its fundamental characteristic is shared with unitary thought: the attempt to discover in the story of social development one general process to which the mind of the individual necessarily conforms in accordance with his own situation. Marx and Engels, in transforming the Hegelian method, were certainly trying to think in unitary process terms. But they could not escape the quantitative-capitalist conceptions of their time. To the capitalist, money-power was a conscious aim, the deliberate purpose of his activity. Marx turned this round and made money the material cause of human action and economic conditions the determining factor in social history. This was a great advance; it transformed the conscious aim of the capitalist subject into the much broader, and often unconscious, causation of the various economic interests. Moreover the increasing pressure of quantity, the struggle of the masses for their standard of living, could result in a change of quality, a new order of society.

But here again the limitation of a process method of thought to unduly narrow economic concepts restricted its power. Marxism is a theory of economic man in the quantity age. It offers no adequate explanation of the manner in which new ideas or social forms come into existence, or of the way in which the conflicts of the economic process can suddenly be resolved in the final achievement of a classless society, or of the processes by which the hierarchy of power changes its character. Increasing economic equality is possible, but on the condition that a new component takes over the hierarchy of power. In a limited sense a society without economic classes is possible, but Marxism is powerless to explain how or why, because it does not recognize the other forms of the hierarchy of power.

The overcoming of the subjective conception of man and the substitution of a more comprehensive objectivity threatened positions which had been established since the origin of European man. This is most clearly evident in the attack on subjective attitudes by dialectical materialism. Marx challenged the most powerful combination of vested interests: the passionately held conviction of the subject in the independence of his mind, and the vigorously defended privileges of those whose proper development had been distorted into the lust for security and money power. Idealist aspiration and inhuman greed, representing respectively the free and the thwarted expressions of dissociated man, had built vast institutions, temples in which the techniques of idealism dissociated from the organic and social background, and of egoism blind to social need, were practiced by the hierarchies of the devoted. Marx attacked both, for he denied their common presuppositions. His assault was deadlier than any theoretical criticism, for it suggested to the masses that in the course of fulfilling their historic mission they would necessarily sweep away these temples of abstract thought and material privilege.

But this was not the only such challenge to subjective idealism. During the seventy years between the Communist Manifesto and the Russian Revolution another movement developed, expressing the same basic tendency but providing an objective conception of man as a part of organic nature rather than as an element in the economic process. Within the limitations of the ancient mind the idea of the evolution of species had been accepted and formulated by Lucretius, and after a long interval of digestion it was reformulated in modern form in several European countries during the last decade of the eighteenth century. By 1858 the world of thought was ripe for the formulation of the theory of natural selection as the method of evolution, which took shape simultaneously in the minds of Darwin and Wallace. Thus during the first half of the nineteenth century European thought was beginning to approach the view that the physical frame of man and its history could only be understood as part of the general order of organic nature.

But the movement had gone further than that. Spinoza and Goethe had already prepared the ground for the further step of denying that even human consciousness represented an independent form of reality, and of seeking the interpretation of human thought and behavior as a type of natural process like any other. The West had already begun to recover itself and to return to the emphasis on the unity of process which had marked early Greek, Chinese, and Indian thought. In 1840, when Marx was studying Hegel's identification of the entire historical process with the development of the spirit, a biologist, Carus, had come to the conclusion that the "key to the understanding of the conscious life of the soul lies in the unconscious." Here we see two aspects of the theme that has preoccupied Western thought during the last hundred years: the discovery of the true relation of thought to material processes. By transforming Hegelian thought from a subjective to an objective content, Feuerbach, Marx, and Engels developed one of these aspects for Lenin to mature in the active re-forming of society. The other aspect, the interpretation of individual experience and behavior in terms of the unconscious, has provided the distinguishing characteristic of the modern schools of psychology which are in course of proving themselves by the re-forming of the individual.

The progress of physiology, neurology, and observational psychology during the second half of the last century had underlined what appeared, in dualistic thought, as an intimate parallelism of mind and body. But until the end of the century the new sciences had not explicitly challenged the autonomy of the conscious mind by denying its supremacy even within its own field, the realm of thought. Now the time had come when the issue which Marx had opened in relation to the history of society had also to be raised in respect of the life of the individual.

The story of the development of modern psychology is complex, but Freud may be selected as a representative of the general tendency. Just as Marx had claimed that his interpretation of the historical process proved that the conclusions of the class mind expressed its economic needs, so Freud asserted that his therapeutic technique revealed the distortion of conscious thought by sexual desires. Marx taught that the renunciation of the subjective idealism of individual thought and the acceptance of the inevitability of the economic process as a guide to action would bring nearer the ultimate redemption of society. Freud taught that if the maladapted individual would submit himself to a psychoanalytical critique, conflict could be removed. If Freud had extended his concept of the libido to include all organic tendencies, or if Marx had not tended to restrict his theory to the productive relations in society, the two systems might together have provided a more comprehensive interpretation of man. But even this combined picture would have been inadequate since neither theory recognizes the part played by the formative tendencies of the individual mind.

Here we touch the fundamental aspect of the parallel between the schools of dialectical materialism and psychoanalysis. Though these two theories drew their power from the fact that they sought to apply an objective historical approach to society and to the individual, and so to offer man some degree of scientific self-knowledge, they nevertheless both limited their scope by denying the constructive tendencies of the mind. It was no chance that the two great advances of thought concerning man which were made after the middle of the nineteenth century emphasized respectively the economic and the narrowly sexual aspects of life and neglected the formative and co-ordinating role of mental processes.

We saw that in the course of the development of the intellect it is the constant or permanent aspects of phenomena which are first mastered; only when these have been exhausted can the intellect pass on to the subtler task of identifying the forms of process and development. It was therefore inevitable that the first scientific conceptions to be developed in relation to the organic world represented factors making for the permanence or preservation of life, just as in relation to the inanimate world the first general ideas were concerned with the conservation of matter and energy. Physical conservation and the tendency to mate, reproduce, and preserve the life of the species are simpler ideas, more readily clarified into scientific concepts, than the idea of a formative or developmental process. Thus when the time was ripe for scientific thought to be applied to man the only conceptions available were concerned with the permanence of the species, economic survival, and reproduction. Those who felt the need for a conception of growth or development which could be applied to man could obtain no aid from scientific thought and were forced to fall back on vague vitalistic ideas lacking any constructive value. The formative aspect of the organic processes was necessarily neglected by Marx, Freud, and every other thinker who attempted to apply objective methods to the study of man, because the scientific mind had not yet recognized the formative processes either in elementary physical systems or in organisms.

The intensity of the reaction from the humanistic faith in the individual mind must not be regarded as due to the activities of these two schools, which are themselves expressions of the more general transformation which was in progress. The separation of subject and object was fading, and the subject was yielding its supremacy to the object. But this change tended to paralyse individual initiative and so to destroy the tradition because, as we have seen, the formative processes in nature, which find their most highly facilitated form in the mental processes of the individual, had not yet been identified by science. The subject had accepted a conception of nature in which his own formative faculties had no place. Man had recognized certain components of his own nature in the conception of dialectical materialism and of psychoanalysis (with its kindred schools) but he found nothing in their conceptions of man to correspond to his personal faculty for constructive thought and action. There was no place for the organizing will of the individual in either Marxist or Freudian man. For a time the concentration of attention on the economic and sexual tendencies actually extended the dominance of these tendencies, and the influence of each of these theories was temporarily such as to make men more like the abstract man which they portrayed.

The last consequence of subject humanism was thus to lead man to deny himself. Those who had a full sense of the significance of the European tradition were paralysed by its decay. They lost their power of initiative, their spontaneity, and their confidence, intimidated by the alien world of material necessity which dominated the new form of the tradition. Genius felt itself frustrated, and failed to guide. The long-foretold disaster was at hand. Europe passed into the hands of those who had deliberately renounced the influence of the old tradition and had thus escaped the paralysis of its decay.

The subjective tradition of Europe restricted further development, and its decay was inevitable. The isolated subject had to die before being reborn as part of nature. This meant agony for countless individuals all the world over, who experienced the dissolution of values in their own and their children's lives. The death of such a grand tradition was bound to lead any high genius who experienced it to visions of unequalled and intolerable intensity. This was Nietzsche's situation. He is still too close for objective interpretation. He experienced, I believe, so much of the universal situation that is here described that a general acceptance of his place in European thought will only be possible after unitary thought has become commonplace. His arrow to the farther shore can be followed only by those who can stand outside their own failure. Europe cannot accept Nietzsche because he represents the death of the European tradition. He is the last despairing cry of the European subject, humanistic individualism outreaching itself in an isolated and dissociated genius, forerunner of the rage with which

Europe would turn its sadism on itself, his man-god as much an illusion as the god-man he rightly repudiated. Until European man had expressed his despairing rebellion in this ultimate challenge, the resources of dissociated subjective thought had not been exhausted.

Nietzsche's dangerous vision is for those who can absorb it without damage, and these must still be few. His main error was the consequence of his role as the last genius of the subjective tradition: to see himself as the divine dynamite that would destroy the world and the divine intuition that would create it anew. The dynamite and the creative intuition were certainly at work in him, as he believed. But he was only one, though perhaps the most representative, of countless carriers of the contemporary transformation. Never again after Nietzsche will it be appropriate for the single individual to take on himself the burden of human destiny. After Nietzsche not merely God, but messianism itself was dead. *Sub specie aeternitatis* it may be said that he died that all after him might be saved from the illusion of a god either outside, or more dangerously, inside the subject. He identified history with himself, not himself with one component of history, as did Lenin. Nietzsche was the last European genius with philosophic vision. Until unitary man is established he must be hated, for he symbolizes the transition which has been so painful to twentieth century man.

7

The Twentieth Century

Science is the image we form of the continuity of nature, and history our image of our own past. In static thought these two are separate, but in unitary thought they become one. Human history is a part of natural history, but a part in which the method of approach has a special importance. The view of natural process given in the second chapter led immediately to a view of man and of the history of European man, and these in turn lead to a view of man's present situation.

To those who have experienced life throughout this century it must appear a long journey from the *fin de siècle* to the "forties." In each decade "the twentieth century" has stood for a different outlook, and the swift changes of this period offer a nice problem for unitary thought. The interpretation of this half-century has many pitfalls for any method that is not well rooted in the historical trend. An able historian appeared to be sure of his judgement when he wrote at the end of the last century, perhaps at the moment when Nietzsche was dying: "the turbulent energy of these new forces (generated in the 15th and 16th centuries) had not yet found the well-regulated paths in which it flows today in such a well-disciplined manner." Perhaps the lesson to be drawn from that example is that any interpretation should be made so definite that if, like his, it does not prove right, at least it may be as clearly wrong.

In every recent century there must have been decades in which men believed they were experiencing unusually rapid social changes. Behind these decades of instability there have been longer periods marked by major historical transformations, such as the transitions from antiquity to the Middle Ages between 200 and 600 AD, from medieval to modem times in the Renaissance and Reformation, and from the eighteenth to the nineteenth century through the French Revolution, the Napoleonic era, and the Industrial Revolution. These transitional periods are in turn set within the background of overriding changes in the biology of human development, which though potentially universal found their most decisive expression in Europe. The most important of these are: first, the development of universal empires, ideas, and gods, accompanied by self-consciousness; second, the discovery in 1600 of the first heuristic method, the method of quantity; and third, the contemporary transition to an age justifying a new heuristic method, the unitary method, in all fields: in the process unity of nature, in the social unity of man, and in the potential unity of every man. In the 1940s the experience of change was abnormal because this decade is not only likely to prove the one marked by the greatest instability within this century, but also marks the coming to man's attention of that third change in the biological development of man from the quantitative to the unitary age.

It is impossible today to escape the need for a general awareness of the phasing of the historical process. In the past great cultures could be created unconsciously, the organic processes forming the new patterns without man's attention being drawn to their wider significance. But the unconscious phase of history is now past. The acceleration of social change which has resulted from the attention paid to specialized techniques can only be controlled by paying attention also to the general formative processes which in earlier times were unconscious. Consciousness of specialized technical methods must be balanced by consciousness of general developing forms. After a certain point in history every people involved in a time of transition may flatter itself with a great destiny. There is no harm and indeed great advantage in that if it implies the acceptance of the path of development proper to man and does not obscure the vision of facts as they are. I do not see how to escape the conclusion which arises from the unitary image of the past and the experience of the present: mankind is at the greatest opportunity of its history since the Jewish prophets proclaimed the ethic of monotheism and the Greek thinkers established the universal idea. The species can now, through the full acceptance of process, realize unity without loss of diversity or differentiation.

The greater the reorganization the greater the pain before it becomes possible. The reverse is not always true, or we could infer from the agony of three decades the grandeur of the world of to-morrow. For thirty years the human mind has suffered confusion, myriads of lives have suffered premature disaster, and the necessities of war still dominate life and thought. Yet this half-century has not been a monotone of evil, but a black and white confusion, bewilderingly paradoxical until beneath its contrasts the underlying transformation is recognized. On the one hand there has been the progressive release from the distorting inhibitions and idealisms of an age-old dissociation, bringing a tremendous sense of new opportunities of functional fulfilment, of material security, of personal readjustment, of love relieved from fear—a sense of the possibility of a development as far reaching as any that already lie in the human past. On the other hand there have been the complementary disasters in the subjective and objective worlds, the failure of personal initiative, lacking a principle of integration and intimidated by the knowledge that thought is conditioned by hunger and desire, and the external anarchy of a society ravaged by the expansive virulence of quantity.

This paradox of emancipating release accompanied by a frustrating disorder is the sign of a transformation from one order to another. The ancient dissociation becomes unstable and the suppressed passions exploit the techniques of the age to wreak their vengeance on the old ideals. At the same time the dimly sensed opportunity of a new integration of life and technique sustains a non-rational hope. The old and the new do not co-operate as a dyarchy in which different aspects of society are reorganized in turn. The old order, already dying under the cancer of quantity, may turn into reaction and angrily seek to retain its hold, while the new steadily shapes itself within the patterns of a society that has not yet become aware of the form of its destiny. The changeover follows no step-by-step logic accessible to analytical reason, but an organic or unitary logic in which the new social organs are developed in the course of their struggle against the resistance of the vested interests, spiritual and material, of the dissociated past. Science, in the form of quantitative technique, creates closer frictions but does not unify. The idea or concept is the instrument of social integration in human communities and until the uniting idea has been passed around, technical knowledge can only intensify the struggle.

This process is no respecter of beauty or persons. The contrast of the old and the new escapes the categories of good and evil, and of better and worse. The scene is dominated by challenge, tension, and development, and in this tension of transition a multitude of distorted forms appear. The second, third, and fourth decades of the twentieth century represent this field of distortion between the last phases of an old and the emergence of a new community. This is the moment of potential anarchy when the community lacks any explicit principle of order which can be effective under the conditions of the time. This is the night of violent and bestial release, the opportunity of the inhibited perversions which can now ally themselves with technical power. The dominance of the dissociated idealisms is over, and the two remaining active principles, sadistic vitality and technical power, join forces in a brief period of dominance. This short reign of Antichrist depends on the fusion of two principles which are both vicious because they represent only a part of European or Western human nature: instinctive vitality distorted into sadism, and differentiating human vitality distorted into quantitative expansion.

Unprejudiced by the illusions of a past age and appearing to the exhausted humanist to possess a strangely objective vision, the distorted man knows that his brief opportunity of power has come, for he alone can be as ruthless as the occasion demands. It seems almost as though a formless world at such a moment would accept the impress of any arbitrary will. But even a ruthless maniac can only enter the records of history if he is the instrument of a general process. Whoever at any moment achieves power must use the symbols which at that moment facilitate the organization of human action. As the distorted man pursues his lust for power he increases the general tension, and thereby hastens the decay of the old. But a new order is in course of development; he must use some of its forms to achieve his own power, and his violence serves to prepare the soil and scatter the seeds. He wields power because he has lost the illusory ideals of the past, and can therefore recognize the technical skeleton which for the time being is the only valid instrument of social organization. This figure of the distorted man is no aesthetically acceptable Mephistopheles, offering man experience at the price of his soul, willing evil but achieving good. It is the spirit of frustration breaking out as lust for power, wrecking an old world and preparing the way for another not better or worse, but different from the old. History cannot be understood if it is sentimentalized as a necessary progress towards better things. No future is necessary unless we are such as to make it, and if we do make it and it satisfies us, this will be because it is appropriate to our condition, not because it is better or worse than what came before.

A human type unprejudiced by old illusions may easily dominate a disordered society, but that alone is not an adequate explanation of the ascendancy of the distorted man of the twentieth century. The gangster and racketeer get away with it in their limited fields and the Nazis temporarily dominated Europe, because by discarding certain illusions they acquired a positive strength lacking in other contemporary types. This arose from the fact that they rejected humanism without adopting in its place any other variant of the European dissociated tradition. The distorted man rejects the entire ethical and moral content of the European tradition, and with it the European mode of organizing the life of the individual and the community. His ascendancy expresses this overcoming of the European dissociation. In this he is in no mean sense a man. He stands firmly on his own ground and in the vigour of his action displays without shame that the past means nothing to him. He builds with the materials at hand for a purpose that is unquestionably his own. This vitality has its attraction for those to whom ideals have ceased to be real and culture become a tradition separated from life. It is courageous, honest in its dishonesty, and adventurous. The idealist, innocent of the deeper ranges of experience, may fail to recognize its significance. But there are moments in the history of individuals and of communities when the catharsis of blind and sensual action must precede the restoration of a proper rhythm.

In the early 1920s it was already evident to some that such a moment had arrived in the history of Europe. The situation in Germany contained features which defied interpretation in ethical or political terms, and implied, if they were maintained, a radical transformation of social life. This impetus might express itself in socialist or nationalist action, but beneath this superficial antithesis lay a common discontent. In destroying the old Germany the Allies had made sure that the new, when it appeared, would not accept traditional European criteria. Beneath such criminal activities as the murder of Rathenau lay the general discontent with a spurious liberalism that no longer had meaning.

In the conflict of vitality and an effete tradition, the gods of history never hesitate. In such a conflict there may come a terrible moment when those who are moved by the immediate historical trend, but fail to see its further implications, are inspired by a religious nihilism that hesitates at nothing. Merely to condemn Nazism implies an appeal to ideals that neither they nor history recognize. One can only condemn with insight what one has recognized in oneself. The Nazi is a symbol of a distortion universal to contemporary European and Western man. He took on himself the radical struggle with a human disease that might be universal. The end of the Nazi system can mean the beginning of unitary Europe and a unitary world, and only the firm establishment of that new world will enable mankind to look back without prejudice to the role of Germany in this great transformation.

It is not long since the madman was thought to be possessed of an evil spirit, and we still can consider a community as inspired by evil. Yet just as madness is the expression of frustrated vitality, so a community thought mad by others may express a formative process in which the new destroys the old. Such a time is of necessity cruel; and unitary man, having outgrown the need to condemn the inevitable facts of a particular phase in history, seeks only to ease the development of the new. But for this, two mutually dependent conditions are necessary: he must have outgrown the European dissociation and he must understand his own time.

I shall return in a moment to analyze the phasing of the history of this century. But for two decades, from 1920 to 1940, this situation remained unresolved: the ascendancy of the ruthless and the silence of the others for whom neither humanism nor Marxism was adequate. The crisis had been long anticipated in the world of thought. The failure of humanism had been clear to Schopenhauer, Dostoevsky, and Nietzsche; the new temper had been evident in the changing quality of socialist thought from Robert Owen to Marx, and from Marx to Sorel; the rationalism of Comte had given place to the vital intuition of Bergson. After the first war it was clear that the principles of the European tradition were losing their grip on men's minds; Marxism had narrowed itself to a form appropriate only to Russia; Europe was looking beyond industrialism for a new motive; for the moment the vacuum of ideas was filled by the irrational leadership of the distorted man. Fascism was ascendant, the others silent. The leaders of world thought scarcely seemed to be aware of the peculiar features of the new situation. Some saw aspects of the situation but all lacked a unitary view. Well's vision, like that of most liberals, was prejudiced by utilitarian assumptions. Rathenau, Unamuno, Huizinga, Ortega y Gasset, Berdyaev, Murry, Whitehead, and many others recognized the moral crisis but spoke in the old language. Marxism claimed a monopoly of process thought and thereby misled young enthusiasm. A generation suffered violence in the world of action and silence in the world of thought.

The strength of the Fascist and the paralysis of the man of goodwill were both due to the collapse of the European dissociation. This had consisted, as we have seen, in the separation of two partial modes of behavior: the socially dominant system of deliberate responses based on static concepts and ideals, and the system of spontaneous, usually instinctive responses to immediate stimuli. The strength of the Fascist arose from the fact that in the breakdown of the dissociation the released tension led to a movement in which action tended to dominate thought, experience was valued more than knowledge, and the instinctive and other vital passions overcame the civilized control of differentiated behavior. Technique became the instrument of the released tendencies rather than of any ideal system of control. The European system had rested broadly on the claim of mind to dominate being; now being—at first in the narrower sense of action—was to dominate mind.

This division of human life into pairs of contrasted aspects: action and thought, experience and knowledge, instinct and intellect, being and mind, is itself an expression of the dissociation. The fact that the Fascist still had to think in these dualistic terms, though he was himself in process of over coming the dissociation, arose from the fact that the movement of release carried the emphasis too far from thought to action, the Fascist finding his opportunity precisely in the absence of any general integrating principal. The distorted man of the twentieth century seizes the moment of potential chaos and imposes on it not the developing order of a valid organizing principle, but the local and temporary order of a personal, national, or racial will. In the absence of the new conception which can co-ordinate the actions of men of goodwill, the Fascist imposes on the social system a form which expresses the resultant of the released passions and of the technical tendencies of the time. More accurately, it is these tendencies and passions which allow the Fascist for one brief generation to hold the instruments of power.

The new philosophies of activism were not an expression of healthy vitality; they betrayed in their ruthlessness a pathological element which could only arise from a denial of some component of contemporary human nature. The Communist Party's will to power was stronger than its desire to aid the men and women who make up the working classes. The appeal of the ultimate millennium of working class power blinded the party to practical tasks at hand, except in the one country where it had already achieved power. The end was more important than the means, humanity more important than individuals here and now. Here again the Communist was a true European, lost in the dualism of means and end, of fact and idea. It is appropriate that it should be Russia's task to translate a European theory into Asiatic reality. Marx pretends to renounce idealism but retains the idea of humanity or the State as more important than the men who actually constitute it, so that the end which is the good of humanity—justifies the means—which is the present denial of a part of human nature. Apart from Germany, the most unbalanced European country, where Communism might have been achieved, this doctrine could suit only Asia, since there it coincides with the ancient emphasis on a single hierarchy in contrast to the European division of social life into balancing components promoting individual variety. Russia adopted the Western doctrine of progress and technical methods, and molded a new developing society appropriate to her own vast collectivity. Such denial of individual variety as this involved was alien to the European, but not to the Asiatic tradition.

But in Europe the new activism lacked the adaptability of a long-term historical movement and displayed instead the fierce will of perverted leadership in a disordered society. If an individual is deeply dissatisfied with himself, he must seek confirmation of his own rightness in a forced relation to the community. He must either deliberately hide himself by conforming to the amorphous mass and so become material for tyranny, or else impose himself on others and become the tyrant. The will to power and the need to conform to the mass through loss of personality appear together, as twin signs of the despair of the individual in a society lacking any order which might permit him to develop his own life.

Tyranny is the result, not the cause, of the collapse of order. The machine gun has power over those whose measure is their own life in the narrow present, and that is all that the isolated individual possesses. But if the individual is not isolated, but part of a true community, the richness of his life will lead him to defy death. In such circumstances the bullet may not be fired, for though it can destroy single individuals it cannot terrorise a vital community. The power of a tyranny cannot rest ultimately on its machine guns, since at one time the tyrant group were unarmed. Society hands the guns over to them because the unreality of the existing order is realized and the masses demand at least a personal symbol of order and call for the leader who will dominate them. When a true order becomes possible they throw him away as suddenly.

The organizing mental processes do not tolerate a vacuum. The formative processes always tend to establish symbols for organizing behavior. The most efficient of these are general ideas, but when ideas fail the community returns to the personal symbol of the father, the magic man, the group leader, the hero. No one can escape this need. In those deeper affairs where no philosophy can offer guidance, even the strongest mind finds peace and the bravest will stability in recalling the great figures of history, the heroes of his innermost thought. But the community always needs symbols, and when the tradition fails it, only the personal symbol remains.

This reaction from civilized tradition to personal tyranny took different forms in different areas. Germany had lacked the balancing influences and long development which the Southern, Western, and Northern ocean-faring peoples had enjoyed. More recently war, blockade, and inflation had undermined the remnants of European idealism. Just as the dominant classes in Germany had been in turn more intensely individualist, Protestant, imperialistic, rationalistic, and scientific than any other European people, so now they became more ruthlessly totalitarian. Germany has over and over again given her soul to some one element of the European tradition, but has never been loyal to the tradition itself or experienced the balance of its varied components. The situation of the

German people today is not the result of astute propaganda. The lie is effective only when society itself is felt to be founded on a lie and no general truth is recognized. The strength of the German nation in the second war has been due to this: behind the unscrupulousness which is so misleading to their opponents, the people have devoted themselves to one supreme task, the total application of technique in the interest of one overriding national purpose.

Here we reach the essence of the totalitarian system as seen in Germany and to a lesser degree in Italy. The European differentiation of independent institutions is discarded and all the activities of the community are centrally controlled in a hierarchy devoted to one major purpose. This co-ordination of effort means that a new criterion of validity is applied to every aspect of society. The economic laws of earlier societies are neglected, quantity symbols are operated only in the interest of the single aim, and reason itself is socially recognized only as the instrument of the community will. The totalitarian society is active and hierarchical, and its stability depends on propaganda to maintain some correspondence between the community desires and the processes already set in motion by the ruling group. The consequence is that such a state can survive only while the community as a whole is ready to support its expansive aims, or such transformed aims as its leaders may devise to meet new situations. Totalitarian tyranny is vulnerable, for though it expresses certain features of the time it lacks any central idea which can provide stability when its initial momentum is exhausted.

We have now traced the course up to the present day of the main components of the transformation: the final collapse of humanism, the development of quantitative anarchy, the growth of a new objective view of man, the gradual dissolution of the European dissociation, and the appearance of totalitarian tyranny. But if we are to diagnose the exact stage reached in the forties, and the prospects for the future, we must examine more closely the phasing of these component processes and the present state of the underlying trend.

In assigning dates to the different phases of these processes we have to bear in mind the acceleration shown by all social processes during the last few decades. The rate of scientific discovery, of its practical applications, and of the consequent social changes has increased steadily since the last decade of the nineteenth century. This acceleration is a result of the self-developing characteristic of scientific thought, which as it develops facilitates to an ever-increasing degree its own development. The importance of this property during the last fifty years has been accentuated by two facts: the finiteness of the earth, and the existence of a limit to the fine structure of nature. The first has permitted a concentration of effort and mutual facilitation between different groups of scientific workers that was not possible while the world remained to be explored, and could not exist in an infinitely extended community. The second fact, the finiteness of the accessible fine-structure of nature (which here means the restricted number of chemical elements, crystal types, organic species, etc.), has meant that new discoveries in one region immediately throw light on neighboring regions, new facts growing easier to discover as more and more facts are fitted into place.

These two facts express a single situation: the human community is in process of adapting to an effectively finite environment, and as the process continues the pace grows faster. In 1890 the world still appeared boundless, while in 1940 man is experiencing its finitude at every step. The outlook of the Western mind has undergone this change during the last few decades, but no corresponding change has as yet been made in its fundamental concepts. The acceleration may be expected to continue until the conceptions and the form of society appropriate to the new conditions have been established. In approaching the phasing of these decades we must therefore bear in mind that while in European history as a whole ten generations could see fundamental changes and one generation represent a critical transition, we are now concerned with an unstable state which might settle into a new characteristic form in the course of a single decade.

We must now pass from these broader vistas to the details of a time of rapid transition and it will be convenient to fix certain dates by noting some of the events that closed each decade. In 1910 Lenin was in Zurich, Lloyd George was creating the new demagogy, Bleriot had flown the English Channel, Bohr was at work on the quantum theory, Proust was recalling his past, Bergson was in fashion, Freud still to be discovered, Wells an unquestioning optimist, Shaw already 54, Mussolini 27, and Hitler 21. These names are evidence that the final challenge to traditional Europe was already in preparation. By 1920 Lenin was in Petrograd, Wilson back in Washington, Zaharoff had founded a chair at Oxford, Freud had become popular, Joyce was at work on *Ulysses,* and Hitler had conceived his mission. The first challenge had been delivered.

For many Europe had died in the valley of the Somme, its beauty enhanced in retrospect but its corruption final. Beside the horror of an ancient civilization destroying its young the daily life of family, religion, and career, inspired by the old ideals, had become a macabre jest, recognized only by the surrealists. Hitler, and others with him, knew that the corpses of Flanders were more real than a society that had not yet admitted the death of its soul. A league of anachronisms inspired by German piety only served to draw a curtain between man and the horrid truth. But daring to look deep into himself the surrealist saw that European man had lost his community, and therefore also his unity, and was obsessed by the obscene symbols of sub-human vitality. Only Russia, safe outside the European cordon, escaped the decay and set its eyes on the future.

By 1930 Mussolini and Stalin were in power, Hitler was awaiting his chance, radio and the mass-man had established their dominance, the liberal economic system was displaying its cycle of indifference, for the first and last time on a world-wide scale. In a vast conspiracy of pretence the vested interests of old money and old ideas continued their frivolous rituals, and left it to the distorted men of unsatisfied peoples to announce that the game was over.

By 1940 Europe had disappeared, and the English-speaking world was at bay in defence of its inheritance. Such was the crude structure of these decades, against which we must now identify the successive phases of the underlying transformation.

In the previous chapter we traced the progressive decay of humanism, and there remains only the task of considering how far European society was aware of this process at different dates during this century. Anxiety for the future of civilization, that is, for their children's future, had already been shown by the masses of Europe, for about the turn of the century three hundred years of rapid expansion of the European population came suddenly to an end. The anarchy of quantitative competition had created a profound sense of unease, but few had given expression to this vague presentiment. Even as late as 1905-10 minds fully competent to deal with superficial historical events could still remain blind to the general trend. But by 1916-18 it was evident to many that technical war had exposed the folly of further confidence in the efficacy of humanistic ideals. Since those years, when Europe first flung its youth to a mass-death, the whole of Western literature has been occupied either in getting to grips with this problem, or in offering an escape from it. Only the dense unimaginativeness of the prosperous concealed it from the "fortunate" sections of European society. The literature, art, and music of Europe evidenced its despair. The life of Berlin openly challenged the ideals of the tradition, Paris maintained a mere pretence, and London its insular indifference. Against these fundamental factors the few desperate attempts to save the liberal polity were poultices concealing the need for the knife.

The next component which we have to consider is the development of the quantitative method. The present status of the quantity principle is a matter of importance since this principle has determined the chief characteristics of the last two centuries. The extension of quantitative methods to new fields of exact science has recently come to an end. It is as though three centuries of increasingly intense application of the quantitative method had exhausted its guarantee of the progressive improvement of thought, because the regions where the method is adequate have already been explored. In experimental physics the attempt to establish quantitative space-time co-ordinates in very small regions has led to the discovery of a limiting uncertainty. If we attempt to pursue quantitative exactitude beyond this limit, we find ourselves left with a form which cannot be localized. In biological problems, such as chemical embryology and the study of the functions of the cerebral cortex, the attempt to split the process into spatially localized factors has failed to yield satisfactory results. The quantitative method of exact space, time localization has also failed to provide a suitable calculus for describing the subtly interrelated hierarchical balance of the nervous and glandular systems. In psychology the theory of the gestalt or form has been developed to compensate excessive analysis. It is scarcely possible to avoid the conclusion that a new method is now necessary to supplement the method of quantitative analysis.

A similar exhaustion of the elementary quantitative method is apparent in many other fields. The analysis of materials is no longer regarded as adequately covered by a global statement of the percentages of the different elements present, and this must be supplemented by a description of the electrochemical and aggregated condition, i.e., of the whole arrangement of the atomic and molecular groups, expressed in activation energies and selective forces serving to attract and orient structures of specific form. The developing pattern is what counts; an elementary quantitative analysis determines only certain basic components of the pattern, and may miss the most important.

The same situation is found in the application of number and quantity to the organization of society. The operation of the quantity symbols merely to increase production is no longer adequate, the essential task being now the organization of distribution to meet known human needs rather than an apparent demand indicated by the quantity symbols of the market. The failure of the financial quantity symbols is far going. Units of currency change their nature with a change of ownership. The money symbols no longer guarantee their "owner" a claim on a determinate measure of goods or services, but are limited by permits and coupons, and sometimes even withheld as treasure for a heavenly future like food buried in an Egyptian tomb. Capital in the sense of quantity of credit can no longer operate in the manner that gave it its original meaning; the state limits all its activities: investment, speculation, inheritance, exchange, and control of production are all restricted. Ownership of the quantity symbols of money has lost much of its meaning.

These examples show that the quantity concepts and their symbols are no longer performing what was once their function: to describe nature with increasing exactness, to organize production, to balance supply and demand, and to preserve value. The simultaneous appearance of this situation in so many fields might be no more than a multiple coincidence, but it suggests that the intense exploitation of the quantitative method during recent decades has exhausted the regions to which it is suited. While the known world was expanding, on the globe, in space, and in the atom, the elementary quantity symbols continued to extend their domain. But if the limits of this expansion have now been reached, it may be that these symbols no longer constitute the appropriate instrument for the further organization and application of knowledge. A complementary non-quantitative technique may be necessary to control the ordering of finite patterns in a finite world, which is the task now before the race.

The power of quantity is already in decline and the emphasis is shifting to a new system of ideas: symmetry, pattern, organization, function, development. The recent rate of extension of quantitative technique has been so rapid that various new fields of application have been exhausted within a single decade, instead of being slowly exploited one after another over centuries, as they might have been had the rate been less. The culmination of the age of quantity can be placed in the 1920s. In 1925 Heisenberg formulated the uncertainty principle of atomic physics which recognized the existence of limits set to space-time measurement in small regions. In 1929 the concentration of credit in single hands reached the maximum for all time: the New York slump of that year was the collapse of a symbolic fiction of credit circulating in the market but unsupported by production.

There is no longer any magic in quantity; physical quantities are what we can measure, finance a calculus to serve human wills. The autonomy of the symbols is challenged; number and quantity no longer exist in their own right as an independent order of reality. Just as thought is recognized as acquiring its significance only as a component of the processes in man, so the quantity symbols are now understood to be valuable only as a means of organizing whatever can be measured or counted. When the quantity symbols fail, either because they are misused or because the things with which we are concerned are not measurable, then they lose their status and must be supplemented by other methods. For this reason physics has resorted to the non-quantitative calculus of groups to describe the atomic patterns, and the emphasis of economic thought has shifted back from the money symbols to the economic processes and goods which they originally represented. It is evident that lack of finance capital does not of itself set any limit to the possible achievements of a community, and that the flow of goods between nations can proceed without the usual consequences of current bookkeeping. The obsession with the quantity symbols is at an end. Thought has penetrated behind the symbols to the process of which they represent only one aspect. Man has measured the limits of measurement, and credit is discredited. The passion for quantity achieved the expansion for which it craved, but at the price of its own exhaustion.

How rapidly the mood of thought can change within a small community may be seen by looking back on some British prejudices of the 1920s. It was then shocking to common sense to suggest that in every situation there is some factor which can override the influence of quantity: "Nothing can be done without adequate finance." "The quantities of economics are beyond the control of individuals." "The individual life is too short; men of goodwill too few." "The subject matter of exact science consists of pointer-readings." These pathetic fallacies, which read into nature man's passing obsession, have already lost their power to impose on the average mind.

So long as quantity was given an absolute status and nature regarded as being essentially quantitative in structure it was not possible for the mind to find its place in nature. Though the concept of quantity is a typical product of the mind, representing the ideal of static permanence, yet the forms of mental processes cannot be expressed in terms of quantity. The prestige of quantity thus helped to maintain the dualistic separation of mind and nature. The present recognition of the limitations of the quantitative method leaves the way open for the unitary method in which mental processes are identified as a special form of the universal formative process.

This leads us to consider the point reached in the next component process: the development of an objective view of man. Here generalization is less reliable, and the evidence of recent trends might at any moment be reversed by new events. Nevertheless certain conclusions will probably stand. On the one hand the progress of biological and psychological science is steadily bringing the field of established knowledge closer to the central problems not only of the physiology of man but also of his character, temperament, and modes of thought. On the other hand the dogmatic views of the orthodox Marxist and Freudian schools appear to have lost their first revolutionary appeal. Between 1920 and 1940 the influence of the relatively small groups that accepted either of these doctrines as an adequate science of man reached its zenith and began to wane. The more society was influenced by these doctrines the less tenable became the view that either of them was adequate. Narrow dogmatic views can be maintained only in opposition to an established tradition; the process of discovering their limitations goes parallel with their absorption into the community tradition. Economic man and sexual man are useful abstractions, but even in combination they fail to describe contemporary men and women.

The development of the objective picture of man had at the outbreak of the Second World War reached the stage at which these two abstractions could be widely recognized as relevant to components of human nature but as neglecting some essential element. We have already seen that unitary thought interprets this situation by showing that the fundamentally static thought of the recent period has emphasized the conservative or life-maintaining components of human activity, while neglecting the formative or developmental component. On this interpretation an objective conception of man has now been sufficiently developed to prepare the community for the identification of the formative tendency which dominates and co-ordinates all the component processes in human nature. Since an objective conception of man based on this principle would necessarily include all the valid elements of the earlier subjective conception, the present phase may also be regarded as the prelude to a synthesis of the subjective and objective methods of approach to man.

One of the most striking features of Western thought during the last two decades has been the clash between idealism and materialism, in the sense of the partial views of man offered by subjective religion and humanist ethics on the one hand, and by dialectical materialism and certain recent psychological theories on the other hand. This clash of two partially valid conceptions, neither of which Western man could honestly reject as false, is the final expression of the European dissociation. Each aspect of divided Western man provides apparent evidence of the truth of the corresponding doctrine and yet the two views are contradictory. Too much is already known of human nature for either view to be rejected in favor of the other. The individual therefore oscillates from a materialistic to an idealistic emphasis, just as the physicist does from particle to wave representations of the electron, both being forced into the dualistic dilemma by the failure to use process concepts. Thus the materialistic and idealistic attitudes, with their common vested interest in the ancient static methods of thought, become allies in delaying the needed synthesis, as Communist and pacifist at one time joined forces in attempting to frustrate the defensive instinct of the average Englishman. But the steadily increasing scientific knowledge of natural processes will, if the unitary view is correct, shortly impose on the tradition a definitive unitary reorganization. The materialist and the idealist will then become anachronistic reminders of the age before the unitary process was recognized.

This recognition of the unitary truth will come about as one aspect of the unitary process operating in man and above all in his mental processes. The formative tendency in thought expresses itself in the tendency to think and act in parallel, to develop action in accordance with thought, and thought on the basis of past action. This tendency to establish the conformity of thought and action may be arrested in a dissociated individual or civilization, but it is an aspect of normal organic integration in a thinking organism, and is known subjectively as the persisting latent desire for honesty in thought and action and for knowledge concerning man. As a consequence of the ascendancy of scientific truth this impulse towards integrity of thought and action has acquired a new importance in recent decades. What Nietzsche foresaw more than fifty years ago has now come true: "Perhaps this coming generation will on the whole seem more evil than the present one—for in evil as in good it will be more straightforward."

This leads us to consider how far the general process, of which these special tendencies are components, has developed during recent decades. This transformation consists in the disappearance of the European dissociation and the substitution of a unitary organization. What do the last thirty years show in this regard? As the appropriate unitary language is not yet sufficiently developed it will be convenient to consider this central question from the three interrelated aspects of emotion, thought, and behavior. How far have the emotions, thoughts, and actions of the Western peoples displayed the breakdown of the traditional dualistic form during this recent period?

The prevailing relativity of moral standards leaves the field clear for a new criterion in the emotional life. The only criterion which can be accepted today as determining the status of an emotion is its genuineness, the extent to which it can express the whole nature. But the mere recognition of this fact does not imply the disappearance of the dissociation. Indeed it is just this desire for emotional honesty which prevents the rejection of either the materialistic or the idealistic view of man—until a more comprehensive substitute is in sight—because each is felt to contain an element of the truth. Yet this unstable dual consciousness, this general awareness of an equal degree of validity in man's material and spiritual needs, shows that the dissociation has lost its justification. For the dissociation expressed the social recognition of the spiritual as more legitimate than the sensual appetites. But in his new straightforwardness man denies such biased discrimination, and seeks only the integration proper to his nature at his own stage of development.

The two dissociated components are now locked in a final unstable clash and this means that the provisional integration of the European system has gone, the latent duality become patent, and the tradition no longer offering to the maturing generations a possible method of organization. The dissociation was often painful but usually tolerable. The condition which results from its collapse is intolerable because it leaves man without even the pretence of the single control which is necessary to every organism. If unitary thought is valid this condition must result either in rapid regression and the loss of all civilization, or in an equally swift establishment of a new unitary organization expressing a unity in man transcending and co-ordinating his varied emotions. Since we are concerned here only with the tradition and its influence on the individuals of each generation, this does not imply the disappearance of conflict in every individual but only the offering by the organized tradition of assistance to every individual in organizing his life, in place of its present dualistic distortion of his potential harmony. In its demand for emotional honesty this century has prepared man for the far-going reorganization appropriate to his present condition.

If this interpretation is correct we must find the same situation displayed in the intellectual component of the tradition. We have already noted that the analytical method of thought, based on the use of static concepts and culminating in the calculus of quantity, appears to have passed its zenith. In many branches of thought the historical method, or the tracing of development, offers the only promising guide through the overwhelming complexity of detail. Exact thought is in a condition of confused suspense; the duality latent in the basis of European and Western thought has come to the surface. Time and space, function and structure, purpose and quantity, freedom and necessity—each concept refuses to yield primacy to its partner. Their disharmony now lies open, and frustrates the proper role of thought, for these dualisms fail to express the returning unity of experience. The same intellectual dualism reappears as the conflict of individual and community, and this, like the others, remains irresolvable within the logic of static concepts. The barrier of this dualism can only be overcome by retracing the development of the intellect and discarding system in favor of a process system of thought.

Finally a parallel situation is evident in the behavior of the community. The relaxation of the inhibitions on the instinctive life, which maintained the dissociation without the substitution of any adequate novel co-ordination expressing the integrity appropriate to human nature, has resulted in a new emphasis on the animal needs of man. A vast sensual demagogy, threatening civilization with its technical apparatus of standardized pleasures, is one of the many aspects of the collapse of the dissociation. Sensual man challenges the ascendancy of spiritual man, not merely in an instinctive rebellion of vitality against restraint, but as the expression of a new honesty. Yet within the challenge of sensual man to a spirituality which he scorns, there lies also a deeper latent rebellion against sensual pleasures which bring no contentment, and hence even from the favored countries men go willingly to war.

It is no wonder that in such a situation the old conceptions should fail as guides. Utilitarian thought, whether liberal or socialist, wrote on its banner, "Feed men, and then ask of them virtue," and under the sign of organic man this could not he refuted. Sixty years ago Dostoevsky recognized that this was the issue, and that organic man could not represent the whole of man. Yet it was not till the 1930s that this issue was decided on a scale for all to read. Britain in the nineteenth century had denied itself current consumption and so built up its great productive capital, but this was a consequence of the operation of the quantity symbols in the interests of the owners of industry, a process to which the masses paid no attention. But in the third decade of the twentieth century Russia and Germany repeated this achievement with the support of the majority of the active sections of their people, Russia to defend the first socialist society, Germany to dominate the world.

The Russian and German peoples, in denying themselves bread to achieve the guns of defence and offence, proved that the utilitarian age was at an end. It is no longer possible to think that men put bread before virtue, if virtue is interpreted, without moral implications, as the co-ordination and control of the instincts by an overriding tendency. Man abhors the absence of integration. He demands integration, and will create religions, achieve heroic self-sacrifice, pursue mad ambitions, or follow the ecstasy of danger, rather than live without. If society refuses him this satisfaction in a constructive form he will seize a destructive principle to which he can devote himself and will take revenge on the society that thought his only demand was pleasure. Vice, in this sense, shares the integrating power of virtue, of which it is merely the negative form. The mass-man readily rejected the utilitarian philosophy which had created him and accepted in its place the new mass-religion of national suicide. This has not been understood by the fortunate Anglo Saxon, who, still retaining habits from the earlier dissociated state, has failed to realize that the utilitarian age is over. The German disease is an intensification of a general situation. The decay of European ideals had left no path of virtue, and the restless German therefore turned to vice. For the moment the entire race finds glory in the vice of war. But a species which places vice above bread may at another time prefer virtue to bread, and then be able to share the loaf in peace. This is a historical possibility, but for that very reason not a moral advance, unless it is moral to display order in a time of order, and immoral to suffer disorder in a time of disorder.

Nothing is easier than to undergo obsession by an idea and to substitute for fact the satisfying pattern of an abstract principle. It is, I find, possible to interpret the contemporary scene as the prelude to a unitary reorganization. In such a matter there can be no proof, and the outline of an interpretation which I have given here can only serve as support for a personal assertion. The purpose of this analysis of the recent decades has been to permit a conclusion regarding the phase now reached in the general transformation and hence to bring the apparent dualism of history and prophecy within one unitary form.

The conclusion to which this analysis has led is that there is no evidence of such a fundamental lack of adaptability of *homo sapiens* as must lead to a reversal of the secular trend of development which has persisted through the earlier local civilizations and has now become general to man. There is no evidence of any lack of potency in the hereditary constitution to permit the further parallel development of the tradition and the individual. The faculty of differentiation shows no sign of exhaustion, though the emphasis may pass from accelerated differentiation to reorganization, adjustment, and a more complete co-ordination of finite systems. Mankind is now ready for the first step in this reorganization: the recognition of the limitations of the European and Western tradition and the explicit formulation of the unitary principle.

8

Nine Thinkers I:
Heraclitus, Plato, Paul, Kepler, Descartes

As the story passes from past to future its form must change. Up to this point the test of unitary thought has been its power to interpret history; that the reader may judge here and now. But the anticipation of the future must be measured by the power of unitary thought to facilitate the development which it foretells. In passing through the present the story loses its contemplative character and becomes an instrument to facilitate action. It is therefore appropriate that the continuity of the story should be interrupted as it reaches the contemporary scene in the fifth decade of the twentieth century.

In the next two chapters we shall take another even more swift retrospect of the history of European thought. The previous chapters have suffered from neglect of the individual. This is inherent in any philosophy of history, and for those who believe that general ideas constitute a higher reality than individual historical facts, it may be no disadvantage. But to the unitary, thinker ideas are components of individual lives and lose their meaning when divorced from them. Moreover while the historical trend in the past may be viewed with detachment, the future trend must be experienced, by some individuals at least, as the passion and inspiration of their lives. Certain aspects of the future can only be developed by the facilitation which results from conscious attention to the task. For example, the intellectual tradition can only be reorganized by attentive thought, and unitary thought cannot be established unless the trend seizes individuals and makes them its conscious instruments. If any individual develops a personal conviction of the contemporary trend, that implies not only that he recognizes it intellectually but that he experiences in his will and ambition whatever components of the trend are appropriate to his personal temperament. The unitary interpretation of the past is therefore incomplete until we have seen how the past trend, in its different phases, became the inspiration of individual lives.

It is not possible here to follow out the structure of the formative process in the complex patterns of daily human life at different periods of history. But every great transformation of the tradition has found its supreme symbolic figure. It is in these representative individuals that the formative processes of history can be most directly seen; in them the dialectic of dualistic tension and the resolution of discord within new characteristic forms are displayed in the life and thought of a single person. The philosophy of history, normally a generalization from countless individual lives, becomes concrete in the thought processes of such representative figures.

A group of nine leading thinkers has been selected and an attempt made to epitomise the story of the preceding chapters in terms of their thought. They have been chosen solely for their fitness to represent the changing form of the organization of European life, as evidenced in the changing forms of thought. In each we shall discover some European prejudice or some aspects of a universal truth. But these thumbnail sketches are neither complete nor objective in the sense of lacking any presupposition. They start by assuming that the majority of these nine made certain fundamental mistakes, perhaps inevitable at the time, but none the less now seen to be mistakes. Each sketch is an estimate in terms of unitary thought of the essential structure of the individual's mental processes, and hence of his reliability as a guide in this unitary world.

In tracing this changing form of the organization of life and thought we can largely neglect the explicit or literal content of each individual's thought and pay attention mainly to its formal structure. This is a great advantage since it is impossible, for example in the case of Paul, to know the implications of a Greek, Latin, or Aramaic phrase for a person living at the opening of the Christian era. Words derive their meaning from their context, which is the entire matrix of social life within which each word gradually emerged as the symbol of a particular situation. Yet the implications which give each word its meaning are linked by the thread of a common structure, or formal similarity, which guides the processes of memory and association. A process word recalls similar processes; a static word rouses thoughts of permanence; what is single is associated with other singleness; symbols of conflict recall similar conflicts. It is this formal structure, common to all that is implied in an idea, with which we are concerned. A particular structure is common to all the dominant ideas of any stable tradition, and characterises it. When this structure undergoes a general modification, we say that one tradition has disappeared and been replaced by another. But this cannot occur without a far-going social transformation.

Though this changing organization is most clearly expressed in the ideas of such representative individuals, we are not dealing with isolated mental processes, but with historical persons, each intoxicated with his own vision of the significance of experience. The temperament of such a person is closely related to the formal structure of his thought. A man's thought may either express or compensate his personal life; there is no necessary identity between the forms of the personal life and the forms of thought. But at the deepest level, where only the most general characteristics of form operate, there is a general correlation. The temperament and passion of a static dualist is never that of a unitary process thinker; their responses to God and to woman, to eternity and time, express the same continuity of form as does their thought. In this ultimate sense the individuals can be taken to represent stages in the development of Europe in their personality as well as in their thought.

Since we are primarily concerned with the systematic structure of a changing tradition rather than with personality there are certain supreme figures which, though of symbolic importance, lie outside the scope of this analysis: Socrates, Jesus, Goethe, Nietzsche. These men did not help to create systems but represented certain universal attitudes in their lives, their works, and their deaths. Of these four I have included only Goethe, whom I require to throw light, by contrast, on the limitations of the European form. The other three set the limits to the story of Europe. What appeared in Socrates and Jesus, the spiritual consciousness of the individual subject, was exhausted in Nietzsche. The searcher and the god-man led of necessity to the man-god, and to disaster for the tradition. The attitude of these three to the divine and to woman reveals the grandeur and the limitations of the European dissociation. Only after the closing of that cycle of experience and the final collapse of the European tradition is it possible for man to recognize objectively the universal source of his own formative genius. It would appear that no true European could help misunderstanding Goethe, whose real contemporaries are to be found either before Plato or in the present century. Yet he was also marked by his time and can lend a part of himself to throw light on the dissociated forms of life which he repudiated.

Jesus proclaimed the rediscovery of undifferentiated innocence; Socrates sought a differentiation of thought which would restore and protect man's integrity; Nietzsche dreamed of the integrity of a new race of men who would overcome the failure of the Christian-Socratic differentiation. This is the frame of our story. The European experiment in differentiation is an episode in the biology of man's social development and the attempt to interpret it must employ the broad vistas of a philosophical anthropology. Man set out on a two-thousand-year trial of a particular method of differentiation, adapting the structure of his mental processes, conscious and unconscious, to a certain general form.

We need consider only the most general characteristics of this form, and for the purposes of this analysis, these reduce to two. Thought may be either unitary or dualistic (since other pluralistic forms may be neglected), and it may be either process or static. These two pairs produce four combinations or types of thought: unitary-process, unitary-static, dualistic-process, and dualistic-static. The first and last are the most stable and common types, the unitary-static and dualistic-process forms are less frequent and may be regarded as anomalous forms appearing at times of transition.

The analysis into these sharp categories of a field as subtle and complex as thought is no more and no less reliable than any other method of classifying the forms of process. Such discrete classifications can throw light on the nature of thought just as the mental separation of male and female types represents a real divergence of two complementary types within the general diversity of human individuals. But just as a trace of the contrary hormone may set the antagonistic process at work and destroy the sexual balance of the male or female type, so each of those four fundamental types of thought may be disturbed by the influence of a form alien to its own. If we were considering a static scheme of human potentialities it would be enough to choose four representatives, one of each type. But to portray the developing sequence of a process which leads from undifferentiated unitary-process thought through the trial differentiation of dualistic-static forms to differentiated unitary-process thought, we require at least twice that number. No individual is ever a pure representative of his type. Each develops amidst the inheritance of his past and the impress of his environment, and forms his own resolution of these varied influences. Each displays the tension of the process, the antithesis of contrary elements from which one general pattern tends to emerge. Yet these representative figures have been chosen to display certain definite stages in the development of the form of the mental process in man, as revealed partly in temperament but more clearly in the spoken and written word.

At the dawn of European thought there stands a dark oracular figure, *Heraclitus* (540-475 BC), whose vision is at once more ancient and more universal than the European. Aristocratic, lonely, and pessimistic, his dogmatic fragments provide a contrast to the subsequent development of thought. Europe neglected him for twenty-three centuries, and it is only now that his stature can be recognized. Heraclitus links the European tradition with the process thought of the early Asiatic civilizations.

In the earlier Milesian and Pythagorean schools, Greek thinkers had already begun the attempt to see nature and experience as a rational whole. From the study of harmony in music and in geometrical forms Pythagoras had come to believe that number was the key to reality. Heraclitus dismissed this view: "Pythagoras, son of Mnesarchus, practiced investigation most of all men, and having chosen out these treaties, he made a wisdom of his own, much learning and bad art." To Heraclitus all was strife and change, and harmony was not to be regarded as static, but as lying in a developing relation between opposites. Change was universal, but there was one pervasive order within it. Man was a part of that order, and subject to its transformations. The unity of nature was to be found in its variety, and in the continuity of the transformation by which life became death, and night day. The harmony of opposites was seen in process of their interplay, and all values were relative.

Though the Heraclitean fragments are sometimes obscure and are not expressed as a system of thought, the emphasis is unitary and the basic conception is one of process. There are no fundamental dualisms in the pervading order; opposed elements are harmonized through their mutual relations, and perhaps also by the process which transforms each thing into its opposite. These are the formal characteristics of unitary process thought, and they are unmistakable in Heraclitus:

> It is wise for those who hear, not me, but the universal reason, to confess that all things are one. This world, the same for all, neither any of the gods nor any man has made, but it always was, and is, and shall be, an ever-living fire, kindled in due measure and in due measure extinguished. Into the same river you could not step twice, for other waters are flowing. —In change is rest. —Craving and satiety. — God is day and night, winter and summer, war and peace, plenty and want. —For men to have whatever they wish, would not be well. Sickness makes health pleasant and good; hunger, satiety; weariness, rest.—War is the father and king of all. —It is hard to contend with passion, for whatever it craves it buys with its life.—[Heraclitus blamed the poet who said, 'Would that strife were destroyed from among gods and men.' For there could be no harmony without sharps and flats, nor living beings without male and female, which are contraries. The harmony of the world is a harmony of oppositions, as in the case of the bow and the lyre. The unlike is joined together, and from differences results the most beautiful harmony, and all things take place by strife.] —Good and evil are the same. —Unite whole and part, agreement and disagreement, accordant and discordant: from all comes one, and from one all. —To me one is ten thousand if he be the best. —A man's character is his daemon. - Wisdom is to speak truth and consciously to act according to nature.

In these fragments we recognize Heraclitus as the father of process thought, as have others to whom we shall refer later. He is the representative of undifferentiated unitary process thought, thought before it separated itself from nature and set out on the search for analytical clarity. I have given these quotations at length because they provide a vivid contrast to the main trend of European thought. Their meaning and content do not call for comment here, but their general form is clear: in place of dualism, there is the opposition of complementaries; in place of static substance, there is the rhythm and strife of process. Heraclitus is aware of himself as different from others, but he is pantheistic, lyrical, and intuitive, not self-critical or analytical. He is subtle and dogmatic, but he does not moralize in the hope of improving. He feels the same rhythm in himself as he observes in nature; the gift of thought enables him to criticize his senses, but it does not separate him from nature. Most men may be blind and life may be tragic, but man, as Heraclitus

sees him, is not a problem to himself. In Heraclitus there is something of the early Greek sense of unity and balance, which was
later lost in Greece and was rejected by Europe. Yet if the fancy be
permitted, we can imagine that Heraclitus might have understood
the two thousand years of error as a stage in the process of history,
for "we all work together to one end, some consciously and with
purpose, others unconsciously. Just as indeed Heraclitus, I think,
says that the sleeping are co-workers and fabricators of the things
that happen in the world." (M. Antoninus.) To the unitary mind it is
as though the achievements of Europe had been a brilliant dream
in the long sleep of static thought, when man was unaware of his
unity.

It is one of the strangest features of history that there are brief
periods, and even individual lives, in which the developments of
many centuries are epitomized. A few generations of Greek history
appear to summarize the history of Europe, and the thought of one
Greek philosopher to carry within it the fertile seed from which has
grown the European soul. To understand *Plato* (427-347 BC) is to
understand Europe, for if we look deep enough we can see in him
not only the separation of thought from the world of phenomena
which it is the task of science to overcome, but also the disillusionment which gave Christianity its opportunity. Plato expresses more
completely than any other thinker the tension which set Europe its
task and was at the same time its prime mover. The disparity of the
ideal and the real created the phenomenon Europe, and in the philosophical realm Plato is its symbol.

But here we can only consider the most general aspect of Plato's
historical situation and personal achievement, and no attempt will
be made to refer to his special doctrines, whether in philosophy,
ethics, or politics. Plato has been quoted enough. His words have a
spurious clarity. For more than two thousand years they have hyp-
notized men with their treacherous lucidity, promising the Socratic
path to knowledge but leaving the soul bemused on a transcendental and wholly fantastical journey. Moreover it would be dishonest
to cite phrases in support of my interpretations, since such passages must either be torn from a Socratic dialectic of enquiry where
the method not the conclusion is essential, or from a Platonic doctrine which changes from dialogue to dialogue, much as Europe

did from century to century, and, like Europe, ends in a bitter intolerance which repudiates its earlier ideals. The tension in Plato and in Europe gave neither any rest; however grand their achievement their common failure proves a deep maladjustment which vitality must sooner or later repudiate.

Plato is the symbol of Europe because he is the expression of the human demand for permanence in a universe of process. This antithesis, which is the most general characteristic of the European tradition, may be identified in every component of the process, in the biological and physiological processes, in the origins of thought, in social and political movements, and in the structure of philosophy. Plato is great because his thought so completely represented both the typical situation of a man at that period and his own personal situation as pupil, lover, citizen, and idealist, through the different phases of his life. This means that we can find this characteristic antithesis represented in every component of his life and thought, but most clearly of all, because he is foremost a lover of truth, in his thought.

To Plato the thinker the world of process and the demand for permanence are represented respectively by the Heraclitean flux and the Socratic search for moral and intellectual certainty. As Aristotle explains, Plato was the result of the interaction of the Heraclitean doctrine and the Socratic demand for a universal ethic. Plato was true to his time and also a true European in accepting the validity of the Heraclitean view as regards the world of the senses, while denying that world reality in favor of a transcendental world of permanent ideas. That was the attitude which the tradition impressed on each maturing generation. Plato sees straight to the roots of the human situation at the time and emphasises the inescapable dualism between the process of the senses and the permanence of timeless ideas. This honesty is the source of his power, and his position has for long been beyond challenge. But he went on to interpret the dualism in a special manner. It was an essential and permanent dualism, and since to him only what was permanent could be granted real existence, the persisting harmony of the ideal world was reality and the confusion of the world of process was illusion. In expressing the antithesis of permanence and process and in granting prior reality to the permanent, Plato speaks for European tradition. This attitude was superimposed on the normal adaptive vitality of the species. Most Europeans continued to believe in the reality of the world of the senses, and to take comfort in the Platonic doctrine only when the facts of process became unbearable at times of frustration, illness, or approaching death.

But why did Plato make this choice? He lived only two or three generations after Heraclitus, yet he represents a different type of man. The transformation of the social tradition at the opening of the third period, which we analyzed in a previous chapter, is concentrated and thrown into high relief by the contrast between these two thinkers. The problems which have preoccupied the modern mind did not exist for Heraclitus, but there are most of them in the *Dialogues*. In Plato there is scarcely a trace left of the ancient undifferentiated unitary man, while most features of the dissociated theoretical mind are already present. These two, in certain respects typical of ancient and modern, appear to be separated by an abyss, and yet they are linked by the continuity of the Heraclitean transformation which led from one to the other. Because Heraclitus accepted process and represents a more universal mode of being it is conceivable that for once the more ancient type might have understood, while pitying, the later.

If they have all met meantime in other regions, I have no doubt that Plato has conceived a heavenly dialogue between Heraclitus and Socrates in which the Heraclitean process and the Socratic dialectic carry the argument from the original antithesis to a joint recognition that the unitary method must now supersede the Socratic. But that dialogue could not be honestly recorded, for Heraclitus would angrily have repudiated its possibility and quite properly thereafter have remained silent, knowing that torn from his historical context he, Heraclitus, could no longer exist. He might think to himself that the whole affair of these Socratic dialogues was an overrated intellectualist fantasy, never leading either to conviction or to action, but he would not trouble to assert what he would know that Socrates could not recognize. So Plato could record no dialogue but only the smiling faith of Socrates, justified by the Europe that drew its inspiration so largely from him, and the grave air of Heraclitus, who, having seen the deeper truth, would certainly be indifferent to the knowledge that, when Europe failed, the world would after all look back to him. The day had not come for a philosopher who would proclaim the joyful wisdom of the acceptance of process, and Plato, after Socrates' death, could not have understood such an attitude.

These two represent the ancient and modern types, the primitive undifferentiated and the European dissociated man, as far as is possible for men who were so close to one another in time, and both pre-eminently thinkers. Why did one choose one form of thought and the other the alternative? What change in social conditions provided the stimulus to a new development in the later of the two? The unthinking acceptance of the forms of ancient life had been disturbed by an upheaval in which both the contrast between one social system and another and the instability of all such systems had been forced on man's attention in the Eastern Mediterranean and particularly in Greece. Social disturbance had unsettled men's minds and the early Greek thinkers were expressing a social need in seeking to recover stability through the discovery of a rational and universal principle of order. We have seen that in the early stages of the evolution of thought the requirement of clarity implies the use of static ideas, and the later and more systematic and logical Greek thinkers of necessity turned to static conceptions. Heraclitus had not been intimidated by the processes of life and the mercilessness of change, but that aristocratic attitude could not be maintained. The common experience was one of discomfort and anxiety; while the old order was no longer respected the anarchy and relativity of the offered alternatives were equally unsatisfying; a general demand for system arose, and with it the opportunity for developing static concepts.

The Socratic method is the subjective and introspective form of what later became the heuristic principle of quantity. Socrates made his life the search for truth regarding the ideal life; intellectual clarity and ethical truth were inseparable, and man should use his mind to seek the truth. Plato took on himself to fulfil this teaching, but it was not enough for him to remain, like his teacher, a humble seeker of truth. Life had disappointed him, Socrates was gone, and he required some established certainty on which he could lean. There were more general physiological and social conditions which facilitated his choice, but in the man Plato it was the evil cruelty of men that compelled his choice. He could not remain with Heraclitus and Socrates in the world of the senses; he refused to accept the ultimate reality of a world which could condemn to death the very prophet of truth; he joined the ranks of those who sought to escape the distress of the actual world in the static harmony of thought. Parmenides had already emphasized the static character of real existence, and Anaxagoras had found this reality in a transcendental world. Socrates, in deadly earnest in his search for truth, had been more cautious. But Plato was impatient for certainty, and the Socratic road to knowledge became the Platonic view of reality: "In the beginning was the Word."

This was the response of an individual to the general social transformation in progress at the time, and it resulted in the establishment of the explicit marks of the European dissociation. But this unitary situation and its results can be identified in the different components of the process: in the physiology of the mental processes, which facilitated the prior development of static concepts; in the social instability which stimulated the compensatory development of systematic thought; and in the bitter personal experience which led Plato to reject the world of process. Platonic thought facilitated a general tendency. In Plato we find the essential form of the European attitude: the intellectual rejection of the phenomenal world of process on account of its sordid ruthlessness and the emancipation of the spirit within its own realm of permanent intellectual clarity and harmony. The ancient, aristocratic, tragic consciousness disappears; man sets out to console his spirit and protect his body by the exploitation of static ideas.

The Pythagorean view of musical harmony had not separated music from life, or number from nature. But Plato appears at some stage in his life to have revolted from sensuous and sensual pleasure, in place of the beauty of nature he came to see only the ugliness of man, and the Socratic method lent itself easily to the separation of the divine music of the soul from the sordid materiality of flesh and blood. With this division man becomes self-conscious, subjective, moralistic, analytical, and critical. Each of these characteristics expresses a static element in Platonic thought. The subjective quality expresses the emphasis on the individual as a persisting entity separated from the processes of the environment; the moralizing tendency expresses the distrust of the processes of organic vitality; and the critical and analytical intellect expresses the impulse to master nature through the application of static ideas. These complementary aspects may be brought together in one observation: the Platonic attitude represented the partial displacement of consciousness or attention from its proper role of the facilitation of development to the vain attempt to modify the real world to conform to the ideal.

The high generality of this interpretation of Plato does not imply any vagueness or speculative uncertainty. It is, I believe, merely the consequence of applying the Socratic method to the Platonic doctrine. An analysis of the logic of many of Plato's arguments, using the radical methods of mathematical logic, would inevitably show that Plato's unspoken criterion of certainty, reality, and truth is always and only persistence and permanence. His arguments for immortality show this most clearly, but the same basis is fundamental to his entire thought. This is the sort of man he is; he can think in no other way.

The Socratic method can lead anywhere; it is the machine tool which can make any kind of tool. In the hands of dissociated European man it leads to dissociated theories, but applied by unitary man to the dethronement of the abstract noun it finally opens the way to proper process thought. Socrates represents the revolt of the human spirit from the relativity of the ancient world, the intellectual search for a supreme sanction in the existence of which man must believe if he is to survive. Unitary thought is the comparable revolt from modern relativity, the search by man for the form of his unity with nature, a unity which his European reason tells him must exist, since life and thought exist.

But in separating consciousness from the material world Plato has to ascribe the formative faculty of the mind to consciousness, whereas the formative processes of the human system are largely unconscious, that is, they operate below the dominant processes of the human hierarchy and only come to attention at special moments. This confusion is inevitable in dualistic-static thought, because the formative element cannot belong to the material world, the criterion of which is mere permanence. It appears, for example, in the Platonic treatment of Eros. There is physiological and philosophical truth in the imagery of the ascent of love from particular and transient beauty to more general and lasting beauty. The nervous system itself is a hierarchy which passes the residues of particular stimuli up to the higher ganglia which respond to more general situations. So thought builds itself up from the particular to the general, and so also man grows from the immediacy of instinct to the broader human vision. Above all in love, which can move the whole man, the formative impulses pass up the hierarchy, potentially creative at every level. But in the Platonic image Eros has no home; the god belongs neither to the flesh nor to the spirit and can only generate in beauty, somewhere between the ideal and the real. Love is no longer a process, with all the power and limitations of a process, but has become an unsubstantial idea. But in truth Eros does not belong to the Platonic system; by his existence he refutes it, and only by denying him proper fulfilment could Plato become so far-going a European. To Heraclitus and the ancient world the experience of beauty was a component of the variety and necessity of natural processes; to Plato and the complete Europeans beauty became a moral idea. The failure of the instinctive integration had made this necessary. Moral ideals were the compensating structures developed by the formative process to sustain a long period of differentiation and dissociation. But ideals are only temporary structures, since their static and universal character denies the diversity of individuals each on his own course of development. Ideals are thus temporary compensations for ignorance of the actual nature of man and of the form of his proper development. Plato and Europe were supreme during the period when man remained ignorant of the form of his unity with nature.

Plato symbolizes the intellectual, and Paul (?-AD 64) the religious self-consciousness. Socrates had developed an intellectual method by his personal example in using the spoken word, and Plato in recording the Socratic conversations had made this method the basis of an intellectual system. In a similar manner Paul's mission was to spread the spoken parables and personal example of Jesus as the inspiration of a widespread ethical community, which was to be developed by his missionary travels and his letters. Socrates and Jesus were lit by a completeness that was only for heroes; few could follow the simple assurance of their gospels. But Plato and Paul, each in his own way a dualistic man denying a part of life, were at once inspired by their respective leaders and touched by common mortality; it was the task of each to spread the knowledge of a noble and tragic life, and to dilute the heady gospel into a socially tolerable ethic. The parallel is valid in so far as it expresses the isolation of primary genius and the role of the inspired but dissociated teacher who alone can convey the new message to the people, but its limits are reached in the different conditions of the two cases. Plato's personal denial was further-reaching than Paul's and he deserted the Socratic ideal to develop fanciful theories; though they alike sought to fulfil their mission in the life of their community, Plato's life ended in practical failure, while Paul created the basis for a universal church and in his own person paid the full price.

From a social point of view Paul is the most characteristic of all European figures. His life and thought spring from a soil in which Semitic, Greek, and Roman elements, partly springing from earlier Egyptian sources, were again combined. While the Jewish tradition was national and separatist, Paul is universally human: "There is neither Jew nor Greek, there is neither bond nor free, there is neither male nor female: for all are one in Christ Jesus." Moreover Paul is an individual in the, European sense; his mysticism was not loss of personality in a passive identification with God, but the sense of a compelling mission, driving him to an active life of preaching, strongly marked by the qualities and limitations of his own person, a form which reappears in the assertive dogmatism of Luther. This European energy sprang from an also characteristically European dichotomy; he did not accept himself, he was not at ease with himself, the necessity was laid on him, woe to him if he did not fulfil it. His combination of strength and weakness, of gentleness and anger, of intoxication and despair, of self-confidence and humility, is a typical sign of the European dissociation. This division is only partially concealed by the longing for unity and permanence symbolized in the monotheistic god of love who brings the assurance of eternal life. But the harmony is incomplete, the unsatisfactory structure of the person speaks through his words, and he is continually disturbed by the sense of failure or inadequacy which so often accompanies good works.

Before we can go deeper into the formal structure of Paul's person and thought we must consider his historical significance. For him there were four historical ages. First, the period from Adam to Abraham, when sin is unconscious, since no right and wrong are recognized. This is the period of primitive man. Second, from Abraham to Moses, when sin is recognized but standards are not defined. Third, from Moses to Christ, the period of the Law. This is the period which we have already discussed, when increasing technical skill and developing awareness enable man to satisfy his instinctive desires, not as necessities for life, but as sources of pleasure. This loss of innocence led to the exploitation not only of pleasure but also of pain, and man became bestial when uncontrolled by social standards. The Law expressed the need and desire of the community to stabilize and order the animal life of man in an ethical system which would control and limit the new lusts. The existence of the Law was thus to Paul a result and an admission of the fact of sin. The Law did not attempt to change man's nature, but only to control it through fear of the Lord.

Paul had experienced bitterly the curse of the Law: man had been innocent until the Law had arisen, the Law had produced the knowledge of sin, but man's sinful nature could not conform to the Law, and was left in a hopeless state of conflict and shame. "Nay I had not known sin, but by the Law; for I had not known lust, except the Law had said, thou shall not covet. —Cursed is everyone that continueth not in all things which are written in the book of the Law to do them. —For by the Law is the knowledge of sin." The breakdown of the modes of life of the ancient civilizations had resulted in uncertainty, license, and bestiality. In the Hebrew community this had been met by the establishment of the Law, but at the price of an inescapable dualism in man's conception of himself. The conflict which man thus forced on himself left him unable to recognize any integrating tendency which he could accept as representing his true nature. "For what I would, that I do not; but what I hate, that I do. —Now then it is no more that I do it, but sin that dwelleth in me. —So then with the mind I myself serve the law of God; but with the flesh the law of sin." The dualism is absolute, and man can make only one choice. "For the wages of sin is death; but the gift of God is eternal life. —For the flesh lusteth against the spirit, and the spirit against the flesh; and these are contrary the one to the other, so that ye cannot do the things that ye would." There is no doubt what is implied in the choice: "And they that are Christ's have crucified the flesh with the affections and lusts."

But those to whom the shame of this conflict has become unbearable, and who have the advantage of the personal example of a new form of life, can be purged of their conscious sinful desires and achieve a new partial integration. This is the role of Jesus in social history. A personal example become a myth serves to transform an exhausting conflict within consciousness into a harmony. But this harmony of consciousness is achieved by a process of suppression which results from the acceptance of a new organizing conviction: the divinity of Jesus come to take the burden of sin from us. The strain of conflict is lightened by the sense of forgiveness, and a new partial co-ordination is achieved, attention being directed to religious sublimations of the instinctive desires and away from the desires themselves. Open conflict is converted into inner dissociation. This apparent victory over sin is the aim of union with the Messiah. As in all sadism the flesh of another crucified is our own flesh crucified, and the battle is won for us: "Knowing this, that our old man is crucified with him, that the body of sin might be destroyed, that henceforward we should not serve sin. — For sin shall not have dominion over you: for ye are not under the law, but under grace. —But he that is joined unto the Lord is one spirit."

Here in the accepted interpretation of the origins of Pauline Christianity we can trace one aspect of the process which led to the European dissociation. The growing complexity of life unsettles the primitive and ancient innocence; man becomes aware of the need for a new order and new standards: these standards render evident the divergence from them of his own nature, and conflict, sin, and shame are experienced; finally a new harmony is established through the relative suppression of certain components of human nature. Another aspect of the same process is seen in the development of the Platonic ethical dualism which separates the real world of ideas from the inferior realm of material phenomena.

It would appear that Paul's thought had been influenced by Platonic ideas, but the whole trend of Mediterranean thought was moving in the same direction and it is impossible to separate its different components. This essential conformity of the intellectual and religious trends becomes evident when we observe that the basic structure of Paul's thought was dualistic and static. The dualism is unmistakable. Even the grace which comes to the believer does not emancipate him from the curse of his divided nature: "I find then a law, that, when I, would do good, evil is present with me. For I delight in the law of God after the inward man. But I see another law in my members, warring against the law of my mind, and bringing me into captivity to the law of sin which is in my members. O wretched man that I am! Who shall deliver me from the body of this death?" The answer is that redemption comes only with the resurrection: "Flesh and blood cannot inherit the kingdom of God; neither corruption inherit incorruption. Behold I shew you a mystery; we shall not all sleep, but we shall all be changed. In a moment, in the twinkling of an eye, at the last trump; for the trumpet shall sound, and the dead shall be raised incorruptible, and we shall be changed.—O death, where is thy sting? O grave, where is thy victory?"

Yet even this vision of final redemption is disturbed by the dim knowledge of the dissociation and of the repressed and distorted components whose eruption is symbolized in Antichrist: "For that day shall not come, except there come a falling away first, and that man of sin be revealed, the son of perdition.— Even him, whose coming is often the working of Satan with an power and signs and lying wonders. —And for this cause God shall send them strong delusions, that they should believe a lie." The instability of the dissociation was evident even then, and the emergence of Antichrist, the distorted bestial man whose lies dominate the time of transition, is foretold two millennia before he appeared.

Beneath the poetry we see the desire for a permanent static harmony. Death is the wages of sin and is the worst punishment; immortality is the reward of faith. Nature is corruption; there is no true development; a trumpet destroys the illusion of time.

A doctrine that has played so great a role cannot he damaged by honesty, if it still has anything to offer. What does this static dualism of orthodox Christianity amount to? It expresses man's failure fully to integrate his progressively differentiating capacities, his sense of frustration, and the consequent compelling demand for the promise of fulfilment in another world. This is psychologically inescapable: if continuity of development is frustrated, continuity of permanence is sought in its place; the ego separates itself from the whole and demands immortality. Those who are frustrated by life or weakened by illness tend to desire their own permanence, but those who enjoy health and fulfilment are free to accept process and to proclaim their less prejudiced view. There is no static permanence. The only lasting feature is continuity of development and when a particular system can develop no further, it can only await its end. Pauline religion was one of many variants of the static dualism of the European dissociation which for long remained the most effective partial integration that the differentiating European had achieved. But it was dualistic and static, and therefore passing.

Yet Paul leaves as a permanent treasure his expression of the brotherhood of man: "Though I speak with the tongues of men and of angels and have not charity, I am become as sounding brass, or a tinkling cymbal. And though I have the gift of prophecy, and understand all mysteries, and all knowledge; and though I have all faith, so that I could remove mountains, and have not charity, I am nothing. —And now abideth faith, hope, charity, these three: but the greatest of these is charity."

Kepler (AD 1571-1630) stands with Galileo at the watershed of the medieval and modern worlds. In Kepler the two most powerful ideas in the history of thought were fused: God is revealed in measured numbers, the numerical harmonies of the planetary motions are an expression of the divine nature. The Pythagoreans had held a similar view two thousand years before, but not with Kepler's reverent loyalty to the facts of the heavens. Greek religious thought was more pantheistic, and Greek interest in number was limited to the harmonic proportions of static figures. Kepler's intense adoration of the one God sustained his long search for the concealed numerical harmony that must, he felt, lie hidden beneath the apparent irregularities of the motions of the heavenly bodies. His passionate monotheism was with respect for detailed fact. He could not doubt that the divine harmony was all pervasive and would ultimately yield its secret to the searcher, provided that his patience and his loyalty to the facts were both inexhaustible. He announced to the world his self-appointed task, and struggled for twenty years to reveal, to the greater glory of God, a simple numerical rule concealed in the movements of the planets.

The two great agencies of the medieval and the modern world, the Christian God and measured quantity, achieved in Kepler their unique synthesis. The glory of his unwavering search brought him to the final fulfilment which transcended his dreams and he broke into triumphant song:

"That which I suspected twenty-two years ago, before I had discovered the relation of the five regular bodies to the paths of the planets; of which my mind was convinced even before I had seen the 'Harmony' of Ptolemy; which I had promised to my friends in the title of this Fifth Book, before I was quite certain of it; which I published sixteen years ago as my task; for which I have devoted the last part of my life to the study of the heavens, for which I came to Tycho Brahe and settled in Prag —*that* have I now at last brought, into the light of day and established more clearly than I had any right to hope ... through the power of God, who fascinated me, inflamed my spirit with an inexhaustible yearning, and nourished my body and mind through the generosity of two princes who gave me the means."

Kepler goes on to describe how delighted he had been to find the same conception of the harmony of the heavens in Ptolemy's work written 1,500 years before, and then confesses the rapture of discovery:

> Nature had revealed herself through interpreters separated by many centuries; in the language of the Hebrews, it was the finger of God that allowed the same picture of the structure of the world to grow in the souls of two men who had given themselves up to the study of nature, though neither had influenced the other. But now since eighteen months ago the first light dawned, since three moons the full day, and since a few days the sunshine of the most marvellous clarity—now nothing holds me back: now I may give in to this holy rapture. Let the children of men scorn my daring confession: Yes! I have stolen the golden vessels of the Egyptians to build from them a temple for my God, far from the borders of Egypt. If you forgive me, I am glad; if you are angry, I must bear it. So —here I throw the dice and write a book, for today or for posterity, I do not care. Should it wait a hundred years for a reader, well, God himself has waited six thousand years for a man to read his work.

Kepler's passion is single. To the Western mind it may appear as a fusion of religious enthusiasm and the exact scientist's passion for numerical discovery. But it was something simpler. Kepler lived at the one moment in history when the religious and scientific passions could be identical. This is not hyperbole. At its root religion is an expression of man's search for unity; so also is science. Before Kepler the subjective element was predominant and there was no exact science. In Kepler the two were balanced; the subjective did not confuse the objective; religious enthusiasm assisted the scientific aim, and the aim of the discovery was a religious offering. But this dual language obscures the true situation; Kepler's passionate belief in a harmony unifying diversity flowed at once into religious emotion and into the scientific organization of fact. After Kepler the objective quantitative element predominated and the subjective religious passion, divorced from the real world of exact science, faded into the background. Objective number is essentially alien to the human spirit and its gods; only at Kepler's time was the state of knowledge such as to bring the two into balance and to conceal their antithesis.

Never before or since has any man searched twenty years for a truth so new as that which Kepler sought and found. Kepler's life symbolizes the process of discovery; a process of long preparation and swift fulfilment; expressing unconscious tendencies, yet subject to the critique of consciousness; using capacities which are neither consciously rational nor irrational, but formative and organic. The formative process in Kepler's mind led him to search for a simple harmony; it was historical circumstance only that gave his subjective experience the form of devotion to a personal god. Indeed in opening a new field to the formative tendencies of the mind, the field of dynamical motions, Kepler and Galileo were doing much to eliminate the psychological necessity for religious faith. Thereafter the formative tendency of the mind increasingly expressed itself in shaping the quantitative picture of nature, and was directed less and less into religious conviction. The harmony which for Kepler was an expression of God soon became a substitute for God.

Yet Kepler's passion for unity was limited in its scope; only through the limitations of its aim could it be effective. Kepler sought a transcendent and eternal harmony, and found it by neglecting the personal life and the world of change. His impulse was, like that of all exact scientists after him, to escape the apparent arbitrariness, confusion, and ceaseless process of the world around into a divine peace and harmony. The dualism of his temperament is concealed, because his emotion and his work are concentrated on the ideal world with the result that he displayed little interest in the world of human process. It has been said that the study of astronomy trained the human mind to understand nature. That is only true for the static aspects of nature and for motions which are stationary in the sense that they display no irreversible change or cumulative development. Kepler never conceived that the solar system might have a history; it had been created once and for all in the image of God, with even the axes of the various planetary orbits in permanent harmonic ratios. Kepler's discoveries contained as much illusion as truth, but in failing to distinguish between them he was true to himself, for his aim was to find the simplest possible reason for the permanent forms of nature being as they were. This emphasis on permanence corresponded to the fact that, as far as he could, he lived in the ideal world. But he believed that in his discovery he had united the real and the ideal, and that illusion made him great.

The supreme moment of Kepler's life was the fulfilment of twenty years of humble search in the final ecstasy of discovery; the comparable moment for *Descartes (1596-1650)* was an evening early in his life when he determined to set out on the search for truth by doubting everything. Kepler's search was guided by a sense of certainty because he felt himself to be the instrument of God, Descartes' by the conviction that amidst the uncertainty of prevalent opinions truth could be found only by the deliberate processes of the conscious mind. Kepler felt that he was guided by the finger of God; Descartes proclaimed the complete autonomy of conscious reason. In a few decades Kepler's temple, so reverently built by him for his god, had been occupied by the human mind.

Descartes determined to take nothing on trust, to sweep away his previous opinions, and to accept only those that could survive the scrutiny of reason:

> When I considered that the very same thoughts which we experience when awake may also be experienced when we are asleep, while there is at that time not one of them true, I supposed that all the objects that had ever entered into my mind when awake had in them no more truth than the illusions of my dreams. But immediately upon this I observed that, whilst I thus wished to think that all was false, it was absolutely necessary that I, who thus thought, should be somewhat; and as I observed that this truth, *I think, hence I am,* was so certain and of such evidence, that no ground of doubt, however extravagant, could be alleged by the sceptics capable of shaking it, I concluded that I might, without scruple, accept it as the first principle of the philosophy of which I was in search.

If Descartes were right, and the value of thought depended on the degree to which it expresses the conscious perception of absolute truth, it would be hard to understand the success of his method. It led to results of the greatest utility to exact science though his first achievement, the assertion of consciousness as a primary, substantial reality, was an error. The religious veil had fallen; man had begun to discover the true forms of nature. He could not fail sooner or later to believe in the independence of his own mind and the supreme fertility of his own consciousness. Nor could Descartes that evening in November, 1619. He represented man torn from his roots, over-travelled, over-sceptical, over-lonely, over-conscious of himself. He sat alone and pondered: man, as conscious subject, alone with the problem of truth, and therefore seeking an absolute philosophic truth separated from the practical life of the senses; man as subject, without conviction, or love, or action; alone with his doubts. The result was inevitable: an exaggerated emphasis on consciousness, and the overcoming of doubt by the new dogmatism of a precise deductive system of abstract necessity. Just as Descartes fled his doubts into a dogmatic system of clear ideas, Cartesian machine-man has compensated his inner uncertainty in a ruthless exploitation of mechanical technique.

To Descartes the consciousness of the self, from which he began, implied knowledge of one's own imperfect nature, and this in turn implied knowledge of a perfect being or god, the idea of whom enabled us to be aware of our own limitations. Kepler's spontaneous conviction of God had already become a scepticism which seeks to still itself with rational arguments for the existence of God, and doubt rather than faith become the means to attain knowledge. Yet Descartes, the sceptic, displays an innocent trust in his own mind. Man could discover the truth, for if he had a clear and definite idea of anything that was evidence of its existence. Since man found himself in possession of two clear ideas, the idea of consciousness or thought, and the idea of spatial extension, these were two realities: mind or consciousness without extension, and matter or extension without consciousness, behind which pair the idea of God was necessary to harmonise the dualism.

The dualistic-static form of thought which marks the European tradition attains its most radical expression in Descartes. Whatever lip service we pay to other ideas, and however certain we are of its falsity, after three centuries we still behave as if we lived in a Cartesian world. The static clarity of Cartesian thought inevitably fascinated and imposed on beings who were so badly in need of harmony and so ready to deny process in the search for it. The very clarity of the method exposes its own errors, but we are accustomed to them and like them, for they satisfy our vanity. It has been evident for a century that unity is necessary to thought, and that process is inherent in nature, but Western man has preferred to perish in his dualism rather than give up the proud autonomy of reason and risk losing his identity in the universal process.

If the clarity of an idea is the criterion of its reality, then the real must be static, since static ideas are the clearest, or at least appear so to European man. Descartes does not say, "I am aware of the intermittent processes of thought in myself, born of the changing relations to the environment which make up my transient life." His demand for clarity leads him to isolate not a component of process, but an existent entity "I"—I think, therefore I am—and so to establish the dualism of mind and matter. Beneath the aim of clarity is the demand for permanent entities, substances which in themselves do not change. The immature intellect, being unable as yet to cope with process, creates these persisting entities for its own convenience. The Cartesian mind was satisfied with a spurious subjective clarity in the form of its ideas and neglected to consider how ideas develop, or what their relation is to nature.

The procedure developed by Descartes is the analytical method which assumes that thought must pass from simple, clear, and local facts to the general and complex. This method would be adequate in a world of changeless entities possessing motion but no history, and contemplated by a static mind endowed once and for all with the necessary clear ideas. In Descartes' thought there is no duration, no history, and no approach to an understanding either of the development of form in nature or of the origin of ideas in the mind. Analytical clarity is a comforting illusion, but a dangerous one because it obscures the profound limitations of static dualistic thought. European hopes were ultimately frustrated because a civilization built on static dualistic rationalism could not control its own development. Descartes reduced form to quantity, and opened the way to the anarchy of mechanism and the decay of culture. Unitary man by recognizing that form is prior and quantity one aspect of form can facilitate the recovery of ordered development.

9

Nine Thinkers II:
Spinoza, Goethe, Marx, Freud

In Kepler the desire for unity had expressed itself in a passion that was both religious and scientific, but was limited to a special field. *Spinoza* (1632-77) displays the same desire in a more general and philosophic form. His passion for unity, at once intellectual and emotional, was so intense that it carried him in certain respects outside the European tradition, beyond the limitations of Judaism, Christianity, and contemporary dualistic science. This was inevitable; Spinoza's intellectual consciousness could not accept a dissociated tradition. His transcendental desire for unity expressed itself in a form that had the superficial appearance both of religion and of theoretical science. But the fifty years since Kepler had broadened the human mind, and Spinoza's demand for a universal unity took him beyond religion and science into the unitary realm. The unity of God was not to be revealed merely in external nature but in the perfection of a complete intellectual system, within which all phenomena, including man, would lose their apparent arbitrariness and be recognized as necessary components in the whole. Within this single order there could be no fundamental dualism; there was therefore no sin in the eyes of God, and there should be no separation of mind and matter in the mind of man. Spinoza thus denied the essential tenets of Christianity and of dualistic science; for him Plato and Paul had betrayed the unity of the divine truth. Yet Spinoza remained relatively infertile, and must be considered as European rather than universal, because his single vision was static, and subject to the limitations of intellectual idealism. For Spinoza the emotional and intellectual consciousness was supreme, and prior to life and action.

Spinoza's aim was the same as that of Socrates: the therapy of man through the divine truth. He sought to reveal the necessary order of nature, and in particular the interrelations of human emotions, thought, and action, so that man could live the life proper to him. The aim of science, the discovery of the natural order, and the aim of ethics, the realization of the life proper to man, were here combined in a conviction of the unity in nature and man, which being recognized must lead man towards the permanent harmony which was God. Spinoza's devotion to this aim resulted in what is perhaps the highest expression of idealism in the world's literature. Europe does not lack its symbolic figures: Descartes is the sceptical analytical rationalist, and Spinoza the fervent intellectual idealist. Yet however sublime Spinoza's enthusiasm, his reading of nature and of human nature was wrong. It was founded morally on a doctrine of self-knowledge which he could not apply to himself, and intellectually on a timeless concept of God-substance-nature which reveals his ignorance of nature and his lack of self-knowledge.

To desire honesty with all one's heart is not enough to ensure its realization, for honesty in thought can only exist beside integrity in life. Spinoza loved his dream world, his vision of God, the blessing of a calm transcendent truth, the emancipation from disturbing emotions—he loved these things too much to be able to confess to himself that the external conflicts which he sought to escape still remained reflected in his own heart. He had renounced the traditional, sectarian superstitions of Jewish orthodoxy, received their curse of banishment, and discovered a universal truth and compassion which was more generous even than the Christian. Like Jesus and Paul he had revolted from the arbitrary rigidity of the Jewish Law. That was wholly positive. But he had also renounced the world of men and women to pursue a lonely harmony. Being drunk with God, he certainly had no choice. Yet if we are to estimate Spinoza *sub specie aeternitatis*—and he himself would accept no other approach—his god was only a part of the whole; his conception of nature of limited validity; his technique inadequate; and his emotion, thought, and life a special form that we can now interpret from a broader and more secure foundation.

In his concept of God-substance he denied process; in his life he avoided relations with others; in his heart he failed to maintain that transcendent aesthetic comprehension in which all things are pure because necessary. Here nature and life are merciless; whoever aspires far, necessarily reveals his limitations. Excellence is indeed difficult and rare. All forms of intellectual idealism express the very human desire for a lasting harmony, and the intensity of one special form of idealism arises from a deep lying emotional disharmony. In one sentence which stands out as alien to the rest of his entire work Spinoza confesses to us what he dared not admit to himself, a clue to the source of his denial of woman, and with her of the fuller life of man. He is discussing "jealousy":

> This situation occurs principally in the case of love of woman; since whoever imagines that the woman whom he loves has given herself to another, will be sad not merely because his own desire is thwarted, but because he will feel disgust with it, being compelled to connect his image of the beloved person with the privy parts and excreta of the other.

To the unitary consciousness organic facts are innocent, but dissociated man may by a shudder reveal that his divine comprehension is no more than an intellectual pretence. The spiritual achievement of Europe is displayed in our ability to recognize the significance of those betraying words; we are learning to recognize the limitations of the subjective consciousness, and to separate in it the valid from the invalid. To the dissociated mind, engrossed in its own subjective ideas, it appears that something is damaged when attention is called to a defect in genius, but in fact only its own illusions are affected. Spinoza remains the same, so true to himself that we can learn not only from his superb intellect, monistic but static, but also from the underlying division which separated his consciousness from the organic matrix of his life. The perverse association confessed by Spinoza is one of the many sources of dissociated idealism. Disgust with any aspect of organic function, whether it leads to over-emphasis or inhibition, expresses the distortion which accompanies a dissociation of the human system. The example of Goethe shows that such dissociation is not a necessary element in a developing and creative personality. Spinoza overcame much of the ignorant dogmatism of Christian morality, but in preferring a static harmony to development, and isolation with his god to the fuller life of action, he reveals a limitation which renders his thought relatively infertile. In this he represents the idealism which has now to be overcome.

Yet in many respects Spinoza was not merely ahead of his own century, but represented an attitude of self-conscious man towards his own life which still lies ahead. Christianity serves to maintain and compensate a dissociation; Spinoza, in spite of the limitations of his static isolation, rejects the moralistic attitude, and the religious emphasis on sin and repentance. Rationalism still divides matter and spirit, and uses different techniques to study the two realms; Spinoza asserts their unity. He is thus at once the symbol of European rational idealism, and yet also far ahead of it. This paradox arises because the form of his temperament and thought constitutes a transitional state; between the static dualism of Europe and the unitary process thought which is now in development, Spinoza represents a mixed unitary static form. This explains why he is at once ahead of and behind contemporary thought. Such conceptions as process, tendency, development, find no place in his ethical geometry; in this he is before Bruno, before even Aristotle, back with Plato and Euclid. On the other hand in his radical monistic emphasis, his inability to see man in any other way than as a part of the general order of nature, and his vision of the divine as a pervasive unity of form, he reaches far ahead through Goethe to Marx, Nietzsche, Freud, and the unitary age. But this far-reaching intuition of a new morality, a revaluation replacing the morality of dissociation, was not the result of any arbitrary prophetic magic. It arose directly from his single outlook, and displays some of the positive qualities of the unitary principle, prejudiced by its static frame. Monistic thought may be static but a unitary attitude of life cannot be; in Spinoza the static element represented a failure to live and think according to his own conceptions. He was a yea-sayer to God and to nature, while denying the fuller personal life.

The following extracts show Spinoza's intransigent monism, in which he parts company with the main European tradition; his pantheism, which sees God in everything and man himself as a part of God which happens to have a thinking body; and his enjoyment of the detailed variety of fact in this pervasive unity. This characteristic emphasis on unity and order links Spinoza on the one hand with Heraclitus, prior to the differentiation of European conceptual thought, and on the other hand with the present age in its need to re-establish order. Yet in his thought we feel the poverty of an intellectual idealism which neglects the development of personality by active experience through which old ideals are transcended. Spinoza's thought is a ghost-like spirit, lacking the time-sense which is indispensable to a more mature and complete life and thought.

"Free is that which exists solely according to the necessity of its own nature, and whose action is determined by itself; *necessary,* or rather compelled, is that which is determined by something else to exist and act in a given manner. —there is nothing arbitrary in the nature of things; but everything is determined by the necessity of the nature, of God to exist and act in a given manner. The order and relationships of ideas are the same as the order and relationships of things. —The will cannot be called a free, but only a necessary cause. —To those who ask why God did not make all men in such a manner that they would live by their reason, I answer, because he had enough material to make everything from the highest degree of perfection to the lowest. —Men deceive themselves when they regard themselves as free; and this view merely results from the fact that they are aware of their actions but do not know the causes which determine them. —There is in the mind no absolute or free will; but the mind is determined to win this or that by a cause which in turn is determined by another and this again by another, and so on without end. —Every man comes into the world without knowledge of the causes of things, but with the instinct to seek his own benefit and full awareness of this. From this it follows that men consider themselves free, since they are aware of their own wills and instincts and do not even dream of the causes which determine them to desire and to will, because they are ignorant of them. Most of those who have written on the emotions and behavior of men do not appear to be dealing with natural phenomena which follow the general laws of nature, but with matters which stand outside nature. Indeed they seem to treat man as a state within the state. For they believe rather that man disturbs the order of nature, than that he must follow it, and that he has absolute power over his actions and is determined by nothing other than himself. Further, they ascribe human frailty and instability not to the general forms of nature, but to goodness knows what crimes of human nature, which in consequence they lament, laugh at, or despise, or more commonly curse. And everyone who can eloquently decry the weakness of the human spirit, is regarded as divinely inspired.—Happiness is not the reward of virtue, but virtue itself; and we enjoy happiness not because we control our desires; on the contrary we are able to control our desires because we enjoy happiness. —Yet excellence is as hard as it is rare. —Whoso truly loves God must not desire God to love him in return."

Goethe (1749-1832) is a unitary man, living in the eighteenth century. All that is universal in him is characteristic of the periods which still lie ahead, while his limitations are those of two centuries ago. Goethe stands beyond the range of personal or literary criticism because, like Socrates and Jesus, he unhesitatingly followed a vision of life which bore within it the germ of centuries to come. Like them he dared to live his vision, not in isolation but in the world of men, and to live it out to the end. The vast difference between him and them, which makes the comparison bewildering unless the mind is held steadily on the major issue, arises from the fact that they heralded the dissociated man whom we know while he foretells a unitary man who is not yet recognized. At the level of philosophic truth the three had comparable inspiration; their differences give some measure of the changes wrought by the two thousand years of that dissociation. Ancient man was innocently at one with nature; the attention of European man was drawn to all that seemed to separate himself from nature; unitary man re-establishes his unity with nature through the discovery of the universal forms of process operating in himself. Goethe is not merely the first unitary process thinker since Heraclitus; he is the only figure of stature who did not lessen but enriched his knowledge and his personality by the recovery of the sense of unity with nature. He is the only adequate example of unitary man.

Those who approach Goethe merely as man or author of the eighteenth century are bound to end in a confusion of values; to dissociated man the forms of his genius and of his personal life seem to invite both reverence and protest. There is only one unfailing clue: Goethe was a sport of nature; unitary man finding himself alive between Newton and the industrial age; compelled to attempt universality, but prematurely; lacking certain essential clues to the understanding of himself and nature; damaged by his failure to achieve in science what he was convinced his method should ensure; driven back in his loneliness to feed arrogantly on his own superb assurance; uniquely wise, and yet so rarely self-forgetful; genius, and yet court official. We need not here look deeper into either his frustrated spontaneity or his satisfactory art of eluding tragedy. Most of these things fall into place; they express the necessary situation of a unitary process nature in Goethe's time.

The foundation of his uniqueness was perhaps a peculiar form of vitality, an intense enthusiasm for life, which prevented the development of any inner dualism and led him to reject the dissociated aspects of the tradition. His vitality was peculiar only because it was, in a dissociated community, abnormally normal. Life and nature were manifestly a process of change and, wherever possible, of development. That was as clear to him subjectively in his

own passionate demands of life, as it was objectively in his observation of men and of nature and in his study of history. The whole
affair was a rhythm of change and development, in which the diastole and systole, the alternations of tension and release, and the
steady intensification of the process, all played an essential part.
The unity of nature as process was beyond question. Nothing persisted unchanged, metamorphosis was universal, and time was necessary for the completion of each stage. Logical systems and
mathematical analysis missed the point; the individual phenomenon constituted by each system following its own development
was the only truth, further symbolism was unnecessary. Each
aperçu could be displayed through individual examples, from human life or nature; in the one case it was in a literary form, drama
or poem; in the other as a scientific description of the significance
which some natural object had for him as subject. The dualisms of
Faust are a poet's recording of dissociated life; he warned Eckermann
not to look there for any general attitude to life.

If the whole of nature is one system in perpetual transformation and development, the attempt to isolate any part is bound to
lead to failure. In particular the separation of man as subject from
the field of objective nature blinds him to the form of life proper
to him. Man can fully understand himself only by fusing the objective knowledge which is gained by observation of the whole
of organic nature with the subjective knowledge of individual
experience. This can bring a new ease and self-acceptance, an
innocence based on knowledge. The negative prejudices of conventional morality are replaced by a positive enthusiasm for developing life, and condemnation by ironic tolerance. Yet this
operative self-knowledge could not be attained by the merely introspective or intellectual analysis proposed by Spinoza. The ancient admonition "know thyself" was suspect, as part of a priestly
conspiracy to distract men from the fuller practical life towards
the illusions of introspection and penitence. "Man only knows
himself in so far as he knows the world, for he only becomes
aware of the world in himself, and of himself in the world." Effective self-knowledge can be gained only in action, and can be
maintained only by being perpetually developed.

To moralists this outlook appears pagan, to analytical minds it
seems vague, and to monotheists it has the quality of a return to

primitive pantheism. Yet it was neither pagan, nor vague, or pantheist. Goethe did not propose a return to the undifferentiated condition of Heraclitus. The development of man led from undifferentiated unity with nature, through a differentiation achieved by separation, to a new organized unity. But this last state would be different from the first; it must contain within its recovered unity all the differentiated knowledge, all the specialized organs and faculties, of two thousand years of development. What appeared pagan was a re-integration of human nature by the self-acceptance that must result from a unitary knowledge of the human system as part of the system of nature; what appeared vague was the outline of a novel world of unitary process thought lacking the illusory precision of static concepts but offering instead an ordered system of thought; what appeared pantheistic, was not, as with Spinoza, the vision of God in everything, but an unquestioning acceptance of the phenomenon itself, of the unity in the variety of concrete processes, which took the place of dissociated man's need of religion. Goethe, as unitary man, had no need of a personal god or of the promise of immortality, except perhaps towards the end of his life, but lacking a unitary language he was compelled to use Christian symbolism to convey his thought. Heaven, he said, would be terribly boring, one would meet so many self-righteous Christians there. The Christian symbolism was the most convenient one available, but it held no monopoly of truth. For those whose understanding embraced both the sciences and the arts, who could recognize objective and subjective truth, there was no need of other religion.

If Goethe is the best example of unitary man, this does not mean that men of the unitary age will model themselves on him. Christians do not copy the life of Jesus, or rationalists imitate Socrates. But he was a man who manifestly expressed a unitary attitude to life. There is nothing vague or obscure about this, and it will bear closer examination. His life was unitary in that it reveals no general or permanent conflict, no neurosis of dissociation, no fanaticism, or moral intolerance, or anger. No part of his nature being denied in consciousness or in expression, there was no such fundamental distortion. The tensions which are evident in his life and work arise from his acceptance of his own nature, and contribute to his fertility. He never allowed the dualities of his nature to harden into a dualism. Moreover his thought was not divorced from his life, but continuous with it influencing it and influenced by it. His thought and creation were the overflow and re-ordering of experienced life. This re-association of thought and life is evidenced in the balance and interplay of professional and personal life, poetic creation, and natural observation. Similarly within his thought there was no dualism or separation:

All effects, of whatever kind, which experience brings to our notice are continuously related to one another; they pass into one another, and undergo the same rhythms. The pedantry of sharp classification and vague mysticism are equally harmful. But all activities, from the most commonplace to the highest, from the tile falling from the roof to the illuminating *aperçu* which comes to one and which one shares with others, are continuous with one another. We attempt to express this in the series: chance, mechanical, physical, chemical, organic, psychic, ethical, religious, genial.

This continuity of experience extends through the subjective and the objective realms, and these too are fused in Goethe's thought. His love for Spinoza arose not from any high valuation of the static analysis of the human emotions and their influence on action, but from his sharing of Spinoza's profound sense of unity. This unity, by including man in its scope, overcomes the misleading antithesis of free will and necessity. It also brings within the field of his poetic gift the whole range of experience, extending from the "divine' to the "indecent." But if the term has any useful meaning it is Spinoza's perversion which is indecent, not Goethe's straightforward vitality. A study of the European dissociation should not devote attention to the divine in man and wholly neglect what a dissociated tradition regards as indecent. But unfortunately the natural health of Goethe's phallic poems cannot be offered as antithesis to Spinoza's unconscious confession of distortion, since contemporary law still expresses the dissociated attitude. Perversion can be admitted by a dissociated tradition, but it cannot rise to a simple acceptance of the naked Eros.

Besides those fields in which Goethe established a unitary form, there were others in which he was necessarily less successful. For example he could not see, what unitary thought must prove, that the analytical, quantitative approach has a special but restricted role as a limiting case of the more general unitary method. To Goethe the two methods stood in absolute contrast, and it was inescapable that he should resent the success of mathematical analysis and seek to limit its scope. It was this situation also which made him seek, prematurely, as we can now see, to bring art and science together. He was right that the formative principle is universal, but wrong in the view which he held so obstinately that it was possible in his time to prove this by using it as an instrument of research. How relieved he would have been to know that one day it would all be clear, and that in this point too the strain he felt was only the inevitable lot of genius, at once in his time and out of it. More light may be granted to us.

It would be easy to give support to this interpretation of Goethe by countless quotations. But Goethe was a poet, not a systematic thinker, and though his writings are rich with the overtones of his philosophic intuition, it would not be appropriate to tear passages from their context of poetry or scientific observation and build them into a theory. Goethe's thought, conscious and unconscious, was of unitary process form, not because he decided that was the right way to think, but because a process of that form dominated his life and person without the distortions which mark dissociated man. There is a deep productive tension in him, expressing itself as the alternating appeal of romantic and classic forms the need of loneliness and the desire for life, the need to experience intensely and then to outgrow each experience. But his profound sense of unity prevented this tension ever becoming a frustrating dualism, and throughout his long life he continued to develop as a person.

The dissociated man, divided in his loyalty between the ideal and the real, may find in Eros his opportunity to recover unity. The ultimate role of woman is to preserve unity and continuity in the chain of life. To herself she is the center and equilibrium of life's development; to man she appears as a complement, stabilizing his own achievements. For the dissociated man woman has this special importance: she can heal him from the damage of a tradition absorbed too earnestly. He may fail to see this, or lack the courage to let himself experience it; to him Goethe's words "the spirit of woman draws us forward" express a sentimental enthusiasm, not the complement to man in a developing unity, which Plato came so near to expressing. The male principle obsessed with its differentiated action and thought too easily loses its unity, and hence its proper path of development, and man too long alone must live and think in a distorted manner. The irony of Goethe's situation was that his faculty for experience and growth was so great that each woman swiftly exhausted her role, and became a tie that thwarted his own further development. Only those without courage or generosity will doubt that in this Goethe was true to himself. He had to accept the limitations of a unitary man living two centuries before the period that would think and feel as he did; there was no need for him to accept further restrictions to his untiring spirit.

We have seen that the peculiar confusion of the last century and a half arises from the paradox that the intensive exploitation of quantitative, static, and dualistic thought has obscured the long-term tendency towards a unitary process system of thought. This antithesis has been paralleled in the social field, where the steadily maturing awareness of the unity of man and its gradual social realization has been accompanied by the anarchy of uncontrolled industrialization and of separatist movements asserting special privileges. Goethe had the good fortune to live before mechanism had seriously threatened the integrity of European society, and yet at a time when the need for process thought, that is, for a historical method of reasoning, had already become evident. His general approach to experience offers the first mature example of historical, as opposed to analytical, reason. Within those human and philosophical fields of which he was fully master his use of historical reason was calm and lucid, because he was convinced of its validity in a way that was no longer possible for those who had to challenge the imposing successes of the mechanical age. Goethe's resentment of Newton was an indication of what was to come, but it was insufficient to disturb his own assured comprehension of the developing processes around him. Since Heraclitus no other man has displayed Goethe's radical acceptance of process. Before Goethe the human mind was insufficiently aware of the historical background, while since his day a complete philosophy of process implied a reinterpretation of mathematical science which has only now begun to come within sight.

I find that it is impossible to leave Goethe without allowing him to speak to the reader, as he did to Eckermann:

> My tendencies were opposed to those of my time, which were wholly subjective; while in my objective efforts, I stood alone to my disadvantage. -People are always talking about originality; but what do they mean? As soon as we are born, the world begins to work on us, and this goes on to the end. What can we call our own except energy, strength, and will? -Whether a man shows himself a genius in science, or in war and statesmanship, or whether he composes a song -it all comes to the same thing; the only point is whether the thought, the discovery, the deed, is living and can live on. -Men will become more clever and more acute; but not better, happier, and stronger in action or at least only in epochs.

And finally:

> "Meyer," said Goethe laughing, "always says: 'If thinking were not so hard.' And the worst is, that all the thinking in the world does not bring us to thought; we must be right by nature, so that good thoughts may come before us like free children of God, and cry, 'Here we are.'"

Within three years of Goethe's death *Marx* (1818-1883) was already choosing his profession, and the sharp contrast between them bears witness to the swift advance of the industrial revolution. Yet in the broad perspective of this analysis their situations are similar. They are both late Europeans in revolt against the dissociation, recognizing process in nature and man, and in their different ways seeking to promote development. Goethe and Marx are alike concerned with the development of man in this terrestrial world, and Marx's revolt against the anarchy of individualist capitalism has the same significance in the social sphere as Goethe's dislike of the disintegrating influence of analytical thought in the personal. Goethe's integral nature maintains its essential unity in spite of all inner tensions, though at the cost of an apparent detachment. But Marx's warring soul, deeply scarred by the social consequences of the European dissociation, projects its own dualism into history and generates his tremendous gospel of conflict.

In Marx himself, and in his thought, necessity conquered idealism. These three words express the strength and the weakness of militant socialism. The illusions of idealism had to be replaced by a broader view of the historical process. Marx accomplished that, and thereafter history could never be the same. But just as Judaism was a premature monotheism, and thereby condemned to distortion, so Marxism was a premature attempt at unitary thought, and therefore similarly distorted. Marx could not at that time, and being himself would not have wished to, replace idealism by a unitary conception which embraced and transcended it. His role was to use the conception of material necessity to destroy a spurious idealism, and though his doctrine rested on a dialectical theory of process, it was dualistic and not unitary. Marxist necessity was one-sided, and lacked the comprehensiveness essential to any universal doctrine. Marxism distorted process thought by forcing it to provide a gospel for militant socialism.

Goethe is the best representative of unitary man, but if our concern had been with intellectual systems rather than the complete man, his contemporary, Hegel, might have served even better. The naive static rationalism of the eighteenth century had placed the emphasis on the conscious discovery of material laws as the main source of further social development; enlightenment guaranteed progress and its prophets did not look behind consciousness to any general historical trend. Hegel revolted from this analytical and materialistic attitude, and drawing on many sources from Heraclitus to his immediate German predecessors developed what is often regarded as a dogmatic metaphysical interpretation of history as a continuous process of development. In fact it was no more metaphysical than the outlook of the French rationalists, the difference being that they were ignorant of the essentially static form of their concepts, while as a rebel Hegel had to make his process form explicit. The Hegelian form was as ancient as the early Greeks but it was alien to the European tradition, and it is interesting to see the same process structure developing simultaneously in Goethe's intuitive *aperçus* and in Hegel's logical intellect. Hegel systematized Heraclitus. The universality of process, the inevitability of conflict between antitheses, their synthesis within the wider wholes of a new level of development, the interpretation of history as the continuous development of the spirit—these Hegelian conceptions were the natural outcome of a Heraclitean type of thought in an idealistic European growing conscious of human history and biological evolution and reacting from the analytical methods of contemporary science.

In transforming the Hegelian dialectic of consciousness into a more general dialectic of natural process Marx broadened its basis and helped to prepare the way for unitary process thought. The religious dynamic of communism derives from its roots in process thought, not from its expression of material interests. Modem man is reborn when he becomes convinced of his role in history, and to many Communism brought that conviction. But Marx forced the method to fit the aspect of the contemporary historical situation with which he was most concerned, the role of the proletariat in the class war against the bourgeoisie. In their calmer moments Marx and Engels knew that their doctrine was not a universal conception of man or of history, but an interpretation of one phase only in the development of a particular civilization. The *Theses* of 1845 are almost beyond criticism from this point of view. The Communist Manifesto of 1848 also states explicitly: "the theoretical propositions of the communists in no way rest on ideas or principles that have been invented or discovered by this or that would-be universal reformer. They are merely the expression, in general terms, of the actual conditions of an existing class struggle, of a historical movement going on under our very eyes."

If Marx is judged by this limited claim, his position is unassailable. But as a general philosophy of history or a universal conception of man Marxism is inadequate. The difficulty in evaluating the doctrine arises from the fact that in it an immature unitary system of thought has been distorted through its adaptation to one burning practical issue. This adaptation led to the creation of a communist state in the pre-unitary world. It is to be hoped that the unitary community now developing will not continue to regard the communist state as an alien body, and turn on it as the European community has so often turned on the Jewish. In each case a community had to isolate itself and to take special measures to defend a premature doctrine. But the parallel implies the relation of the unitary world, and the more swiftly that is achieved the less the risk of a clash between the American West and the Russian East.

The confusions of Marxist thought arise from the prejudiced application of dialectical thought to a social situation charged with intense emotion. Marx was aware that his concepts did not fully parallel reality. "The concept of a thing and its reality run side by side like two asymptotes, always approaching each other but never meeting. This difference prevents the concept from being directly and immediately reality, and reality from being immediately its own concept." This dualism of concept and reality is alien to process thought and appears in Marx only because, thanks to his partisan mission, he is bound to use static concepts and to betray the unity of process thought. Marx must treat as absolute at least for this phase of history, such concepts as "the proletariat," "the class war," the "productive relations," "the economic structure." But these terms beg the question, by assuming that the classes retain their separate and characteristic identity, and that economic production is a separable and permanently dominant element in society.

Marx and Engels repeatedly assert that the productive relations are only one component of a total system in process of transformation, in which everything influences everything else. But this attitude is never developed, for the good reason that it would rob Marxist dogmatism of its authority. Nowhere in Marxist literature is there a consistent development of dialectical materialism as a general method of thought, and there cannot be, since the resulting interpretation of history could not be Marxist. True dialectical thought, in the sense of a system of Hegelian form based on natural process, cannot provide either the dualism of right and wrong or the economic emphasis which are essential to Marxism as a fighting doctrine. To justify its appeal to force, Marxism requires the moral mission of the proletariat to redeem humanity, and so has to distort the tension which is inherent in all processes into an absolute dualism of good and evil. But a lucid development of dialectical thought would reveal this error and rob militant socialism of its logical foundation.

In a dissociated age it is not possible for a lonely thinker to discard the illusory security of sharp categories and to trust the formative power of unitary thought, and least of all for a man who is himself divided. On the one hand Marx was inspired by the magnificent dialectical interpretation of history, which had grown from the Hegelian unitary form. But he was a man whose passionate sense of justice had led him to identify his entire being with the struggles of the poor. The form both of his thought and temperament tended to separate him from his contemporaries, and this external division was echoed in the ruthless demands he made on others for the sake of his own work. For Marx morality was concerned with social relations rather than the control of the instinctive life. Denying himself normal co-operative relations with others he had to find compensation in a fierce doctrine of social morality. The dialectical process of history ceased to be an objective vision of a natural development; it was the story of the mission of the proletariat against the exploiting capitalist class. The dualism of good and evil is an expression of the need for sharp concepts through which the division in his own nature could express itself. Had Marx himself not been so divided, or had he lived in another time, he might have accepted the historical process with less moral distortion, and have seen, in place of a battle of good and evil supposed to culminate in the sudden achievement of freedom, the perpetual interplay of special privilege and general development.

For reasons which were partly personal and partly due to his historical situation, Marx needed clear-cut, black and white, and therefore static concepts, even though his system was one of process. The same dualism is expressed in his emotional nature, an Old Testament morality repudiating his understanding of the necessity within human motives. Moral exhortation and historical thought are incompatibles; a dissociated temperament cannot use process thought properly. Marx could not escape the old error of idealism to treat one component (in man or history) as right and the other as wrong, and thereby seek to measure the future by the ideals of a dissociated past. It led to the charmingly naive expectation of a sudden leap into freedom on the beautiful tomorrow when Marxism, which Marx hated, would no longer be relevant. Here again we find the irony: the most intransigent fighter must after all go down on his knees and confess that the ugly struggle of good and evil is not the whole truth, and project into a sentimental future the state he cannot himself attain today. It is true that there is a developing rhythm in history and that the economic age has now come to an end, but it is doubtful whether Marx would recognize in the unitary hierarchical community of tomorrow the classless society of his idealistic vision.

To read Marxist literature is to be torn between the brilliance of the general method of thought and the inadequacy of its conclusions as regards either man in general or society as we know it today. Marx's role was to facilitate the development of one component of unitary man, his awareness of the economic basis of life, with all that such awareness implies. Marx, Lenin, and Stalin are the great realists of that partial movement, each of them narrowing the universal truth a stage further in order to carry forward its practical realization and survival. Thus step by step the comprehensive generality of the dialectical method is betrayed, till the gospel of the historical process finally becomes the patriotism of one community. Throughout this process unrestricted dialectical thought was the deadly enemy. Just as the one god which pretended universality was a jealous god, so the Marxist line had to claim a monopoly of true historical thought. But revolutionary socialism could not avoid admitting its indebtedness to that ancient and aristocratic philosopher who first gave form to process thought. It is impossible to facilitate the historical process without thinking about process, and any revolutionary seeking logical justification had to copy the thought forms of the earliest Greeks. Lassalle emphasized Hegel's debt to Heraclitus in a book which stung Marx to abuse. But the connection was clear to Lenin, and his editors, secure within their socialist state, could afford gracefully to acknowledge Heraclitus as "one of the most prominent dialecticians of ancient times." At the judgement day of the intellect the last trump will find Heraclitus, Lao Tse, Bruno, Goethe, Hegel, and one half of Marx in lively intercourse, speaking the language of process. But the other half would be elsewhere with the orthodox Marxists and Christians in the confusion of their sharp divisions.

We have seen that by 1850 the subjective character of the European tradition was growing inadequate. The subjective emphasis had become explicit in Descartes, had been developed by Kant, and culminated in Hegel's absolute idealism While Spinoza had reached a static intellectual unity by his choice of God-substance, nature as the one primary concept, Hegel by a more arbitrary choice of mind as the primary reality was able to formulate a unity of process. The one-sidedness of the European subjectivism here reached its extreme form, and gave Feuerbach, Marx, and Engels the opportunity of turning it inside out. Hegelian subjectivity became Marxist objectivity, and the dialectic of mind that of matter. But this inversion was illegitimate; the formal structures of the mental and material components of process are wholly different, mind is formative while matter is not. When Marx asserted that matter was the name of an objective reality in perpetual dialectical transformation, his intention was correct but he failed to identify the formative principle which was necessary to emancipate matter from static mechanical determinism and to allow mind its proper role. Thus in spite of dialectical theory Marxist concepts remained dogmatically static, and in accepting a materialistic dialectic the individual mind committed suicide. Not only was humanism destroyed, but socialism lost all faculty for leadership in the areas that had experienced the centuries of humanism. Only in Asia, where individualism had never taken root, could the doctrine find its adequate leaders.

It was through Marx that the European dissociated tradition suffered its first systematic attack. As Marxism grew in influence large numbers began to think in terms of process, to try to understand their own role in history, and to realize that human thought is not an arbitrary process but a part of man's attempt to survive and develop and therefore influenced by his situation. During the previous centuries men had thought that the faculty of consciousness and of discovery would guarantee the further development of man. Man as subject would come to understand nature and so further the realization of his ideals. Marxism gave the first shock to this innocent assumption by showing that the forms of consciousness, the nature of man's ideals, and his actual behavior were all components of a social process through which alone they could be understood. Only through the study of his social history could man come to understand the full significance of his own ideas, and realize that his ideals may sometimes be the enemies of his further development.

In his early studies of the Greek philosophers Marx recognizes two main types: the earlier objective philosophers of natural process, and the later subjective philosophers of consciousness who laid the basis for the European subjective tradition. He knew that his own part was to recover the objective approach, and here unitary thought is in full agreement with him. But it can accept neither his distortion of process thought into a moral dualism in which the end justifies the means, nor the neglect of the human individual within his vast abstractions.

Freud (1856-1939) also displays the awkward situation of the original thinker in the pre-unitary period. Like Marx he rejected the subjective view of man, seeking to discover behind consciousness the factors which make man think as he does. Both lacked a unitary method of thought appropriate to their material, but they adopted opposite ways of overcoming this difficulty. Marx, being concerned with the one field where historical or process thought had already been developed, was able to take over Hegel's system, though distorting it into a dualistic form. Being supported by so powerful a system of thought he had few doubts regarding either his own historical role or the validity of his theories. But Freud, finding no such system awaiting him in the field of psychology, had to develop his own method step by step, often modifying or discarding his previous convictions. This tentative approach, however proper in a scientific pioneer, was reflected in his uncertainty regarding his own place in the history of thought and his scepticism regarding his own theories.

Freud knew he was on the right lines because his technique had opened a virgin field to knowledge and could sometimes restore the neurotic to health. But he did not know why his technique had that therapeutic power. The fact that until his death he experimented with new fundamental concepts of the mental life shows that he was not content with his own theories. From the point of view of this study, every successful psychoanalysis provides evidence refuting Freud's picture of the mind. For his conception was dualistic and lacked any general principle of development which could account for the recovery of personal integration. Freud admits that he found the integration of the ego "very remarkable."

The theoretical method which Freud adopted was that which must be used by any scientist breaking into a new field. He had to begin, as systematic thought always must begin, by seeking to identify permanent elements in the mental life. Just because he was approaching the treacherous ground of an objective critique of consciousness he had to start with the most elementary static abstractions from the apparent confusion of mental processes. His Super-Ego, Ego and Id, however inadequate, served him and science better than a premature application of the Hegelian dialectic. In challenging the supposed supremacy of consciousness Freud was engaged in a struggle as difficult as that of Marx in challenging the supposed idealism of the propertied classes, and each needed the clear-cut divisions of a dualistic system in order to maintain his attack.

Thus Freud, as a scientist opening up a new field in the late nineteenth century, was bound to neglect the beginnings of process thought in history and philosophy, and to use concepts which were not only dualistic, but static in the sense of lacking any co-ordinating principle of development. The Conscious and Pre-conscious were opposed to the Unconscious, and Freud never formulated any principle by which their harmony might be achieved. The same lack of any integrating principle marks the Super-Ego, the Ego, and the Id, which broadly represent conscience, perception, and instinct. The Eros Instinct, which unifies and develops life, provides a strange antithesis to what Freud called the "Death Instinct," which expresses the profound conservatism that seems to lead life not only back to earlier states, but back to the inanimate. The Pleasure and Reality Principles express the same inescapable dichotomy. Man's fate is that he is divided, and Freud sees only one irrational hope. If he can educate himself to reality, learn to know himself as he really is, something may come of it. Objective science is his only guide.

There is nothing in the literature of science more moving than Freud's late essays in which he implicitly confesses the despair of a genius and idealist, aware of the pessimism of his own doctrines but recognizing that they are only provisional and retaining an ungrounded hope that courage and science may yet bring real enlightenment to man. There is a bravery, honesty, and dignity in Freud which dwarfs all those who challenge him without recognizing what he accomplished. Unitary thought can look back on him because it builds on his work, recognizing it as one component of the self-discovery of dissociated man.

That it certainly is, the uncovering of the logic of human distortion. That is the purpose and result of his technique: to reveal to the analyst, and through him at the appropriate moment to the patient, the way in which the distortions of the past continue to distort the present. "Repression," "projection," and "displacement" are names for processes whereby distorted forms persist and are extended, though their origin may not be admitted. Such distortions must arise from conflict, and in identifying the source of the conflict Freud accepts the European dualism and treats as absolute and universal to man a dichotomy which is but the temporary result of a dualistic tradition.

This error was perhaps inevitable in a thinker placed as Freud was. To simplify his task he had deliberately restricted himself to what he could recognize as making up the "mental" life of the individual. Thus the physiology of man was excluded, though he knew that "all our provisional ideas of psychology will some day be based on an organic substructure." The price paid for this narrowing of the field was that his concepts are essentially unbiological. In biological development dualism or conflict is always superimposed on a prior unity. The existence of an organism capable of survival implies integration, and unity is therefore always prior to inner conflict. Conflict may arise as the result of an inappropriate adaptation, and it may prove fatal or it may be overcome. But the recovery of organic health never involves the synthesis of fundamentally opposed principles, since these cannot co-exist in an organism. It only seems to do so because the actual condition of the organism has been misinterpreted in using a dualistic language. The historical process does not involve the synthesis of pre-existing logical opposites, though it may appear to in the confused language of immature dialectical theories. The recovery of organic health in the individual and the recombination of separate tendencies in the social process take the form of the restoration of an earlier unity which has been partly prejudiced by the development of conflict in the process of adaptation.

Freud's technique is successful when it sets free the formative process in the patient; his theories are inadequate, judged by the austere criterion of science, because the dissociated tradition working in Freud's own mind prevented him recognizing the formative process. But this contrast of theory and technique is only partially valid. The technique often failed, because it left the patient without the self-knowledge, which is only possible through a unitary form of thought. On the other hand some of Freud's concepts will long continue to bear fruit.

It is appropriate that in coming to grips with Freud unitary thought is forced to develop something of its own conception of the structure of contemporary personality. It is no part of my task to attempt here even an outline of the unitary psychology of man. The theme of this book is limited to the general effect of the tradition on individuals, and much of the Freudian material lies outside its scope. Yet Freud was mainly concerned with the neurotic European and here the unitary interpretation of the tradition is relevant. The dissociation underlies some of the special symptoms which

Freud describes, and is partly responsible for their frequency and intensity in Europeans. The Freudian discovery of the neurosis is, as I have said, an aspect of the self-discovery of dissociated man which has now been proceeding for a century. The main Freudian concepts therefore bear a close relation to the unitary picture of dissociated man. But to see this we must first recall the unitary view of normally integrated man.

The individual man, like any organism, is a hierarchical system of processes in an oscillating equilibrium in which the internal and external formative tendencies dominate successively. The internal component of the rhythm consists of all the downward tendencies of the separate parts and organs towards lower potentials, the katabolism or breaking down of organic materials, the systole, the breathing out, the release of inner tensions, the relaxation of the organic system towards the static perfection of inorganic structures. The other, external component consists of the tendencies of the wider environmental system, which sustain the organism, the anabolism or building up of organic materials, the diastole, the breathing in, the renewal of sources of energy, and the maintenance of the organism through its development as part of the physical, organic, and social environment. This developing balance of alternating tendencies is what is called life, and it can only be understood as a part of the development of the wider environmental system which includes the organism. But dissociated man, having lost normal hierarchical integrity, found that dualistic concepts were well adapted to describe what he experienced as a double separation, of himself from the environment and of conflicting tendencies within himself.

The dissociation consisted, as we have seen, in the separation and coming into conflict of reason and instinct. Reason involved attention or consciousness. The separation of instinct therefore meant that much of the instinctive life tended to be repressed from consciousness in those who took the tradition seriously. The formative process operating at the dominant levels established a dissociation between the religious and ideal discipline of consciousness and the instinctive tendencies whose spontaneity and accessibility to consciousness tended to be thereby thwarted. The dissociation resulted in a persisting separation between the Conscious and the Unconscious, producing a dislocation which is absent in integrated man.

Dissociated man also displays a sharper separation of the internal and the external tendencies. These correspond respectively to the Pleasure Principle, pleasure being the release of inner strain, and the Reality Principle, which represents the external tendencies which dominate the organism and result in its adaptation to the environment. Freud, having separated the life of the organism from its environment by the use of non-biological concepts, finds difficulty in seeing how the Reality Principle comes into existence, how man ever learnt to control his instincts. Adaptation can only be interpreted by a system of thought which explicitly recognizes the fact that "life" is a consequence of the molding of the organism by the environment. Freud denied the existence of dry instinctive urge expressing itself in the Reality Principle, and he was right in ascribing much of organic development to the external, disturbing, and distracting influences of the environment. But his theory, because it lacked an organizing or formative principle, could not explain how those influences resulted in an integrated development.

Freud's use of the term instinct is misleading, but his "Death Instinct" corresponds closely to the inner tendencies which, when isolated from the environment, retain the organism in its old habits, lead it back to earlier states, and ultimately back to the inanimate. As soon as the organism is isolated the profound conservatism of nature dominates. If "life" refers only to the processes of the isolated organism, then the goal of life is death. Dissociated man, being divided within and without, reveals this death-seeking and death-promoting tendency in many forms, both concealed and open. Europe has not only reproduced more rapidly, but also killed more in war than any other continent.

On the other hand the Eros or Life Instinct is an expression of a particular form of the universal formative tendency. Eros binds and unifies. In integrated man Eros, in the most general sense, is the expression of the formative tendency in the wider system of the individual and his social environment, the supreme factor linking each person with these around him. But in dissociated man suffering from the double separation, Eros degenerates into what is generally understood by the concept of sex, the specialized pleasure principle of the isolated internal tendencies. The peculiar significance of Death and Eros arises from the fact that those two factors alone can exert an overriding influence on the organic processes at

every level in the hierarchy of the human system. Death dissolves
the entire system and leaves each structure to complete its separate
tendency; it is final and unambiguous. Eros can raise vitality at
every level, strengthening the unity and intensifying the course of
life. There is thus a continuous gradation of forms of process related to the Eros principle which may be expressed in a series of
concepts of rising generality: sex, libido, Eros, and the formative
tendency uniting the individual to his community.

In individuals and communities not suffering from dissociation
all these processes are at work. But as dissociation sets in, the higher
unity of the community and individual life decays. Eros declines
into sex, joy into pleasure. Egoism and sex, which are normally
developed and fulfilled within the life of the whole, are then exposed as isolated tendencies seeking exhaustion in death.

Being himself a dualist, Freud mistook this situation and like
the Christian dualists adopted the view that culture is built on
instinctive renunciation. That is true only of a dissociated civilization during the phase where idealistic reason and moral discipline are in the ascendant. It is untrue of other civilizations, and
untrue aiso in certain phases of European history. During the periods when Europe made an attempt to recover the earlier Greek
ideal of an harmonious and complete life, culture was promoted
by a relaxation of the dissociation and a partial restoration of balance. Even in the nineteenth century Arnold knew that culture
might be furthered by a Hellenic spontaneity of consciousness
rather than by a Hebraic strictness of conscience. The same is
true now. Those whose conception of life is moralistic and superficial may fail to see in the contemporary "paganism" an integrity
and fullness of life which promise well for man. The culture of
the future, if there is to be any, must be built on the re-integration
of instinct and reason. That was perhaps Freud's hope, though it
implies that his technique must be guided by a unitary interpretation of man superseding his own.

The resistance which new ideas meet is sometimes in part due
to their limitations. Freud knew there were good reasons for the
unpopularity of his work. A determinism based on sex was doubly
fearful to dissociated man; he was afraid to lose his sense of freedom from material causality and afraid also to lose that insecure
emancipation which alone seemed to separate him from the beasts.

That was clear. But Freud did not see that his doctrine struck an even deeper resistance. In the heart of every neurotic there is a hope, whether expressed or repressed, that some sudden magic can set him free. He may be attached to his illness, but beneath neurosis lies the prior background of health where this hope always remains latent. Somewhere there is the place, the person, the work, the secret that can restore health. That conviction may be deeply buried but in the young it is normally still accessible. Those who suffer from hereditary or psychotic disease may be beyond regeneration. But in others the conviction can assist recovery because it expresses an important truth. If the dissociated tradition has damaged the development of an individual, the unitary method of thought can be used to facilitate the regenerative processes which are latent in every organism. The neurotic hope for a sudden healing magic has this much justification: the changeover from dissociated to unitary thought has the quality of an emancipation from the habitual failures of the past. But Freud did not offer the neurotic any such rebirth. He led him into a dualistic and static world, to the doom of a determination which denied all hope of integrated spontaneity. Freud's world of thought lacked the formative principle which could set the spirit free to recover its sense of freedom within the necessity proper to itself.

A true therapeutic method will attract rather than repel the mildly unhealthy. Only the hopeless neurotic would commit spiritual suicide by accepting a determinism without a formative principle. The guilty subject was ready to commit this suicide and to accept the Freudian doctrine in order to receive absolution, just as the Calvinists had accepted predestination in order to have God once again carry the burden of their sins. As the theory did not provide a formative principle, the formative tendency appeared in the form of Eros and the patient sought to identify himself with the analyst. This anomalous situation deflected the restored vitality of the patient from his normal life and the restoration of independent health was the more uncertain.

Freud's theory provides a logic of human distortion but neglects the logic of development. In revolting from the subjective picture of man which naively accepted the conscious mental processes, he developed an objective view which neglected the formative processes expressing themselves in the will of the individual. Jung made an attempt to restore the balance by once again stressing the subjective aspects of individual experience and of community tradition. But in emphasizing the subjective formative tendencies, he tended to neglect the decisive facts which Freud had established. Adler recognized the formative will of the individual, but failed to relate it to the organic processes. The rapid succession of these complementary views suggests that the time is ripe for an approach which is neither subjective nor objective in emphasis but recognizes the single form of all processes. What is needed is not a psychosomatic science which assumes the coexistence of psyche and soma, or mind and body, but a unitary method in which no basic dualism is admitted. The truth lies not in a constructed synthesis of partial conceptions, but in a single vision of what is single in nature.

In these glimpses of the thought of nine men I have attempted to epitomize the changing structure of the European tradition. Before 2000 BC individual personality had rarely left a characteristic mark on the tradition, and until about 600 BC there are relatively few outstanding individuals in world history. If the unitary view is right the outstanding individual will tend now to merge again into the continuity of the social background, but in a new manner. Personality will mature further, but one aspect of this maturing will consist in an awareness of the social and hereditary continuity which expresses itself in the thoughts and ambitions of the individual. Thus the special individual who contributes to the development of the tradition will not appear as an arbitrary or autonomous subject bearing a separate burden and responsible for separate achievement, but rather as one of the many formative organs of the social process. This will enable the individual to be more straightforward in asserting his vision, since he can recover something of the innocence of the ancients whose creative powers were not disturbed by undue awareness of themselves. The burden of European subjectivity can now be discarded, the formative personality being aware not only of himself, but of all the social tendencies which make him what he is. The subjective loneliness, and its companion the messianic temptation of genius, may thus lose their intensity.

If these nine figures stand out in this image of European thought it is only because the continuity which they expressed has been

deliberately neglected in order to do justice to European individualism. The communities of the future will recognize the continuation of the sequence of this chapter in a general process of thought
developing a universal tradition, rather than in a further series of
selected figures.

10

Unitary Man

A view of the future can acquire a reliability greater than that of interpretations of the past, which in the last resort must rest on the support of informed opinion. Those who believe they are molding the future need not always wait for the judgement of others, since they may be able to test their view in action. If a view of the future develops successful action, and is itself further developed in the course of that action, it becomes what I shall call a conviction. Though it may contain spurious elements, a conviction must in some degree conform to the structure of the contemporary historical process. A conviction is a principle which develops itself by organizing emotion and action as well as thought. No form of thought can enjoy a more complete relation to its social setting than such self-developing conformity to the historical process.

Such prophetic convictions have been the guiding threads of European history. Though only rare individuals have been conscious of the major trend, yet at critical moments communities have chosen their line of development by becoming aware of the path corresponding to their general tendency. This has been possible because specially placed individuals have continually made correct anticipations of the future which could be recognized by others. Amidst the clamour of conflicting views the reliable voices can often be recognized by their unhesitating assurance. Marcus Aurelius had them in mind when he wrote of the early Greek thinkers and "their kindred spirits, bold, soaring, unwearied, revolutionary, and sublimely confident." Such voices appeal because they convey the sense of a resolution of earlier tensions within a new harmonious rhythm. There is nothing mysterious in this. The significance of the new conviction can be recognized by thousands who cannot discern the future for themselves. Those to whom it is appropriate cannot but follow it. The power of prophecy thus becomes a commonplace in unitary thought: the attention of the many is held by any conviction which facilitates their developing tendencies; they are fascinated by any principle which offers the relaxation of some general tension within a new form of life. It is because the ways of history have been well and truly paved by prophecy that the peoples could move on while paying so little attention to the way they went.

But the prophetic conviction cannot be widely recognized until it has begun to do its work. The community can always, through its informed specialists, attempt to weigh the truth in any interpretation of the past, but it has no technique for a rational estimate of anticipations of the future. The prophet cannot be challenged in the field of thought, and if his assertions are viewed as abstract thought his self-confidence must appear as irresponsible dogmatism. It is the action, not the intellectual response of the community, which provides the test of his conviction.

I have suggested that the ultimate source of the achievement of Europe is not exhausted and can serve as a guiding principle for the species. A general truth which was only partially recognized by Europe can now become explicit and universal. This forbids any wholesale rejection of the old traditions. The European tradition must be recognized as an inadequate version of a more general truth whose full significance can now be recognized. The tradition has to be reorganized so as to reintegrate the anarchy of Western civilization in a new form appropriate to all peoples. That new form will have many variants; the broad continental tendencies, the regional differentiations, and the local specializations finding their common sanction in a universal tendency characteristic of man at this stage in his social development.

The formulation of this universal human norm is not merely an immediate need, it is implied in the continuity of history which unitary thought traces forward from the past. It appears to offer as great a promise as that offered in the past by Christianity, humanism, or quantitative science, but it must fail, as they did, to fulfil this promise in every individual life. Yet this reorganization of the tradition is assisted by clear limitations of its scope. The reorganization is a social task to be achieved in this century. It can neglect both the extended processes of natural selection and the limitless variety of individual lives. It is no more and no less than the transformation of the dominant human tradition, the tradition of European and Western civilization, into a form appropriate to the world community of the decades immediately ahead.

An advanced stage has already been reached in the transition from the recent anarchy of contrasts to this new universalism. This transition is expressed in a relaxation of the tensions which arose from the exaggerated contrasts between races, nations, and classes. But that release of tension could not come about by a conscious or rational reconciliation, since thought itself was prejudiced by two thousand years of search for separate persistent identity rather than for unity in process. The relaxation has therefore taken the form of violent clashes resulting from the separatism of different races and doctrines, often expressing the conflict between exclusive privilege and general development.

The terrestrial globe is a unit gradually settling down into a hydrodynamic equilibrium; in this process strains are set up which cause eruptions and earthquakes. Mankind is experiencing a corresponding development, but as a community in course of discovering the process equilibrium appropriate to its present state. The strains of this process cause social disturbances which echo through the whole system. The old separating traditions are thus ground down upon one another until prejudice loses its power and the conception of the one species with its common history can emerge to dominate the life and thought of man. This does not mean the making uniform in every aspect of life of what was previously varied, but the bringing to awareness of a unity of situation previously neglected but now becoming dominant. This transformation is not merely subjective and internal, or social and external, but a unitary development involving all aspects at once.

I suggest that one conviction alone can serve as the central principle of the reorganized tradition, the conviction that a formative process pervades nature. Man needs this principle to organize his thought. He needs it equally to organize his feeling, and through his thought and feeling his action. This conviction is on all grounds indispensable to the recovery of man. It is a biological need which once recognized cannot be denied. Man can understand himself only by viewing himself as a system in which a dominant formative process organizes an organic hierarchy of such processes in an environment of similar processes. Distortions and maladaptations in the development of man, whether as individual or species, represent disturbances to the balance and integrity of this hierarchy. The European tradition represents an inadequate social adaptation which for a period facilitated man's development. The next stage is marked by the recognition of the complete co-ordination proper to man as organism and social community. This implies a norm for man: the recovery of animal harmony in the differentiated form appropriate to man at this stage in history. But the clue to this recovery is the conceptually formulated conviction, at once subjective and objective in origin, that the form common to all processes is that of a formative tendency. When this conviction has become the basic principle of an objectively established universal tradition the period of unitary man will have begun.

Visions of similar promise have continually haunted men's minds and hearts, particularly at those seductive moments when everything is fluid and all things appear possible. The messianic hope of a new world near at hand seems to be necessary at certain periods to enable man to tolerate his lot. Through the centuries countless individuals, consumed by a sense of what man might be, have lost themselves in esoteric doctrine, introspective mysticism, or mania. But mid-twentieth century man has a unique advantage: he is supported by the sane tradition of a progressive body of knowledge that is now beginning to throw light on man himself. Today science brings the individual a double protection from illusion: it enables him to scrutinize both the subjective and the objective sources of his ideas. If a vision is seen to be only the compensation of a personal failure, the warning is patent. If an idea is incompatible with scientifically established fact, it can only be followed at risk.

This double check was not available when the visions of the past were formed. But today if anyone is tempted to live in a dream there will sooner or later come a moment when he can question its validity. Then science can save him provided he desires either subjective integrity or objective truth. If he cannot overcome his dream he may become either the permanent victim of an illusion or the instrument of a conviction which will transform him into a willing agent of history. Time alone can decide which, but the question does not exist for him. As far as unitary thought is concerned, the situation is unambiguous. What is put forward here is without authority. No science and no tradition supports it. But it is positive and explicit. If need be it will be quickly disproved by events. Moreover if any reader is tempted to accept the doctrine of unitary man without appropriate reserve, let him select any conflict in feeling, thought, or action and attempt to realize the unitary solution. Optimism is quickly lost.

Unitary man is marked by his conviction of a universal formative process. —The integrating convictions of past civilizations have also been of high generality, expressing a particular conception of god, nature, or man. But they did not develop from scientifically disciplined thought nor were they subject to the challenge of science as they spread. Hitherto science has tended to disintegrate rather than to develop general convictions and hence also to damage the unity of society. But the unitary conviction is more radical than those of the past, since it must ultimately either transform or reject everything which does not conform to its universal pattern. Subjective attitudes have to be tested against it and the facts of analytical science re-interpreted through it so that the duality of subjective and objective knowledge may disappear. From this restoration of the unity of thought there comes a new vigour: knowledge from science becomes inseparable from knowledge for action, and thought no longer delays but kindles action.

Viewed historically, unitary man is the universal type which begins to appear about the middle of the twentieth century as the result of a reorganization of the tradition based on the unitary conviction. The coming period in history, the fifth in our analysis, is thus characterized by man's awareness of the formative process which unites him with nature. Subjective religion and neutral objective science represent components of the process of social development in the past which stand in contrast to the comprehensive unitary conviction which grows out of them. The unitary form of life cannot be described in the partial terms of a dissociated civilization. It is not religion, for it is based on the socially recognized facts of science and it neither seeks nor promises eternity. It is not objective science unconcerned with its influence on life, for it is one with feeling and action; its criterion is not an objective neutrality, but the development of life by truth. The unitary form transcends the modes both of dissociated and of less differentiated societies. The human need for unity first created subjective religion, then objective analytical science; now it corrects the partiality of these attitudes by substituting one complete doctrine.

Regarded as an instrument for reorganizing knowledge the unitary conviction that nature is a system of formative processes constitutes a second heuristic principle which transcends the principle of quantity. The fourth period of our analysis, from 1600 to date, has been the age dominated by the idea of quantity; we are now entering the age dominated by the idea of development. But since we are not concerned with knowledge in isolation the unitary conviction is more than a heuristic method. The reorganization of a tradition involves a challenge to traditional social forms. The second heuristic principle is explicitly a revolutionary principle, just as the first was implicitly. Society is already in course of rapid transformation; the unitary principle, when recognized, will facilitate the process of social development by revealing that this process has the sanction of the biological nature of man. The second heuristic principle does not merely promote the discovery of neutral truth, but also the discovery by man of his own potentialities. In doing so it must challenge privilege.

The conceptions of god, nature, and man which served as the integrating convictions of past civilizations did not lead directly to practical conclusions regarding particular situations. In contrast the unitary conviction leads on from a general conception of nature and man to the development of a detailed system of thought applicable to the diversity of individual phenomena. It is able to do this because it is not a new method of thought appearing in a virgin field, as was the principle of quantity in 1600, but a method for the reorganization of a vast body of existing knowledge. In chapters 2 and 3, I have already given an outline of the unitary conception of nature and of the general characteristics of man. There remains the description of unitary man, of man when he becomes aware of the unitary process and organizes his community and its tradition in conformity with that awareness. We therefore now turn to consider the unitary individual and community as conceived by unitary thought. If unitary thought is valid, it is this form of human life which is now in course of development.

Unitary man's conception of himself is based on a norm of human life at this stage, that is, a general form to which the individual conforms in so far as he has not been distorted by special features in his hereditary constitution or his environment. The conception of such a norm implies that there exists one general form of development proper to man in the coming period. The norm is not restricted to any section of mankind, but is potentially universal as the dominant type of the period. The unitary norm extends the principle of organic or animal harmony by applying it to a species with the degree of differentiation and intellectual development characteristic of the new unitary man. It thus comprises, in addition to the conception of animal harmony, this unitary human principle: the individual becomes mature only through his recognition of himself as a component in the unitary system of nature and in the developing system of his community.

This knowledge is the essential feature of the unitary norm, yet it is not an arbitrary intellectual perception but the recognition by man of certain facts about himself, with all that that implies. It comprises realization of the fact that in the course of development of his community he is himself led to facilitate its general development and also the development of all its components including himself. He recognizes in his own formative passion, that is, in his vitality, his love, and his whole-natured organic will, the expression of the persuasiveness and continuity of the formative process. Dominated by his conviction of the universality of this process, he seeks to identify the characteristic form in course of development in every system around him and to facilitate its development. In every situation, including his own, he seeks to identify and facilitate development.

By adopting this conception of himself unitary man automatically preserves of Christianity, humanism, and Marxism whatever is proper to his nature. If there are elements in the present influence of these earlier doctrines which do not facilitate the development of man, these will be rejected by unitary man. But everything which can still serve his development is not only preserved but enriched by re-orientation within the comprehensive unity of the new conception. Unitary man need not judge earlier doctrines; their present adherents judge themselves by their attitude to him.

The main difference between the consciousness of unitary man and that of his predecessor is that unitary man welcomes development while dissociated man fears development and substitutes the pursuit of ideals which he seeks to regard as universal in their scope. Of all human capacities dissociated man regards compassion, or sympathy for the suffering of others, as his most precious. Compassion is the essence of Christianity, the mark of its noble failure. Dissociated man hates and pities himself; he also hates and pities others. Sometimes he appears to project on others his self-hatred and his sentimental self-pity, while at other times it seems that it is his attitude to others that determines his attitude to himself. But in unitary thought neither need be regarded as determining the other. Dissociated man reveals his thwarted integrity in his attitude both to himself and to others.

The failure of idealistic thought lay partly in the fact that it did not recognize that every ideal is linked to its shadow. The Christian cross is a symbol not only of the compassion of Jesus, but of the sadism which he provoked. This ambivalence, which appears paradoxical to minds trained in a static rationalism, is an elementary consequence of process thought. If a formative process is divided it falls into contrasted components. Whatever is incomplete is thus always complemented by its contrary; the penalty for any principle which fails to express the whole is the necessity to co-exist with its opposite. Partial love implies partial hate; spirit, sensuality; self-sacrificing compassion, sadism. The denial of any aspect sharpens and preserves it, while its acceptance transforms it by bringing it within the process of the whole. By proclaiming the ideal of universal compassion the dissociated Christian tends to neglect the complementary fact of the sadism of every dissociated nature. The more romantic the worship of compassion the deeper must be the division and the suppressed sadism.

If suppression implied disappearance, the history of Europe would have been different. But ideals which seek to deny their shadows eventually exhaust their own power, when the dissociated balance becomes unstable and the dark component seizes control. In recent years many have experienced this in their own lives or in the tragedy of Europe. The dissociated culture has failed to maintain itself and failed to realize its ideals. Platonic ideas have failed to organize thought; Christian compassion has failed to organize the brotherhood of man. For all its superb aspiration Christianity has not lessened war, disease, or hatred. It could not, for compassion is dishonest in dissociated man; there is no honesty where unity is lacking. Integrity of thought is possible only with integrity of the person. Dissociated man has denied his potential unity and lacks the vitality to recover it; he finds balm in the service of others. But the logic of fact is relentless. In rendering his own dissociation tolerable he tends to perpetuate it in others. When self-sacrificing service expresses flight from personal despair it is abortive, for it works to achieve its own doom. The builders of the European tradition made sure it would collapse.

The blind cannot lead each other, and one dissociated man cannot guide another to the experience he most needs. Compassion cannot cure sadism, its own complement. The dissociation is the fact behind both; if compassion fails and sadism seizes control, the fault lies only in the division of man's nature. Unitary man escapes these confusions through his recognition that one factor is of supreme importance: the maturity proper to man can come only through the experience of adult unity. This experience may come in many ways, but it means that the individual has, for the moment, outgrown the sense of any division, either within himself or from others, through a mature relation to at least one other person. Tension is inherent in process, but tension does not become frustrating conflict if the overriding unity is realized. The experience of adult unity is unconsciously awaited all through life until it is achieved, when it becomes a memory which guides all subsequent development. This fact is grounded in the general form of all process and in the special form of the dominant organic processes in man. The system of the person is transformed in such experience; the long prepared is achieved. Eternity, as far as it can be known to man, comes within reach, for long anticipations are fulfilled and undeveloped potentialities foretold in this metamorphosis of self-discovery. This fulfilment may never come, or it may be repeated many times in a life of continued development. But only such experience can dissolve the sadistic impulses of the dissociated nature and transform the sentimentality of a compassion based on ignorance into a conviction which facilitates development.

The Christian religion, seeking to preserve the source of its limited control over dissociated man, has never accepted integration as the criterion of conduct. It has demanded in addition that the integration shall be of a particular kind, thereby begging the question and prejudicing the possibility of a whole-natured harmony. In this prejudging of the issue Christianity has displayed its lack of acceptance of nature and human nature, its fear of life and its repudiation of man. This fear of man is implicit in the conception of repentance, which normally covers a slipshod evasion of the necessity for the individual to understand himself. An understanding of past conflicts may aid future development, but a contrite heart, broken by fear of its own sin, is further than ever from being whole.

Fear lies deep in dissociated man and leads him to place a mistaken emphasis on security. The Christian seeks spiritual, and the utilitarian material security, but neither achieves his aim because security is unattainable when regarded as an end in itself. Honest Christians know that doubt is an essential element in their lives; the true Christian is one who discards all hope of security and devotes his whole nature to the struggle with doubt. On the other hand even the mass of the people do not put material security first; a vital community is always ready to desert material aims for the sake of an adventure which offers unity in devotion to a single aim. Even the aim of national security to protect the life of the people is illusory; so long as this is put first the people's homes will continue to be ravaged by war.

Security is an impostor; little can be achieved while each seeks his own freedom from want, from war, or from fear. The general nature of all fear is the awareness that development is threatened. Fear and its consequences can be eliminated only by action leading to continued development. Action can bring the assurance of a development which is more welcome than either spiritual or material security. Only through the pursuit of a general development can species acquire the unity of purpose which may, as one of its secondary consequences, eliminate unemployment and war. In the individual life the same is true: only in unitary development can fear be overcome. Every individual experiences countless shocks from his first breath to his last, and these challenges are necessary to his development. But a unitary tradition can assist the members of each maturing generation to turn these challenges to advantage and to retain their basic integrity.

Yet unitary man knows that there is no guarantee of continued development. "Who so truly loves God must not desire God to love him in return." Life is finite and death is final. To the European seeking comfort in illusions death was an anomaly which he did his best to neglect. But death is as frequent an event as birth, though it plays little part in the literature most characteristic of Europe. To the unitary mind death is the chief symbol of the limitations without which life would lose its dignity.

The European aspired to the infinite; unitary man is content to shape his finite life. But in the unitary period any individual may, in following his own course of development, seek to escape the limitations that are proper to him as human organism and to express some universal and permanent form. In doing so he recovers the possibility of tragedy. Tragic drama expressed the inevitability of the frustration of the individual will following an inner necessity. The hero is a man who has discovered that his finite life can express the universal only if he stakes it without reserve. Integrated man by his mere existence challenges fate. His integrity is resented by the divided, and sooner or later his difference from the rest destroys him. Socrates and Jesus did not call out love only from their fellows. Socrates understood this and unhesitatingly welcomed his fate; Jesus, according to report, did not and appealed to be saved from the end he had made inevitable. But his complaint was laid at the wrong door; it was man who had forsaken himself.

Only two things are certain for unitary man: the universality of the formative process and the inevitability of death. To be a unitary man is never to lose awareness either of the diversity of nature or of the limitations of one's own nature and yet to be able to say with Bruno: "Unity enchants me. By her power I am free though thrall, happy in sorrow, rich in poverty, and quick even in death."

It is in the structure of his thought that unitary man is most clearly distinguished from the Western and European. We have reached the historical moment when consciousness, using dualistic-static thought, can no longer guide action. The policy appropriate in any situation, whether political or personal, is wrongly described as either idealistic or materialistic, humanitarian or self-interested. These false antitheses obscure the need for a common development. Unitary man renounces such dualisms and relies on mental processes which are themselves examples of the process forms of nature rather than on the spurious clarity of static thought. He seeks to think naturally, in conformity with nature, rather than to trace the logic of sharp classifications. Unitary thought overcomes the mental inertia that tends to degrade thought into static forms which assume the existence of unchanging entities which may be labelled once and for all. This is the chief failure of the immature static intellect: to assume that a thing or person is now what it has been, and is in one situation what it is in another. Each identification has its own vested interest in challenging further change. It requires a vitality of mind which analytical thought does not foster to be ready at every moment to discard preconceptions and to remain receptive to fine adjustments of continuing development.

But analytical thought not only tends to deaden such sensibility, its static concepts obstruct the recognition of the sequence of developing forms. Only with a process system of thought can the reasoning mind follow the structure of such transformations, whether in the processes of the inanimate world or in the development of organisms, persons, or societies. Guided by process thought the mind loses something of its inertia and is carried forward by the same formative impetus as it recognizes in the processes of nature. Process thought moves forward as a component of the processes which it symbolizes. It views nature from within, using its own process forms to look forward along the avenues of development. It may be said to make intuition rational, supplementing the intuition which recognizes forms by the rational use of past experience to foretell their development. Process thought also helps to make theory practical, for its concepts are no longer static abstractions valid only in limiting cases, but process forms isomorphic with nature and leading through to action. It cannot betray the individual into the frustration and disillusionment which was so often the consequence of European idealism in those who took it seriously.

Yet the conformity of unitary thought with the process to which it refers cannot always be complete. There are points at which such intimate similarity of form is inappropriate and it is more convenient for thought to make use of a static symbolism. This is a proper use of static and hence of quantity symbols, provided that one condition is satisfied: the result of the thought sequence must be translated back from the static symbolism into process forms before final conclusions are drawn and action invited. For example the damage which arises from the humbug of finance can be avoided provided that the money symbols are used only as methods of correlating human processes, i.e., of maintaining a developing balance between the processes of production, distribution, and consumption. Unitary thought requires that the cycle of every process of reasoning should be completed so that it begins and ends with process concepts. The precision which was the ideal of static thought is replaced by the completeness of unitary thought. It would be an aid to proper thought to print all static concepts in a late Greek or Gothic type as a reminder of the fact that they refer only to the static aspects of process and have therefore only a limited validity.

Yet the significance of this change of aim, from analytical precision to general order, depends on the criterion of truth in unitary thought. What is truth for unitary man? Is it the correspondence of thought to fact, or the coherence of thought within its own system? It cannot be mere correspondence, since in unitary thought there is no ultimate dualism of thought and fact. Nor can it be coherence within a system which serves practical needs, for this conception also retains the dualism of thought and practice. The unitary criterion of truth must arise from the relation of the form of thought to the form of the whole process of which thought is a part.

Truth is thought which conforms to the form of the whole. Conformity to the whole is the criterion. The unitary truth is that which conforms to the whole process of which it is part. The truth is a form embedded in the whole complex of processes in the human organism and its environment, symbolizing and organizing them. A particular truth may not represent the entire structure of a situation but only those aspects which are relevant to thought at a given stage in its development. The truth is a system of symbols whose structure conforms to the whole pattern of feeling, thought, and action, and integrates all the processes which link the reception of stimuli and the moulding of the ultimate responses. This is not a pragmatic criterion, since unitary truth does not merely serve special needs but unites the whole system in a conviction which is at once emotional, intellectual, and practical. Since both the community and the individual are in course of development so is the truth itself, but the truth is not relative to individual judgements. Truth, in conforming to the whole, must express the universal principle, and itself facilitate development. The false sooner or later frustrates development; the truth always leads on. One man's truth may be behind or in advance of the accepted truth of the tradition, but while a society survives its truth must develop. When it ceases to develop, the society decays and gives place to another.

The source of the power of unitary thought is now evident. The unitary conviction of a universal formative tendency is one which satisfies this criterion of truth in a comprehensive manner. First, it cannot stifle development but leads thought on to discover the forms in course of development. Next, it invites the individual to discover the special form of his own development and so to achieve a developing emotional balance. Finally, it leads him on from thought and feeling to the action which facilitates development. The unitary conviction is a necessity to unitary man; he cannot believe anything else. This is no verbal trick or tautology; it is the expression of the fact that only the idea of a process of development can provide the general symbol which can facilitate every conceivable form of development. Intellectual, emotional, and pragmatic truth are combined in the central conviction of unitary man; hence its peculiar power.

We have already seen that European thought in general lacked this power to facilitate the unitary development of the person. The human system comprises component processes which tend in certain circumstances to diverge into apparently independent tendencies, such as those of man's "spiritual" and "material" nature, and European thought by recognizing those separate tendencies and failing to identify any integrating tendency tended to maintain and develop the dissociation. The contrast shown in this respect by unitary thought is best seen by considering how it overcomes the intellectual dualisms that have expressed and strengthened the tendency to dissociation. One of the most important of these is the antithesis of the "ideal" and the "real." An analysis of the contrast and limitations of the idealistic and realistic attitudes will carry a stage further our examination of the failure of idealism.

Ethical Idealism is the attempt to identify certain aspects of the formative tendency which is expressed in all behavior, before the human mind has developed sufficiently to recognize, the true form of that tendency. An ideal is a sign of ignorance. It neglects its own shadow, the component complementary to it. Even when idealism admits the existence of the complementary component it offers no principle which can resolve the dualism of good and evil which it has discovered in man. Not yet aware of the limitations of static concepts, idealistic thought attempts to use them to define the form of those tendencies which it values in human nature. The ideals of truth, beauty, and goodness represent attempts to interpret the process of development as a group of tendencies permanently directed toward certain permanent and universal ends. But human behavior is not directed towards unchanging ends, nor even towards those temporary ideals which each community sets up for itself. The formative tendency is displayed, not in any steady process of definite orientation, but in a rhythmic sequence of transformations which cannot be represented as tending towards any particular final condition. The attempt to interpret this process rhythm as a dualism of ideal aspirations and material needs implies a radical misconception of the nature of man.

A further error in the idealistic approach arises from the attempt to measure behavior from the outside. The processes of human life cannot be understood as directed towards any external or general standard such as a universal ideal. The human community, as a part of organic nature, develops its characteristic forms, and the individual develops his own. Man carries within himself the clue to his own development as part of his community. Ideals which the community brings to the individual cannot bring him more than a partial self-knowledge. But when the community tradition says to the individual: you carry within yourself the characteristic form which your own life must develop through the formative tension between yourself and the community, then the splints and crutches of idealism become unnecessary.

The idealistic misinterpretation has persisted through the history of European civilization, because it correctly described, though wrongly treating as universal, the dualistic tendencies which the social circumstances at the origin of the European tradition, and later the tradition itself, imposed on the successive generations. But this dualistic view is no longer adequate now that man's self-knowledge has begun to reach regions deeper even than this ancient dissociation. These regions, which are imagined as deep lying, are the most general characteristics of behavior and the processes which in the long run determine the form of behavior. The most general is frequently the most elusive, and this is particularly so when the strongest emotional habits of the spiritual and sensual components of dissociated man tend to prevent him recognizing the simple truth. But thanks to the broad movement of thought in which Marx, Freud, and their followers have collaborated, the dualism is already bridged by the knowledge that even when the subject believes his thought to be disinterested it may be unconsciously guided by economic or instinctive needs. Yet this bridge is only a provisional short cut which does violence to human nature; the spirit of man cannot properly identify itself with the objective continuity of process until its formative characteristics have been explicitly recognized. The final elimination of the dualism can only come about through the realization that the need to formulate ideals, and in so doing split man asunder, is itself an expression of the very human but futile desire to escape the uncertainty of process and to find spiritual security in the aim at least of a permanent harmony. Unitary man can achieve this realization, and see himself as a whole, because he is ready to accept his personal life for what it is, a transient development through changes which cannot be foreseen.

When dissociated man lacks the vitality to recover his unity, the formative tendency may turn outwards in one of two forms which seek to impose on society the dominance respectively of an idea and of a person. The first temperament endeavours to make the community adopt a mode of life in conformity with his own ideals. The second seeks to achieve power for himself. The former is normally progressive and theoretical, the latter conservative and intelligent. The tendency for these two attitudes to diverge and to form distinct types is evident throughout European history and is, like all such dualisms, an expression of the dissociation. The idealist operates through general principles and tends to neglect the complexity of human motives. The realist works through individuals, relying on personalities to dominate groups and tending to neglect rational analysis. While the one proclaims abroad the desirability of this or that objective, the other privately debates the relative importance of individuals. Action based on ideals appears satisfactory in anticipation, but is usually unsatisfactory in performance, while the activities of the realist may bring him satisfaction but fail permanently to enrich the tradition.

The European tendency to separate thought and action is evident in the divergence of these types. Yet the leaders who have the greatest influence are practical and constructive, not theoretical nor conservative. Their aim is to understand their time and to facilitate its development. They are not concerned with what may subjectively appear desirable, but with what is possible. They do not measure human action in terms either of idealism or self-interest, but as an expression of the formative vitality of the species which shapes the course of history. Such leaders may appear noble or terrible according to the character of the historical movement of which they are the agents. Caesar, Lenin, and Hitler have this in common: each facilitated the course which was inherent in the situation of his community. This factor is the source of the exceptional influence of these figures. Without some element of self-identification with the historical trend the myth cannot grow, and during a period when fear and hate prevail even the Antichrist may be acclaimed as inspired.

In the coming period, however, a new type of leader will be necessary. The great social leaders of the past were almost exclusively local figures, either tribal, national, or at most continental or imperial, and their lives reflected this limitation. A few stood for universal conceptions which might permanently enrich the tradition by aiding its continuing development: Socrates, Jesus, and Lenin are perhaps examples. But they were exceptions, and it is only now that the world community requires its universal leaders, agents of the common destiny of the race, each symbolizing a special aspect of the general situation and facilitating special components of the common development of all men. These world leaders will specialize in particular aspects of the universal tendency. Local communities will continue to pursue their own courses within the general tendency. The unitary conviction is not merely tolerant of diversity but promotes it, unlike the fanatical convictions of the dissociated. The intolerance of religions or races, whether Jewish, Christian, German, or any other, is transcended in the unitary conception of the species. The world representatives of the coming period, being assisted by the unitary conviction in overcoming personal frustrations, will be less liable to impose their personal or national limitations on the world, since they are offered the greater satisfaction of becoming the instruments of its common purpose.

While overcoming the duality of the idealistic and realistic attitudes to society, unitary thought implies also a changed conception of the relation of the individual to the community. We saw that at the beginning of the European tradition the separation of the subject from the objective world expressed the desire for permanence and the tendency of thought to separate static entities from the general process. This resulted finally in the extreme individualist view which asserted the paradox that the individual could best pursue his development in isolation, that he, needs his "freedom" to develop. Here even Spinoza went astray, as must any static thinker who rejects life and substitutes an intellectual god. "Free is that which exists solely according to the necessity of its own nature, and whose action is determined by itself." This is the liberal, intellectual, and idealist mistake; a nature free in this sense could never develop, never learn, never meet those challenges through which the potentialities of life can alone be realized. Goethe did not fall into this error. In unitary thought such a conception of freedom is logically excluded, philosophically absurd, and biologically false. No development ever continues in isolation, and the development of the individual, in the sense of the formation of novel and more highly organized forms, can occur only as part of a wider system. The concept of inertia is relevant to man in a special sense: man cannot grow by his own efforts in isolation, he continues in his old path except in so far as he is part of a wider system which draws new responses from him. In subjective terms: man prefers his old ways, only the challenge of suffering can change him. Or more accurately: man continues normally to develop along stabilized lines, and suffering is the strain of adaptation to a novel situation calling for a new form of development. Here is always some degree of tension between the individual and his community, and this tension is the source of individual development.

Each individual expresses the universal tendency through the special form of his own system as developed by his ancestry and his own history. Each is unique and yet an expression of the same universal form. This recovery of the sense of unity with nature, which man lost when he became self-conscious, does not carry him back to pagan innocence. In the process of becoming self-conscious he separated his imagination from his senses, and his conscious will from the natural processes around him. But while the pantheistic primitive discovered spirits like his own throughout nature, unitary man inverts his identification and recognizes the general form of natural processes in the workings of his own spirit. This fusion of subject and object is possible because nature is interpreted as the expression of a tendency which has the same formative property as that which man recognizes in his own nature.

The contrast between unitary and dissociated man may be viewed from yet another side. The European based his mode of life on the deliberate pursuit of activities which expressed only one side or other of his divided nature. Denied activity which could express his whole nature, he sought a substitute in the deliberate cultivation either of new sensations, or of the moral will. The deliberate attempt to attain intensified states of consciousness is typical of dissociated man and bears no relation to the trend of human development. Don Juan and St. John of the Cross are equally martyrs to this endless pursuit of intense experience, sensual or mystical. The opposite mode, the attempt to deny feelings in the discipline of the will, is as futile. The moral will of the dissociated nature does not express a proper development of integration, but the dominance of a dissociated and therefore distorted component of the human system. This form of will is angry, intolerant of self and others, and reflects the failure of vitality either to maintain or to achieve integration. Paul and Luther are the martyrs of this will which lacks integrity. Unitary man replaces this spurious discipline by the health-bringing exercise of normal functions in their proper timing, and where need be by the therapeutic techniques of the science which springs from his conviction.

Discipline ceases to be the attempted denial of dissociated and distorted components of the person and becomes education in the appropriate timing of these functions. The dissociated tradition has laid down morally permissible occasions not only for love, conception, and death, but also for mass murder and social theft. Unitary man will discover that these traditional moral rules do not adequately serve the developing integration of individual and community. European morality was directed towards maintaining the dissociation and was therefore mainly negative and superficial. Its principal motive was fear, whether conscious or unconscious; it asserted what should not be done, and it could only be obeyed with a part of human nature. The unitary conviction does not preach a negative. It asserts the formative tendency proper to man and leaves it to the individual to experience it as his own conviction.

The general antithesis of individual and community is resolved in unitary thought, but this fact does not of itself sufficiently assist the individual to follow his proper course. We have seen that the clue to the European achievement lay in the establishment of universals which were conceived as being in direct relation to the individual and which thereby facilitated his development. In his continual struggle with society the individual found reassurance in his immediate sense of these universals: god, truth, justice, nature as a whole. Sometimes this relation became one of experienced identity, mystical unity with the whole. More often the universal offered not an avenue of escape but a source of stability in meeting the tensions of daily life. The universal assumed the guise of a neutral adviser to whom the individual could appeal amidst the conflicting pressures of his own inclinations and the demands of the community.

But we also saw that these universals were fictions designed by man's own thought to satisfy the requirements of his dissociated personality. European thought therefore failed to establish the true relation of the universals to the individual, and as a consequence the individual failed to find stability. He hesitated between the appeal of two principles: the unity with God of pantheistic and mystical religion, and the enjoyment of the variety of personality in the humanistic and Protestant outlook. The first principle corresponds to the need of a universal order controlling the anarchy of finite persons, the second to the sense of a responsible will seeking to develop individual personality to the full. Europe foundered on this dualism, losing itself in its inability to choose between the two modes, or to find the unitary principle which could transcend them. With the decay of religion an absolute social collectivism came to be substituted for the unification of the person with an absolute god. But this substitution of society for god robbed the individual of his guide; the universal had ceased to be neutral and had come down on the side of the community. The source of the European inspiration was thus temporarily exhausted, the individual lost his self-assurance, and leadership passed into the hands of distorted men.

The unitary view restores the proper relation of the individual to the community, by re-establishing a universal principle of the kind proper to man's present condition. The relation of the individual to the community is again balanced by his recognition of an absolute, the universal formative process. His knowledge of the universal form of process provides him with a criterion in his endeavour to find his own role in society and an opportunity to overcome personal frustration. The sense that he is one with all nature yields a metaphysical comfort, his own impermanence being no longer resented. Conflict is eased because the general form of everything is understood. This comfort is no illusion, but expresses a transformation of the person which must confirm itself in action.

Socrates held that it is enough to recognize the truth, since right action must follow. The error of this intellectual idealism lay in the belief that static, analytical, intellectualized knowledge was a sufficiently integral part of the person to transform him. In establishing its static concepts human thought had lost that complete unity with life. But unitary knowledge is in such conformity with the forms of the organic processes at all levels in the human system, and has such power to organize experience within a single order, that it tends to become more than intellectual knowledge. Unitary knowledge by transforming the elements of daily experience ceases to be abstract knowledge, and acquires the status of experienced life. It is not enough to recognize any aspect of the truth for right action to follow at once.

But Socrates was thus far right: if the unitary form of the truth is recognized a metamorphosis is set in process tending to lead to unitary action.

This outline of unitary man's conception of himself is as yet incomplete, for we have not touched the cardinal distinction between European and unitary man. Since man became self-aware two factors have competed in his thought: the experience of freedom and the recognition of necessity. As subject he knows that he is free to choose, while as observer he recognizes necessity in nature. For unitary man there is no conflict between these two approaches to a single situation, but dissociated man was compelled by his inner division to experience a contradiction between them. He could not recover his own unity, therefore he could not recognize it in his thought. Having split himself into a spiritual and a sensual nature, he was bound to interpret the experienced freedom of his mind as separate from, and in opposition to, material necessity. His most precious experience of freedom had arisen through his self-emancipation from the unrestricted dominance of his animal instincts. It followed that the experience of freedom meant to him the power of the mind to choose a path contrary to the processes of the rest of nature. For dissociated man to have accepted the conception of a natural necessity expressing itself within his own act of choice would have meant the renunciation of his hard-won European consciousness.

So long as European man was afraid of himself this situation could not change. It is not far from the truth to say that his fear of his lower nature supported the dissociation and inhibited unprejudiced thought about himself. In fact the fear, the inhibition, and the dissociation developed together. The emotions, the thought, and the dissociation of the European are inseparable, and the collapse of this system came not from a change in any one of these components but from the consequences of his progressive differentiation. When this finally upset the stability of the dissociation, man ceased to be afraid of himself, because the worst secrets of his animality, his self-seeking, and his sadism were already out. The way was thus prepared for unitary man to view himself without prejudice.

There is irony in the case with which European man deceived himself. Not being free, in the sense in which he thought he was, to think objectively about himself, he was compelled to assert his subjective freedom. He had to believe in his freedom, just because his mind was not free to determine the whole behavior of his dissociated nature and had to compensate this fact in thought. During periods when he was unaware of inner conflict man found no difficulty in holding that subjective freedom and external necessity were compatible, because they could then appear to operate on different planes —like the two sides of his own nature. But when the inner conflict grew troublesome he became intellectually concerned about the apparent antithesis of necessity and freedom, and could find no intellectual resolution, any more than he could find a personal solution of his own conflict. Finally with the collapse of the dissociation and the restored dominance of the vital energies, man lost his intellectual belief in arbitrary free will, just as he had lost inspiration and initiative in his personal life. Material necessity appeared to have recovered its dominance.

But this simplification of a complex historical process neglects the formative tendency which guided the entire transformation and is now re-forming a unitary integration within the organic system of man. Unitary man, escaping both the earlier dissociation and the more recent disintegration, develops as a co-ordinated person capable of seeing himself whole, and therefore of recognizing the single truth which is expressed in freedom and necessity. But to avoid ambiguity this recognition must be formulated afresh in unitary terms.

To unitary man freedom means the power of the subject to choose, not arbitrarily or in opposition to the course of nature, but in accordance with his own nature, that is, in continuity with his past. On the other hand the necessity in nature does not imply compulsion or constraint or even the determinism of a mechanical causality, but the continuity of form in natural processes. The experience of freedom and the recognition of necessity can therefore be translated respectively as the sense of being able to think and act in continuity with one's own past and the perception of the continuity of form in natural process. To unitary man there is no distinction between such freedom and such necessity. Continuity of development is the form both of objective necessity and of subjective freedom. The continuity of natural processes has the character of the development of form. The recognizable identity of each person lies in the continuity of development of his own characteristic form. Free will, the exercise of choice, selection-these lead to the course which develops the person's characteristic form. There is nothing arbitrary in free will and nothing constraining in natural law; continuity of development is common to both. Freedom and necessity are the subjective and objective, the spiritual and material, aspects of this continuity seen by dissociated man.

Many European thinkers have escaped excessive distortion by the dissociation of the tradition and have been able to recognize the true relation of freedom and necessity. But even today the misinterpretation persists together with the dissociation. This delay in accepting what is an essential condition for integrity in life as in thought has not merely been due to the unconscious fear that in admitting himself to be part of the general order of nature the subject would lose either the reality of freedom or his precious sense of freedom. To isolate one such motive and treat it as a limiting factor in development is to misinterpret the social process. So fundamental a transformation as the recovery by man of his place in nature can only come about as the culmination of a general process expressing itself in every aspect of life. The continuity expressed in the personal exercise of free will might at any time have been identified with the continuity displayed in natural processes. But the emotional inhibition which hindered that identification was reinforced by the intellectual difficulty that the processes of the conscious mind were obviously formative while natural necessity was regarded as a pattern of mechanical motions lacking any formative property. In unitary man this intellectual obstacle disappears simultaneously with the psychological resistance, as a result of the unitary conviction. This conviction allows the individual to recognize the universal formative tendency operating in his own mental processes and hence the necessity within his exercise of freedom.

But the dissociated man's sense of freedom was limited. The intensity with which monotheism and idealism were maintained was partly the expression of a compulsive neurosis: man had to maintain the pretence of possessing what he lacked in fact. He was not free to realize his ideals, or to be what the dissociated tradition made him wish to be. "For what 1 would, that I do not; but what I hate, that I do." Everyone who has shared in the common experience of the continent of Europe during the last twenty-five years has known in some degree the deadly paralysis of neurosis, the deep failure of ideals, the frustration of the soul, the dark moments before despair is complete. The ideals are gone; for the moment man is lost in the shadows. This experience has been more widespread than ever previously in the history of Europe or of the world. It expresses the final failure of the Platonic-Christian subjective ideals, the exhaustion of the illusion of the autonomy of the conscious mind.

Man needs unity, but the conscious mind had claimed freedom to challenge or deny any components in human nature which it found alien to itself. This denial of unity meant that even the European sense of freedom was limited. At times it seemed to blossom in great achievements but the recurrent conflict returned until at last it dominated everything and robbed the European of the sense that he was free to control his own fate. Antichrist reigned in the shadows. It was not the machine that mastered man, but the uncontrolled tendencies of his distorted nature breaking through the superficial control of his immature consciousness. A stabilized dualism had collapsed into a momentary formlessness which gave the perverted their opportunity. The sense of subjective freedom had disappeared, while the recovery of the sense of freedom through identification with nature was not yet generally possible for the European or Western mind.

Spinoza had identified man with nature, but in a static system which could offer no general guidance. Goethe had made the same identification, but he could not then be followed by others, for his method challenged the validity of analytical science. Hegel interpreted freedom as the acceptance of necessity, and Marx developed this recognition as one of the axioms of his view of history. But the European mind still could not accept this interpretation, since the mechanical and material processes of nature appeared to be of an essentially different character from the formative tendencies which he regarded as the supreme characteristic of his own mind.

In Asia the individual mind was less conscious of its distinction from other minds; the sense of the community was stronger, and the ground was appropriate for the new philosophy. A less differentiated people was thus the first to accept the new identification. Russia could take the step from a subjective religion to an objective collective doctrine, because it had not experienced the individualism of the Renaissance, the Reformation, and the liberal age. It was possible for Russia to accept a relatively immature materialist view of history, because to the Russian this did not mean the loss of individuality which it would have meant to the European. The communist doctrine was successful in Russia and carried that country rapidly forward, while it failed in Europe. Russian communism is of limited validity and essentially alien to Western values, but in spite of present appearances it may represent one line of development towards the unitary view which alone can provide a universal doctrine. The discovery of freedom in the acceptance of the material economic process is not open to all peoples, but for some it may be a stage towards the discovery of freedom in identification with the universal formative process. Soviet freedom, in so far as it exists in so fiercely centralized a regime, consists in a positive act of acceptance and resolution, not merely in a negative security from fear or from want. Negative freedom is an illusion; only the positive impetus which arises from an integration of the person can bring the experience of freedom.

In unitary society the community and the great majority of its individual members share the same characteristic form of development and there is no room for fundamental conflict. The aim of the community is to develop its members, and all the special liberties and rights of man derive from this dominant purpose. Each community develops the political and social system appropriate to its own situation, and the differences between these are of little consequence if development is facilitated. But the aim of government is no longer merely to protect the voluntary activities of the people. It must be based on an explicit conception of the nature of those activities. The life of unitary society is organized so as to facilitate the development of its members along lines which coincide both with their mature, spontaneous choice and with the socially accepted aim. If this is possible the society will maintain its unity through the process of its development; if not, the society will disintegrate. The health of the community thus depends on the individual being able to realize his own freedom within the necessity of the community.

The dissociated idealist is unable to understand this experience of necessity as freedom. He looks for the fundamental conflict which he is convinced must always exist between the compromises of social life and the standards of the individual conscience. This is just the trouble with the idealist; the conflict does exist for him, he cannot escape the antithesis of the real and the ideal which reflects his inner dissociation. His misinterpretation of his own situation is maintained by the fear which prevents his accepting the uncertainties of process and development. The idealist seeks the security of a static harmony, and therefore considers every tension evil. Unitary man recognizes tension as an essential feature of the formative process operating in man. Man creates in resolving tensions, but never brings them to an end. The contrasts of past, present, and future forms provide an inexhaustible source of tension. In every society there is a wide scattering of individuals at all stages of development, just as the tradition comprises ancient myths, contemporary platitudes, and prophetic vistas. The individual who can understand and accept the long-term development of his community may have to stand alone.

Yet beneath all tension and conflict a new unison marks unitary society. The universality of the formative process, once recognized and accepted, casts its spell over man. Every element finds its place in the system of nature, and every particular form symbolizes a general form. Man is himself the supreme symbol, the richest of all natural systems. Words are symbols spoken by man, but in the unitary world every form is a symbol and speaks to man. This unison brings the new light, not merely of deeper intellectual comprehension, but of a more profound organic realignment. Minor frustrations disappear, displaced elements fall into their true relations, the central and autonomous nervous systems move back into balance, cortex and thalamus accept a new integration, and the qualities of this harmony are reflected in the social order. Such recovery has happened before and can happen now. It does not imply the establishment of Utopia, but merely a natural readjustment after the strain of transition.

It has been suggested that society is moving towards a new medievalism, a condition in which every component has its appropriate place in the general order and therefore symbolizes certain aspects of the whole. Medieval society was marked by a social system of hierarchical structure, a mode of thought that expressed itself in concrete symbols, and a blend of universalism with sharp contrasts. These elements reappear in unitary society, but with a changed significance. The medieval order was a relatively stationary pattern deriving its sanction from a static divine authority; the unitary order rests on an explicit recognition of the universality of process and is so constituted as to facilitate the development of society by furthering that of individuals. The medieval features thus acquire a contrary significance in unitary society. What was static becomes formative; the largely unconscious reference of concrete symbols becomes the explicit representation of typical forms of process; the threat of the dark background of the Middle Ages is replaced by the open conflict of great continental modes of life competing for universality.

But throughout both the medieval and the modern age Europeans were haunted by a sense which the symbolisms of art and of science could not adequately express. Within the pageant of daily life, and beyond the reach either of religious tradition or personal introspection, there lay hidden the promise of an important truth, like the memory of some forgotten experience or the anticipation of one not yet known. Both external nature and man's experience of his own nature seemed to hold an emotional implication perpetually elusive but of great, significance. The adolescent experiences this sense of hidden beauty, and some adults realize its meaning at least once in their lives. One such experience, filled with the discovery of whole-natured life, is a draught of eternity as deep, sometimes, as a finite lifetime can absorb. The anticipation of the adolescent is valid, if it is not misinterpreted as the assurance of a lasting harmony. The yearning of dissociated man is also valid; it is rooted in the fact of a human harmony temporarily lost in the process of maturing and capable of recovery through further growth, a unison of development sustained by the rhythm of tension and ending only in death. The enlightenment, at once intellectual and organic, of unitary society arises from the fact that tension and harmony, which are incompatible in static systems and static thought, are the complementary and indispensable aspects of form in development.

By openly recognizing the inescapable rhythm of harmony and tension which is the form of all human processes unitary man achieves a far-reaching emancipation. Much that was concealed can now stand in the open. The neutrality and objectivity of the quantity symbolism seemed to dissociated man a guarantee of the liberation of the mind from anthropomorphic and subjective illusions. But at a deeper level it expressed merely the desire to escape inner conflict in a harmony of static form. This escape was wholly illusory; the superficial neutrality of science left it open to abuse, and the spirit of man has been punished for its attempt to escape struggle in an intellectual harmony. Unitary man renounces such separation and partakes in the development of the whole. Man finds himself in the universal process, by finding the universal process within himself. Tension continues, but henceforward his struggle is with, not against, the processes of nature.

11

The World Trend

Unitary thought has a forward impetus. It is oriented from earlier to later stages, and from the past towards the future. In recognizing any form in process of development, unitary man looks forward to what will develop if circumstances permit. He cannot identify a system without thereby making a conditional prediction regarding its future course. This peculiarity of unitary thought is appropriate to the present stage in the development of thought. Static thought divided scientific prediction into two parts: the identification of a system, and the discovery of its laws. But unitary thought, by postulating one universal law, combines these into one: the identification of the particular form whose development characterises the system. In the course of the development of thought more extensive prediction has become possible; in unitary thought prediction becomes a component of all thought. Unitary man cannot think about anything without viewing it as a component of a developing process.

This means that a picture of unitary man as a particular type of *homo sapiens* must be set at a definite moment in history and include unitary man's anticipation of the trend of his own further development. The outline of unitary man given in the previous chapter is static, and therefore abstract and incomplete. Unitary man not only has a general conception of himself as a universal type following on European and Western man, he also has a conviction of his proper path of development. Unitary man of the 1940s can only become aware of himself when he has identified the intellectual and social forms in development around him sufficiently to enable him to guide his own development for the decades immediately ahead. Unitary man comes into being through his recognition and acceptance of the world trend.

The Christian, the humanist, and the Marxist believed they knew certain aspects of the future. The medieval Christian foresaw the continued victory of evil until the judgement day and the resurrection. The humanist was confident of the continued moral progress of mankind. The Marxist was certain of the main line until the advent of the classless society. But these views lacked a formative principle. Unitary man sees the formative tendency everywhere, though circumstances may prevent its realization in particular systems. He can say with confidence: I have recognized this system; if it develops at all, it will be towards the development of its characteristic form within the processes of its environment. He becomes a full citizen of the unitary world in accepting and facilitating the trend of the world community.

But unitary man's view of his further social development is inseparable from his view of his mental development. The organization of human life is unitary; there is one trend common to its social and mental components. To appreciate this unity we may imagine the world dawning afresh on the mind of unitary man in the 1950s. The world is new to him, for he views it through new eyes. Like an adolescent upon whom maturity has begun to cast its magic he surveys life afresh, seeking to reinterpret everything in the light of his discovery of the unitary principle. He absorbs both the records of the past and the changing forms of the contemporary world, and seeks to find in every situation a characteristic form in course of development. The discovery of development in nature is continuous with the discovery of it in contemporary man. But though this impulse is single, we must distinguish four aspects and consider them in turn.

Unitary man, confronted with the contemporary world and its records of the past, seeks to identify the special forms of the formative process:

in the development of physical systems;
in the history of the universe and of life;
in the history of man; and
in the contemporary world trend.

The task of identifying the formative process in the history of the universe (which includes the development of physical systems and the history of man) constitutes the unitary reorganization of knowledge of the past. The identification of the contemporary world trend constitutes the recognition by unitary man of his own historical situation. But this separation of the past from the present and future is an arbitrary division of the single task of unitary thought. The task is the unitary reorganization of the tradition, and this has, according to the view presented here, to be achieved in this century. The following description of some components of this task is not the outline of an arbitrary 50-year world plan, but the formulation of the only possible path of development for unitary man.

The Development of Physical Systems

Physical systems are those which tend to develop a static or stationary form, in contrast to organic systems, which tend to develop a process form. The task of unitary thought in this field is to apply the conception of a formative process to physical systems so as to provide a unitary foundation for quantitative physics. This must rest on a theory of the process of measurement and- a derivation of the physical numbers (quantities) so obtained, including the universal (pure number) constants of physical theory. Unitary thought has to show how European man, in his search for permanence, put numbers into his conception of nature. Every quantitative physical process has to be reinterpreted as an aspect of the formative process characterizing the system in question. Unitary thought can justify itself only by thus establishing the priority of process over quantity.

Chapter 2 outlined the first steps of an approach to this unitary synthesis of physical law.

Each of the major occasions of history is marked by a seemingly irrational moment when the tide of the past is broken into spray upon the rock of a single event and a new rhythm begins to accumulate in its place. A new phase in the historical process remains ambiguous until it defines itself through some sudden local event. In a voyage it is the sighting of the shore, in war the breaking of victory, in science the establishment of a new symbol of truth, which sets its irrevocable stamp upon the course of history.

In the anticipated derivation of the laws of quantitative physics from process concepts we have reached the special event through which unitary thought must ultimately prove its title. The entire fundamental content of exact science, that is, the essence of relativity, atomic, and quantum theory, is symbolized in one number, the "fine-structure constant." This number, a (alpha), whose measured value is 1/137.03 . . . represents the culmination of two millennia of static analytical thought and of three and a hall centuries of quantitative science. Minds which are ripe for unitary thought cannot believe that the value of so significant a number is arbitrary and meaningless. In the unitary view there is no scope for any arbitrariness of measured number, because the structure of nature is not quantitative, but man puts quantity into nature by applying the process of measurement. It must therefore be shown that a (alpha) has this particular value because in a world of process man has made certain measurements in certain ways. a (alpha) quantizes process, but we do not yet know how. Unitary thought can only acquire the sanction appropriate to its scope through a unitary derivation of this fundamental number, providing the key to a comprehensive scientific synthesis.

This is the most severe of all tests that can be demanded in advance of a system of thought. Such earnestness is appropriate to a doctrine claiming universality. Ultimately no doubt can remain. Unitary thought is the vision of a world. Either that world is a fantasy, or it is this world recognized by unitary man.

The History of the Universe and of Life

While the development of any particular physical system is a process which has been (or may be) repeated indefinitely, the development of the universe is unique. It comprises the history of all stellar universes, of the solar system and the earth, and of the development of physical and organic systems including their mental components. This covers the whole of knowledge. All processes are to be interpreted as forms in course of development.

The book outlines the aspects of this task which are relevant to the diagnosis of contemporary man.

The History of Man

The unitary interpretation of the history of man amounts to a comprehensive anthropology dealing with the evolution and social development of the species, its general or permanent characteristics, and the varied individual characteristics which appear in the adult through the influence of different social and physical environments.

Chapters 3 to 8 outline the aspects of this task which are relevant.

The World Trend

Here we pass from the reorganization of existing knowledge, which has already been outlined in the previous chapters, to anticipation of the future.

The unitary conviction implies that a period has already opened in which men may once again recognize and accept the social tendencies of their time. During the first decade of this century many Europeans were still confident of continued moral progress, though there had been warnings of the impending breakdown. Now, after thirty years of doubt and despair, it is possible to establish a more reliable interpretation of the historical trend, by discarding the emphasis on moral progress and concentrating attention on the process of development which runs unmistakably through the history of man.

This was not possible even ten years ago. The unitary view has been developing for long, in many minds and in many forms, but only since 1939 has scepticism regarding the inherited tradition grown sufficiently to prepare the general mind for a unitary interpretation of the world trend. War appears to hasten the processes of history because it brings long-term and normally hidden tendencies into closer relation to current events. In a decaying culture the vast majority continue to live like puppets in a dead world until the collapse of institutions forces them to recognize the painful truth. Few understood Nietzsche while he was alive, but countless millions have now seen the collapse of France and Italy, the German psychosis of fear and cruelty, and the grandeur of Russia. It is no longer madness to look from the European Christian idealist to a new type of man; the conception which was the monopoly of genius fifty years ago can today be formulated in a manner which many can recognize as a description of what is now happening under their own eyes.

In 1918 the Western world intoxicated itself with a Wilsonian idealism which was the last and the most hopeless effort of the old Europe to achieve its own survival. It failed in its practical aim, just as all Europe's ideals failed, because that aim was the expression of a dissociated tradition and neglected the repressed organic and economic components. The prophecy of this chapter will be realized, because it is not the moral aspiration of a divided vision but the unitary recognition of the developing continuity of human history. The historical trend which is now forming the unitary world is the expression neither of idealism nor of animal self-interest, but of the formative vitality of the community and its members. If this picture of the future appears morally better than the recent past that is because we happen to be moving from a phase of disintegration of convictions and institutions into a phase of reorganization, from disorder to order in the social and intellectual fields. In a generation this transition may already lie behind us, a historical step as unmistakable as a scientific discovery or a social revolution, for it will be the equivalent of both.

The cardinal feature of the new period is the existence of a general trend of development which men can recognize, accept, and facilitate, each in his own way. The conviction of the inevitability of such a trend implies that all its necessary conditions are being realized by the historical process. One of those conditions is the determination of an increasing number of individuals to organize their thought and lives in terms of the unitary conviction. Unitary man does not leave the task to others; he wills what the unitary process in himself leads him to will. He knows that he can develop himself only by helping to develop the whole. He does not sit back and allow an abstract historical necessity which he does not himself experience to do the work, since then he would fail to share in the general development. Each can only do what he is suited to do, but if he fails to do that, neither nature nor the community will spare him inevitable frustration.

Moreover individual action will only be effective in so far as it is in accordance with the trend. With its support everything will seem

possible; against it everything will seem to fail. Goethe said that
the chief reason for Napoleon's extraordinary personal influence
was that under him men were sure of attaining their object. On this
account they were drawn to him, like actors to a new manager who
they think will assign them good parts. No one serves another dis-
interestedly, but he does it willingly if he knows he can thus serve
himself. In the same way the world community will feel itself drawn
to the unitary conviction, though unitary thought denies the validity of this dualisim of selfish and unselfish motives. The distinguishing mark of a period dominated by a constructive trend is that
the interest of the individual and of the community can no longer
be separated. Unitary thought says to every individual: to know
yourself is no longer adequate, because static knowledge is not
possible. You can realize yourself only as a developing component
of the community. You are a man, with human heredity developed
by the human tradition. If you are not distorted from the normal it
is possible for you to achieve your own development within the
development of the community. Such a life may involve struggle,
but it is spontaneous, non-purposive, and self-justifying. In a limited sense it is possible for the mass of the people in all periods.
The special feature of the period we now enter is that this identification of personal with community development again becomes
possible for all sections of society.

The transition is therefore from a phase in which the basic historical trend has been largely unconscious to one in which the trend
dominates the attention of man. The earlier dualistic dialectic of
left and right in politics is overcome. Historical change is no longer
ascribed to the interplay of these supposedly fundamental antitheses in which morality is called in by one side or the other to justify
an exclusive prejudice. Left and right programs achieve little except when the historical trend makes one of them its instrument.
History normally passes on between them. The trend of a new phase
can never be defined in terms of the conceptions of a previous
phase, and traditional parties and institutions can never express the
new. But as the new trend draws attention to itself and begins to
dominate men's thoughts, then a new orientation appears. In place
of the lateral dialectic of one side versus another, there is the polarization of the men of the new world against the men of the old.
There will be as many place-seekers amongst the new as place-

holders amongst the old. But those who look forward will win because they express the developing condition of man.

What, then, is the trend? What are the characteristics whose progressive development will mark the coming period?

The trend is towards a single order, unitary, balanced, and universal; the passage from an apparent anarchy of exaggerated contrasts, by a process of mutual adjustment and adaptation, towards a unitary order; the transition from unrestricted expansion towards finite order.

This trend towards a unitary order implies the following *general*
  aspects of the trend: i.e., increasing
recognition, acceptance, and facilitation of this world
trend;
recognition of the interdependence of all elements in
the world system;
 spread of the unitary conviction;
 recognition that the solution to every problem is to be
    found in its expression as a unitary process of development;
  development of a unitary science;
 operation of the social hierarchy of power and of
    unitary skills in the interests of general development,
    with the continuing reduction of human frustration
    by poverty and privilege.

In addition to these general aspects, the adjustment of exaggerated contrasts implies that the most important *special* aspect of the trend will be:

the industrial development of Asia and the rapid raising towards Western standards of the Asiatic half of the human race.

Recognition and acceptance of the world trend implies that the historical process facilitates itself by dominating the rational mental processes in man, i.e., by becoming conscious in a stable world consensus of opinion and will. The existence of such unified opinion is henceforward the condition of stability in any new phase of the historical trend. The recognition of world interdependence implies that a pre-existing interdependence has forced itself on the attention of the species, so that sectarian thought having become ineffective goes out of fashion. The spread of the unitary conviction replaces neutral objective science and subjective religion as the basis of the form of mental organization appropriate to the unitary period. The development of unitary science means that a comprehensive science comes to grips with life and mind, and permits the proper control of birth, life, and death. Finally the operation of the hierarchy of power and of the unitary techniques in the interests of general development implies an expanding world income distributed less towards owners of property and increasingly towards those whose work and skill contribute to the general development. With the ascendancy of the concept of development the concept of the ownership of property loses much of its significance.

All these general features of the trend express its pervasive character as the progressive elimination of exaggerated contrasts within a single developing world order. The representative man of the period will be conscious of the interdependence of the whole world as sharing in a recognized general trend; his life and thought will be stabilized and organized through the unitary conviction supported by a unitary science; he will accept the place appropriate to his faculties within the hierarchy of the new society, because the operations of those around him who wield power will in the main be guided by the aim of general development. The facilitation of development will constitute a social norm superseding Christian, humanist, and capitalistic ethics.

The period will be marked by a universalism facilitating local diversity. The cruder contrasts of East and West will disappear, but their diversity will remain. For two thousand years Europe has combined unity and diversity; now that example is translated on to a world scale. The world community will be consciously hierarchical, the hierarchy of power passing from the holders of money or property to those who exercise the skills which facilitate the development of the community. This hierarchy of unitary techniques will ensure social stability and so permit increasing equality of religious political, economic and educational opportunity. Moreover this universal hierarchical community will require a new type of leader, not speaking for a particular nation on all matters, as do contemporary political figures but specializing on particular aspects of social life and speaking on them for the whole of mankind. But this universalism, hierarchy, and leadership will derive their sanction from the incomparable emancipation brought by unitary science. The first age of scientific enlightenment led to disillusion and disaster because its static and analytical methods were inappropriate to the study of the historical and organic matrix within which consciousness operates. The prospect of a unitary science embracing man provides a more favorable opportunity.

This world community will develop because it expresses the condition of a type of man now ripe for development. If this is indeed the trend of the general continuity of history, our children and our children's children will live in such a world. This is no utopian dream, but the organic norm for *homo sapiens* at this stage of history. The liberal idealist may not recognize the new world, for it is not the realization of his ideals. It substitutes development for moral progress, formative tension for static harmony, continuing transformation for permanence, the unitary social hierarchy for the ambiguous conception of democratic equality, and unitary balance for the subject-object dualism. It replaces the illusory ideal which neglected its shadow by the proper spontaneity of integrated man.

But this raises the question whether this transition can be accomplished without sudden acts of adjustment, such as the Russian Revolution of 1917. Many countries still display the grip of sectional interests on the instruments of power. Is it possible for the prevalent disorder to develop towards the unitary order without critical moments, both in individuals when they are converted to the unitary view and in each community as it undergoes the corresponding transformation? So profound a metamorphosis would appear to imply a long prepared process culminating in a swift adjustment which must separate the new men and the new communities from the old.

There is no general answer to this question. A deep continuity links the Christian idealist to unitary man, and at that level the historical process may show no sudden change. But the new is none the less sharply distinguished from the old, and the concentration of unitary wills must provoke the consolidation of reaction. At the intellectual level the contrast is explicit: unitary man thinks in process concepts, achieving his own development by facilitating the general development, while the reaction thinks in static concepts, seeking through its dualistic thought and action to preserve separate privilege from the general process. Other intermediary types will tend to disappear and in some communities this polarization may disrupt the social system while in others it may be concealed within a continuous and widely accepted readjustment.

A gradual development through so profound a transformation is possible because, though the thought-structure of the two types is sharply contrasted this does not mean that the unitary principle and its predecessor, the European principle, are in fundamental opposition to one another. The unitary and European principles cannot come into pure opposition, because they represent responses to different situations and provide answers to different kinds of questions. They stand for methods appropriate to communities at different stages of development and can never be practical alternatives. The unitary principle accepts the past, but goes further by bringing to man's attention forms which had not previously been noticed. It transcends and does not challenge more primitive attitudes. It is the child of Christianity and exact science and from its greater strength can tolerate their narrower views so long as they do not frustrate development.

Unitary man recognizes and honours European man, but rejects the sentimental illusion that there can ever be understanding between them. The creation of the unitary world implies a conviction which can grow only where the European ideals have failed. But the fact that the two attitudes correspond to a different condition of man means that unitary man can live beside and co-operate with others who do not share his own conviction. His comprehensive outlook embraces and co-ordinates the special religions and idealisms, not merely tolerating but actively using their more limited aspirations. Only the misuse of the hierarchy of power for sectional interests calls out his challenge.

Violent revolution is not therefore a necessary feature of the transition to the unitary period. To discover whether it is probable in particular countries, we have to neglect the conventional political approach and to recall the form of social development during the European period. We saw that the continuing differentiation of man led society through a sequence of major periods. In the fourth of these, the European period, the main feature of social development was the progressive transformation of the hierarchy of power from religious to political, and from these to economic institutions and persons. The transition to unitary society, which marks the close of the fourth period, is accomplished through the shifting of the hierarchy into the hands of those possessing techniques for facilitating the general development of man. The degree of continuity which is possible in any particular community as it completes this transition can only become evident through a consideration of the relative importance of the different components, family, religious, political, economic, and technical, in its existing social system. The general trend is towards a unitary society, but each great community has a different history and approaches the universal form along its own path.

The following analysis of the social structure of four important communities does not imply any relative valuation of their different systems. Unitary thought is concerned to facilitate the development of each along its proper path within the whole, and not to make ethical or other relative valuations which neglect the differences between the histories and present situations of one country and another. The analysis is a formal study of the role played by the different components in the constitution of the social hierarchy in each community during the 1930s. The term finance is here used to include the separate interests of the great industries.

Great Britain had the most balanced social system. Family, church, politics, finance, and to a less degree technical skill all played an important role in the hierarchy of power. This feature gave British life its characteristic complexity and balance. No one aspect of life was allowed to dominate. There was a place for every element that had contributed to British history, and the balance of British life expressed this deep sense of continuity. We may take the British situation in the 1930s as a standard with which other countries can be compared.

Germany's situation was simpler. Technical skill was valued more, and family, religion, and politics relatively less than in Great Britain. Political forms had never played an important role in the life of the German peoples, and the place of family and religion had been undermined by the strains of the first war and its aftermath. The respect for efficiency, for scientific method, and for novelty for its own sake all contributed to the relative dominance of technical skill. With the seizure of power by the Nazis the importance of finance probably tended to grow less, and the hierarchy of power passed more and more into the hands of those possessing skills which would serve the aim of war, or were believed to contribute to that end.

In the *USSR* the valuation of skill had for long been even more clearly dominant than in Germany, since family, religion, politics, and finance all counted for less relatively to the overriding national aim. The primitive religious collectivism of the 19th century had provided the basis for a national unity more widely effective than the enforced unity of Germany, and devoted to a constructive purpose, the technical development of the community. A skill applied to this end could, in most circumstances, outweighs the influence of any of the other four components. The singleness of aim gave a religious intensity to the life of the community and the result has been a unique development which, in two decades, has made Russia the second world power.

The *United States* always placed a high value on the technical ability which was necessary to develop its virgin land, but in place of the religious collectivism of the Russian tradition, the American community was built by individuals revolting from an older tradition in search of freedom to follow the life of their own choice. Skill was valued for its results, but finance came first, the dollar being the symbol of the individual's success in competition with his fellows. Money was relatively more important than in Great Britain, because of the larger role given in Britain to the family, the church, and political institutions, and more than in Germany, because the United States recognized no uniting national purpose.

In spite of the complexity and subtlety of national characteristics this definite picture emerges because process thought offers a clue to the form of contemporary social development. Within the special approach of this analysis Russia had gone furthest in the direction of the trend towards unitary society, though taking a path appropriate only to her own situation. Germany comes next, since after Russia she values techniques most highly. The United States follows, her valuation of skill being restrained, more than it is in Germany, by the continuing power of money. Great Britain is the last of these four, an apparent laggard through her love of continuity and balance.

The pattern may be checked by cross-comparisons. The U.S.A. and the USSR represent the two sides of the European dualism of individualism and collectivism, each component having had to escape from the other to find its ideal soil outside Europe. The Protestant pride in the responsibility of the individual to develop himself flowered in North America, just as the mystical desire of the individual to lose and find himself in an overriding unity found an extreme expression in the Russian social collectivity. Europe flung its two components apart to the West and to the East.

Another comparison provides a further check. Britain and Germany express two contrasted principles: maximum continuity, variety, and balance in the one; in the other an unbalanced single-component fanaticism. Both countries lack the recognized constructive purpose which gives stability to the Russian system. Britain in the 1930s was stable, because her system rested on many components, Germany was unstable because resting on a single component devoted to an aim which could only be temporary. If both countries ultimately accept the unitary aim, then Germany might represent the model of a pure or "fanatical" unitary society devoted without reserve to a German conception of development, while Britain might provide the antithesis of a unitary society of great richness and variety, in which the other components still play a secondary role. English elasticity would then contrast with the German single-mindedness in pursuit of the development of the areas under her influence. Both would contribute to the variety of the unitary world.

If we compare the state of these four countries, as shown by this analysis, with the forms of unitary society, we can estimate the degree and the direction of the structural change which each must undergo, Each country will retain much of its distinguishing characteristics, since these arise from its geography and history and can find a place within the unitary system. But each must move towards the universal form if it is to share in the common development which lies ahead.

The Russian system cannot form a component of a world order until great freedom, a tolerance of variety, is permitted. The German system requires a radical transformation of aim, and some degree of stabilization from outside, but no fundamental change of structure is necessary. The United States of America will have to control its dollar individualism if it is to provide leadership in world affairs. The technical apparatus is ready, but power has still to pass unequivocally to those who will use it in the main for the development of the world community. This change may be delayed for some years, because the U.S.A. entered both wars relatively late and is distant from the Eurasian land bloc. Moreover a co-operative policy in world affairs might for a time be combined with persisting financial individualism at home. Thus in none of these three countries is an immediate change in the structure of the hierarchy of power to be anticipated. All three value technique highly; two have already in differing degrees subdued the power of private finance and achieved an effective consolidation of social purpose (though in one case antagonistic to the unitary trend) while the other is not yet confronted with the necessity of challenging the existing hierarchy of finance.

But the case is different when we turn to the gracious laggard, Great Britain. This book is not written for British readers in particular, but to establish the unity of unitary minds everywhere. Yet it is written in Britain, and I believe my country still has an important contribution to make in world affairs. In all the realms of quantity Britain's relative importance will steadily decline during the coming decades. But in matters of geography, experience, and quality Britain can still offer the world something which is unique. Thanks to the fact that her own courage was supplemented by the aid of her allies, the continuity of Britain's developing tradition is still preserved. But in the coming decade no ally can help her. Britain can retain her place in the future only if she recognizes what the world trend implies for her. I shall therefore consider Britain's position in greater detail.

The world trend implies for Britain a steady decline in relative importance, as compared with the great communities of the future, in most matters susceptible of quantitative measurement. The existing trends already put it almost beyond question that Britain's proportion of the world's total population, economic production, and naval strength, will decline during the critical decade from 1950 to 1960. Britain's tremendous war mobilization was fed from abroad, and constituted a dramatic climax which partially obscured the increasing relative importance of the United States, the Dominions, Russia, and China. The War industrialization of the Dominions and the United States will be followed by the peaceful industrialization of the East, and as the thousand millions of Asia begin to apply their new energy, the days of Britain's quantitative supremacy will quickly be forgotten. Britain must now cultivate her imagination, and turn her rich tradition and special experience to better account. The blind courage of 1940 must be followed by a new courage of the imagination, if its fruits are not to be lost. The truth may be painful but Britain must take it, if she is to survive.

In the Britain of the recent past the hierarchy of power was, as we have seen, in the hands of four main elements: the old families, the church, the political organizations, and finance. Beside these the possessors of skills needed by the community had only a secondary place because the country acknowledged no common purpose. Social development in Britain had normally occurred gradually, by a slow, unconscious process. The British dislike for rational abstractions had saved the country from adopting a rigid, i.e., static, political system which could change only by sudden and violent adjustments. The passion for continuity had not prevented a slow process of unconscious organic development. But today those four pillars of society are inadequate. The process of development which has hitherto been neglected by the national consciousness now demands attention, and the innocent love of continuity must now grow into a conscious acceptance of a course of national development, if it is not to decay into mere reverence for the past. Britain can retain her soul only by transforming it. The British balance can be maintained only if family, religion, politics, and finance (in so far as they are merely traditional in a static sense) admit the superior claims of those who are consciously devoting their skills to the development of Britain within the unitary world. The hierarchy of effective power must in the main pass to those who know how to wield that power for the development of the community.

This transition may come about with little stir, like a long-prepared adjustment. The change in ideas of the 1940s may be followed by a corresponding change in laws and institutions. Violence would destroy the British balance, which remains the clue to the special quality which she can offer the world. The British solution to every problem depends on the reduction of contrasts, and not on the choice of one of two or more apparently incompatible methods. Britain will not tolerate either a centralized socialism or an anarchic individualism, but will develop her own method, which may appear to other countries as a non-rational compromise. However perplexing this procedure is to the logical mind or to the fanatical partisan, it is organic and proper, the secret of the British ethos. Moreover, it is also the clue to the special role of Britain in the unitary period, which is itself a time of the adjustment of exaggerated contrasts. Thus Britain in remaining true to herself can offer an example to the world in something more important even than heroism. The unitary age expresses the overcoming of quantity by order. The irony of history offers Britain this incomparable opportunity of a renaissance: the hour of her own quantitative decline coincides with the decline of the importance of quantity in men's minds. Between the past and the future, between the West and the East, Britain can play a special organizing role. This, I submit, is no national conceit; the world needs Keynes, Beveridge, and their successors. May this new tradition prosper.

In the past Britain has always been coy in the face of the new, hesitating to admit into consciousness a formative principle, a theory of change, or a dynamic idea. While Catholic Europe worshiped being and systems of static ideas, Britain rejected the dominance of ideas and placed the emphasis on the life of action. In the future her contribution will still, as in the past, lie in the practical field, where ideas are inseparable from personal character and life. Neither Asiatic mysticism of process nor Teutonic theories of process ever attracted these islanders. But it is possible that unitary thought, in which ideas are inseparable from life and unity facilitates diversity, may appeal to Britain.

It is easier to foresee the general world trend and the industrialization of Asia than to guess the future of Britain. But the alternatives are clear. Any government that fails to base its policies on a correct reading of the general trend will fail in all its major actions. Any community that continues to tolerate such a government will lose the opportunity to share fully in the benefits of the coming world economic expansion. Britain's future will depend on the extent to which her leaders and her public opinion recognize the meaning of the world trend.

We must now return to the general situation. Our analysis of these four communities from the point of view of the power hierarchy suggests the following conclusions: In Russia little change is necessary to enable her to maintain her role within the unitary world.

In a world which had subdued the power of finance, she would find less difficulty in overcoming her relative isolation from the West. In Germany scarcely any change of structure is necessary, but the techniques which occupy the positions of power must be transformed from nationalistic, separatist, and military skins to those which will co-operate in a world development. Such a transformation need be neither difficult nor protracted in a country with so little stability of tradition, but the results of Nazi rule, military defeat, and Allied policy cannot yet be estimated. In Britain a far-going change is necessary from the condition of the 1930s, but this is already in progress. The question remains open whether this change will proceed rapidly enough for Britain properly to assist in post-war international organization, and to recover her appropriate share in the goodwill and trade of the East.

To estimate the special position of the United States in this transformation we must restate the nature of the world trend. The form of human society is changing from a group of relatively independent communities of limited territorial extent controlled mainly by financial power-hierarchies, to a universal society whose power-hierarchy will in the main be occupied by the skilled personnel trained to facilitate unitary development, that is, the development of their local communities within the general trend of world development.

This total development will find its special historical instruments, of which the most important will be the United States of America. Washington will be the greatest centre of power in the coming decades, with a secondary center, in Moscow, for the Asiatic continent. With the U.S.A. leading the three hundred millions of the English-speaking peoples and South America, and Russia the majority of the thousand millions of Asia, their relation becomes the major factor in world politics. If the U.S.A., assisted by Britain, can develop a world policy facilitating the proper development of each continent, American power will symbolize world unity and will not be resisted. The half century ahead is the epoch of the rise of Asia, but it is primarily America, as the dominant power, that must accept and facilitate this peaceful development, if the two hemispheres are not to fall into conflict.

To the contemporary mind, trained to think analytically, from the small to the large, and statically, without any sure principle leading from what exists into the future, this uncertain prospect looms dark with the threat of recurrent wars. It is true that no man can know how the American people will allow their power to be used, but the reason why that cannot be known in advance is that the problem is wrongly formulated, and presupposes a situation which does not exist. The American individual (or group) does not enjoy freedom to think or to will arbitrarily, that is, independently of the factors which mold his thought and action. Thought and will are vital responses to specific developing situations. Given a recognized world trend Americans cannot escape thinking and acting within the context set by so pervasive and universal a fact, any more than they could escape pursuing the dollar while that was the accepted symbol of enterprise, character, and achievement. America will choose in accordance with her own situation and tradition, but in relation to a world situation whose main characteristics will soon be unmistakable. Being offered the opportunity of so profitable a role, America must sooner or later overcome her love of competition and accept the trend.

For it is not America but Asia that is the main determinant of the world trend. The trend is towards the adjustment of exaggerated contrasts, and Asia will say to the world: we are half the species; we are going to raise our standards of life; help us if you will, but obstruct us or exploit us at your peril. The divided idealist without conviction might well doubt my prophecy of a unitary world if it had to be brought about by an idealism that represents only one distorted facet of the whole man. The unitary world will be formed because it is implicit in the continuity of the historical process. Nor is this particular prediction the expression of an individual's desire. The unitary world trend will be realized because the time has spoken to a thousand million men. Soon there will be a consensus of opinion in Asia, and in parts of the West, such as has never been seen before. This is no apocalyptic misuse of language, but a sober deduction from present social, economic, and technical facts. Russia has already proved its possibility, China is awake, and India is stirring. It is within the setting of these major facts that the next generation of the English-speaking peoples will have to shape their lives and thoughts.

The United States will have its own internal problems of North and South, of black and white, and would serve its own interests by conforming, in its foreign relations, to a world trend become unmistakable. The U.S.A. can wield supreme power, or seem to do so, on the condition that she allows the world to teach her. The rate of industrialization in the 1950s will far surpass that of any period in the past, and the industrialization of Asia will be a portent. To share in that expansion, the United States will have no choice but to restrain its financial individualism in foreign lands. If Britain fails to learn the same lesson, these islands will decay and the world move on with the same indifference as Britain showed to the decay of Europe. But if America were to fail also, new world conflicts would swiftly arise, foretold by fresh unemployment and despair. The American interest is now identical with that of the world as a whole.

When a historical movement is analysed into supposedly separate components, such as the economic and political, these appear to interact in a subtle and unaccountable manner in producing the final result. One reason for the difficulty in anticipating the development of the world in the years immediately ahead lies in this habit of analyzing a unitary process into supposedly separate parts. Two special problems which appear to confront the world are the political problem of the adjustment of national sovereignties within the unitary world system, and the economic problem of the compensation of the American export surplus which will be necessary to re-establish and develop Europe and Asia. These complementary problems are created by an inappropriate division of the unitary process, and history will appear to "solve" them by the unitary development of American power. In this process the U.S.A. will find itself compelled by circumstances to make free gifts and to accept new rights and responsibilities. In the development of its own power as the dominant center of the new world, the U.S.A., in order to maintain internal employment and world stability, will barter its export surplus for legal and political rights. The process may be concealed within the operations of an international investment authority. But after a decade of military and economic assistance to Europe, Asia, and Africa the United States will find itself —directly or indirectly —the legal tenant of military bases, ports, factories, and plantations in all continents. The rest of the world will have sold a part of its birthright in return for the opportunity to develop, and all countries will have renounced something to one another in order to achieve a general economic expansion. The exchange of goods for titles which is necessary to lay the basis for that expansion will progressively forge a world unity marked by the fading of the conception of sovereignty and the emergence of one dominant center of world power. So long as the expansion is in the main guided so as to facilitate the development of all peoples, the dominance of one or more centers will not imply domination, and the process equilibrium will be stable.

The controlling principle of this distribution of goods must therefore be one acceptable to all communities, and in a period of movement towards an ordered balance this principle must be the raising of all peoples towards a common standard of life. A limit may be set to the speed of this process of levelling-up by the requirement of stability. But this unitary aim implies the fair sharing of a steadily increasing real world income, which in turn requires fullest employment, maximum efficiency in the use of labor and materials, and the distribution of an increasing proportion of that income to active workers of all kinds as against the passive owners of property,

In the course of this process employment in richer countries will be maintained by the assistance given to poorer areas, and their effective and contractual unity will thereby be strengthened. Europe will be fed and rebuilt, Asia industrialized, and Africa aided in the development appropriate to her condition. Within Europe the same principle will operate, poorer regions receiving priority until minimum standards of nutrition and health have been established. The application of this principle is indispensable for the further development of the species, and those communities which reject it will suffer by sharing less in the general economic expansion. Each area has the choice of partaking in the general development, or following a path of isolation and relative decline. As the economic standard of the English speaking peoples is ten times that of the masses of China, the demand arising from Asia, if it is allowed to operate, will be sufficient to maintain a general upward trend throughout this century. The upward equalization of nutrition and industry will ensure economic expansion. In making her demand to the world Asia will act as the agent of the new historical trend.

Only within this world picture is it possible to consider the situation of Europe, or what is called the German problem. Germany is the unstable barometer of the European and world trend. In a period of anarchic expansion Germany comes in late and attempts to beat the world at its own game; in a unitary world a Hitler could never develop, but there will certainly be great German planners of the development of Europe and the world. Political leaders are seldom fully responsible agents. Their countries make them what they are. Only the general restoration of man's faith in himself can solve any national problem, whether it is the problem of British traditionalism, of German violence, or of the stability of American policy. The age is over when local solutions were possible to fundamental national problems. Technology has brought the world together, and it will now be united by the recognition of a common trend which will transform every local problem. This universal movement will not be deflected by the lip service to national vanity which will accompany it.

Yet each continent has its own past and future. The ages ahead will look back on the two world wars as the deliberate abdication of Europe from world supremacy, the final suicide of a two-thousand-year-old culture wasting its energies in internal conflict, hastening the decline of its population, and accelerating the development of the other continents. Europe can be reborn as part of the unitary world on one condition: that it can establish a form of unity which will facilitate the diversity which is proper to it.

Asia will establish more uniform and relatively despotic collective communities in each section of the great land bloc, united by their common emphasis on a socially controlled industrialization. North America and the English-speaking world, relatively rich and developed, will in different degrees control their individualism within a new social leadership stimulated by the opportunities of the unitary period. Africa will accept a phase of suzerainty until it develops its characteristic forms within the new world system.

During the first half of this century Europe abdicated its supremacy to the United States, but the second half will be marked by the rise of Asia even more than by the predominance of American power. The coming shift of emphasis from West to East is, however, the compensation of an ancient lack of balance rather than a mere swing towards the opposite state. Moreover the new role of Asia is not merely one of greater weight in world affairs and a fuller life for its own people, much as that means.

In becoming Westernized European man lost his integrity but laid the basis for the universalism of science which was a necessary prelude to unitary man. While discarding the forms which characterized him during the period of his world supremacy, the European retains the knowledge that he has made the world what it is today. Europe and its descendants constitute one third of the race and no man can think without using European forms of thought. Asia missed the long journey through Christianity, rationalism, and exact science, and if Europe can now give expression to a universal principle of development transcending these and proper to all men, Asia cannot but accept it.

But this acceptance by Asia of a universal form of thought generated in Europe involves no betrayal of Eastern tradition. Unitary thought and unitary man represent a return to universal forms from the long deviation of European man. At the time of Heraclitus and Lao Tse men in all lands saw one process in nature, in society, and in the individual. The formative tendency in European man led him to desert this process unity and to seek to master himself and nature by imposing on the universal becoming the sharp categories of being. To that effort the race owes its greatest achievements, but those achievements did not bring the emancipation for which the European hoped. In the twentieth century man behaves with the same stupidity, disharmony, and sadism as he did before the two thousand years of monotheism. Today the West cannot but admit its ugly failure. Measured by the Eastern criterion of unity and harmony the West has not merely failed to succeed, it has failed even to try. Unitary man recognizes this and accepts from Asia its deeper aim of harmony as proper to all men. Enriched by the grand failure of Christianity, static reason, and quantitative science, a new type of man emerges combining the unity of the East with the differentiation of the West. The separation of East and West is over, and a new history opens rich in quality and majestic in scale.

This increased range of community life, both in the differentiation of new faculties and in social scale, permits the unitary techniques to take over the control of society without wholly displacing the earlier components from their share in social organization. The family survives as the basic unit process, even where new methods of insemination are encouraged in order to control the quality or numbers of the community. The local religious institutions con-

tinue to play their role, though the hygiene of the unitary conviction, life, and science, robs the Christian symbols of their once
compelling attraction. Political democracy, no longer a moral ideal
pursued in ignorance of its limitations, will in new forms continue
to facilitate the mutual education of leaders and people. Passive
ownership, whether of real property or of symbolic claims, will
mean less and less beside the new emphasis on development, but
in restricted fields property will remain important as a title to exercise initiative in individual enterprise. These four components will
remain effective in varying degrees in different countries, but will
be subordinate to the unitary skills in all communities which conform to the world trend.

Yet the growth of such a world system will bring occasions for
conflict on an unprecedented scale. Once unitary man is aware of
himself that awareness will create problems that did not exist previously. The balance of the world community is determined by
three interrelated factors: the present distribution of population, the
process of industrialization and the distribution of consumable
goods, and the movements and net reproduction rates of the popu-
lations in the different continents. These present a master problem
already in process of solution by the algebra of the historical trend.
For the coming half century two types of solution are possible:
unitary planning, or total conflict between East and West. Soon the
white peoples will realize what is involved in the higher birth-rate
and increasing industrialization of the East, and they may see that
their own interest in their own development renders co-operative
planning essential. In a world of competition and fear lacking the
expansive background of the nineteenth century there can be no
hope of a major recovery in the Western birth rate. But the prospect, of a unitary world would at once render the rise of Asia less
ominous, and tend to stimulate Western faith in the future.

Europe committed suicide mainly through its failure to control
the disintegrating influence of money when the age of expansion
was already over. During the coming decades the West may repeat
this act of self-destruction, and hand the world over to the more
numerous Asiatic and colored races. I suggest that it will not; that
the threat from the East will compel the West to subdue finance;
that the emergence of a practical sense of world unity will put power
in the hands of those whose aim is to fulfil their own development

in a unitary development of mankind as a whole; and that within the unitary doctrine East and West can co-operate.

Man is now ready to accept a unitary order which will facilitate diversity. He lacks only the unifying idea, and the enemy that calls out united effort. A new idea has little power over man unless an old tradition is already challenged. As war turns to peace the vitality of all undistorted men will rally to the principle of a unitary development against the threatening influences of inertia and privilege. The failure of past methods will force man to accept a new conviction lest the old Adam destroy him.

Postscript

The story continues. The role of thought is to facilitate development and its value is measured by its power to lead on. Quality of thought arises from the emotion which it expresses, and the quality of the emotion from the action to which it leads. If attention has been drawn to the true form of process, then action must follow on thought, and man be aided to achieve his unity. If speculation can guide life, then it is more than subjective fantasy. Here I could afford to be dogmatic. I have nothing to lose and the truth itself cannot lose. For I am sure there is enough error here to prevent its being misinterpreted as absolute truth, rather than as a first vista of unitary truth in course of development. If there is folly here, those who persist in it will surely become wise.

This process of the self-development of life by thought is self-justifying and requires no sanction. The developing tendency of life cannot be measured by the values which it itself creates. From the underlying unity of form which unites unitary thought and the forms of human life it follows that unitary man accepts life with a spontaneous and radical comprehension. This acceptance is inescapable. Unitary man may not exist, but if he does, he must welcome complete life. In the unitary period every appraisal of the formative tendency in man is a judgement on the judge. To interpret development as moral advance is to admit failure to outgrow the illusory security of idealism and to see life as it is.

The genius of man lies in his growing faculty for enchantment without illusion. As man develops, the less need inspiration feed on illusion. Every fresh inspiration is born of a new discovery of unity, and every major step in development from the discarding of illusion. According to the state of man this process may appear in two contrasted forms: as the rejection of old limitations or as the acceptance of new ones. Traditional restrictions may prove illusory and the spirit of man may break through them in a proud outburst. Or an old freedom may be discovered to have been an illusion and a new limitation be accepted as the condition of a more extensive achievement. Humanist man was an explorer; he tore aside the veil of religion and rejoiced in the expansion of his powers. Unitary man is an organizer; he sets out to order his finite world. The unitary consciousness, in discarding the conviction of its own autonomy and permanence, may appear to betray the infinitude of the Christian-humanist spirit. But that dream of infinity ended in the concentration camp, and the austerity of unitary man has no room for sentimental worship of what has been outgrown. Beauty is integral with its matrix and cannot be recovered. Unitary man cannot escape his knowledge that the personal life is finite; he must find eternity in the passing moment, for it can be found nowhere else.

The discoveries of the explorer rejoice his expansive vitality, but man's rediscovery of himself by adjustment to real limitations may also bring the sudden blessing of a new inspiration. Already during the nineteenth century European genius had lost its illusions and set about the task of readjustment; now in the first half of the twentieth the peoples have lost their old faiths and are ready for a new conviction. But on this occasion the new is not the projection into history of a fanaticism born of conflict. The inspiration of unitary man is tolerant because it is subjectively humble and draws its assurance from the unchallengeable movement of science as common knowledge in course of development.

But if it is to retain its validity the unitary truth must be protected by a scepticism which can penetrate optimistic naivety to the level of the real. None can wholly overcome the appeal of security, but in this some are more mature than others. Unitary thought, if it is to remain fertile, must be aristocratic as well as popular. Yet this distinction is contingent, not absolute. The many require authority; unitary thought will provide it. It may be that they require mystery and illusion; but a unitary mode of life will reduce this need. When the unitary development of an individual is frustrated, he creates a dream as substitute. This dream does not represent his proper fulfilment since that is obstructed and cannot be conceived in advance. The dream is therefore an illusion, but its existence is the sign of a potential completeness. The demand for illusions is evidence that man is not content. This fact makes his failure less miserable. So long as man dreams, the sordid pattern of his life is not his full measure. But so long also must the unitary conviction of a universal form be protected by a deep scepticism regarding the particular, if the truth is to be preserved from debasement.

In the course of history every universal truth has been misinterpreted and used as the instrument of privilege against the general development of man. The misinterpretation which makes this abuse possible is partly due to the limited faculties available to each individual in applying the general truth to his own situation. But it arises even more from the dissipation of the austerity of truth which results from the demand of the many for mystery and authority. Yet in the course of the development of man each one of the sequence of universal truths has been less liable to misuse than its predecessor. Each successive principle has been effective over a wider field of human behavior and has influenced a greater proportion of the human race. Magic was the dominant principle in the organization of primitive communities, but it did little to facilitate general development, Monotheism symbolized a component of unitary truth, since it integrated and enlarged the world of the individual and promised to each a path of spiritual development if he accepted the guidance of religious authority. But the interpretation given to this truth by religious authority was exempt from any general scrutiny and was freely misused to protect the privileges of a few. Quantitative science, by limiting its scope, established a standard of objective truth which could not be degraded or misinterpreted. This was important, not only for knowledge and its material benefits, but also for the unity of the species, since it established a universally accepted method of thought within that limited field. Yet the achievement was incomplete because exact science could be freely misused, only its interpretation, not its application, being subject to general scrutiny.

In unitary society the application, as well as the interpretation of science, is subject to the test of a universal standard. Thought must be appropriate to the general structure of nature, and its application appropriate to contemporary human nature. Unitary man asserts that there is a universal norm for the application of science which the entire species can accept: the development of the species in all its members. The developing orthodoxy of neutral science as a body of abstract knowledge thus enlarges into the developing social authority of a reorganized universal tradition. This actively developing tradition based on the scientific self knowledge of man will generate its own standards of austerity and scepticism. Moreover the unitary tradition will not only satisfy the need for authority, but assuage the demand for mystery by revealing to a generation hungry for magic the scientific miracle of an unsuspected unity in nature.

There are moments in history when it seems that a transformation of special importance is under way and the community experiences a heightened sense of the passage of time. After several centuries of a maturing sense of history this consciousness of time has now reached its culmination in the postulate of a universal method of thought. But a vivid awareness of time need not hamper recognition of what is changeless. The formative process is as permanent as nature, and certain aspects of human life are as permanent as man. The entire rhythm of human life from birth to death co-exists at every moment, and throughout history the pattern of unity and conflict, of fulfilment and frustration, is always present. Human potentialities change, but the degree to which they are realized remains the same. Human life is a web of general invitation and rare integrity. History alters the scope but it does not change the quality of man's self-expression.

To he alive may mean to float with the stream, to recognize and further the processes of history, or to withdraw and live alone in what is eternal. This apparent choice is fixed for each by his own stage of development. Each is what he is: asleep, awake, or exhausted. At a late stage in the cycle of a local civilization it may seem that with increase in knowledge there comes a general fatigue. Over-differentiation and loss of vitality appear together because they are two aspects of one condition. But there is no evidence that knowledge and vitality are always incompatible. Europe lost its vitality in the disintegration resulting from its dualistic static thought. Unitary thought offers a mode in which rich variety of thought and full vigour of action are inseparable. The race may have worn out its ancient guides, but it is not itself exhausted.

Ontogeny repeats some of the features of phylogeny; the development of the individual from conception to physical maturity passes through stages which marked the evolutionary history of the species. (The parallel is not complete, for evolution has its short cuts; the later need not repeat the whole sequence of the earlier.) But physical maturity is not the end of the development of the individual, and as he matures socially, that is, in knowledge and character, he may recapitulate features of the social development of the species which followed its evolutionary history. This book, which is the history of one aspect of the social development of man, may also reflect the story of the social maturing of an individual. In fact the story of the development of a tradition may parallel the story of the effect of that tradition on a particular individual. Moreover the personal experience of that individual may be the source of his interpretation of the history of the tradition. The late European in seeking to understand himself must seek to understand the story of the Europe which has made him what he is. An interpretation of history may be faulty, but if it expresses a personal experience of the tradition which is shared by others then it satisfies the only available criterion. All we know is the influence of the past on ourselves and on our contemporaries, for the past itself is past. The sublimation into philosophy of a personal experience of the tradition is the most that can be attained, until thought passes into action. If it is recognized by others as an image of their own experience and aids their further development then it is a component of the developing truth.

This book may appear to claim power for an idea. But what is power? One who does not fully partake in the life of the many may find himself forming in thought what they are occupied in developing in their daily lives. His idea will then facilitate their actions. The behavior of the many will seem to have been caused by the idea, which thereby acquires the semblance of power.

Appendix

Glossary of Unitary Thought

The following glossary of unitary process concepts is arranged in sequence so that the definition of each concept uses only terms already defined, apart from a few whose meaning is taken over unchanged from contemporary English. The system of thought develops itself from the fundamental concept of development by applying it to increasingly complex and specialized situations. The concepts occurring earlier in the sequence are the most general, and the later concepts represent their application to special types of system. Ten fundamental concepts which form a logical sequence are printed in italics.

This formulation of the basic concepts of unitary thought is a first step towards a non-quantitative system of inference. But it is not a positive deductive system of the kind appropriate to a developed scientific theory, since it is neither logically perfect nor scientifically complete. At least four essential elements are lacking. Asterisks (*) indicate points at which constructive additions are necessary to convert this provisional method of thought into the foundation of a unitary science. When thus developed the method should lead to the general descriptive morphology anticipated in *Critique of Physics* (1931).

Though the following concept sequence is incomplete, it provides support for the text as a further stage in the progressive clarification of ideas which must precede a definitive formulation. Moreover it goes some way to show that the language of unitary thought used in the text is self-consistent and is not dependent on alien conceptions derived from other modes of thought.

It is intended to continue the development of the method elsewhere and to examine similar methods which have already been proposed. The absence of references to such methods does not imply that any part is regarded as original.

The history of an unfinished task is relevant to an understanding of its purpose. This attempt to develop a unitary method of thought was stimulated by a sense of the inadequacy of the basic concepts of contemporary mathematical physics to provide the foundation of a comprehensive unitary science or even of a unified physical theory. *Archimedes, or the Future of Physics* (1927) gave a semi-popular survey of the opportunity for a reorganization of scientific thought in term of a process asymmetrical with respect to "t." *Critique of Physics* (1931) presented an analysis of the contemporary methods of theoretical physics, and outlined a program of research directed towards the establishment of a unitary theory which would use non-quantitative basic concepts to provide a theory of measurement and of measured quantities. The present work offers a provisional formulation of the basic concepts of such a unitary process theory. But it applies the method to the prior task of interpreting the present condition of man.

Glossary
(* See footnotes on page 273)

Change	
Form	Recognisable continuity.*
Process	Form within change.
Nature	The whole process. Continuity within change and unity in diversity.
Unitary	Of one general form (of process).
Dualistic	Of two incompatible forms.
Development	Decrease in asymmetry.* (The simplest type of development is the separation, persistence, and extension of symmetrical form.)
Formative	Displaying development.
System	Whatever displays development (in process, arrested or completed).
Tendency	The process of the development of a system, which occurs if it is compatible with the development of the larger system of which the system is a part.

Structure   An internally developed system tending to persist and to extend its form (by a repetition of the process by which it was formed). (Structure is not sharply distinguished from process but is a process which approaches a symmetrical static form.)

Facilitation The tendency of a structure to extend its form by a repetition of the process by which it was formed.

Record   A persisting structure preserving the form, and facilitating the repetition. of the process by which it was formed. (A record which is not static, but still formative, facilitates new forms of process.)

Dominance The relation of a structure to the processes which it facilitates.

Hierarchy A system of processes connected by relations of dominance.

Organism-Environment

An oscillating equilibrium between the processes of a hierarchical system (organism) and of the wider system (organism and environment) of which it is part, resulting in the development of a characteristic (organic) process form.*

Proper   Facilitating the development of characteristic organic form.

Organic structure

A structure forming part of the system of the organism, facilitating a process (its function) which develops it further.

Organic function

The process which an organic structure facilitates.

Differentiation

The development of an organic structure developed by and facilitating a process proper to the organism.

Integration The arrangement of organic structures and functions so that a single characteristic form is developed.

Organization   The system of dominance relations in an organism or group of organisms.

Organizing process

> The dominant process in the hierarchy of an organism.

Attention

> "The attention of an organism is directed to A" means: the form of A is impressed on the organizing process of the organism.

Brain

> A record of the forms of organizing processes, facilitating new delayed responses.

Material

> Related to the permanent aspects of processes.

Mental

> Related to the facilitation by a brain of the formative aspects of organic processes
> *hence also:* in which a record of organizing processes facilitates delayed responses.

Instinctive

> Formed by organizing processes resulting from the maturing of inherited forms.

Intelligent

> Involving the facilitation by a brain of individually learned responses to particular situations. (Animal intelligence.)

Word

> A part of speech either formal or associated with a situation or thing and acting as a symbol for it.

Intellectual

> Involving verbal symbols (spoken, written, or operating without immediate motor activity). (Human intellect.)

Concept

> A generalized verbal symbol.

Organizing principle

> An organizing process in conceptual form.

Time sequence

> The class of asymmetrical relations characterizing change.

Space frame

> The class of symmetrical relations derived from structures.

Process concepts

> Time-like concepts, i.e., those referring to the time sequence.

Static concepts

> Time-less concepts, i.e., those not includ-
> ing the asymmetrcal time sequence in
> their reference.

Quantity   Measured relations.*

*N.B   The main additions which are necessary to convert
this descriptive language into the foundation of a
unitary science are:

1. The formulation of the conditions which determine
    "recognizable continuity."
2. The precise, but non-quantitative, formulation of the pro-
    cess of development in a form applicable to all systems,
    and of the conditions under which the development of one
    system may arrest the development of another.
3. As a special case of 2, the formulation of the process of the
    development of cellular organisms.
4. The description (in unitary terms) of the process of mea-
    surement, and hence the mathematical derivation of the ba-
    sic measured "quantities" (universal non-dimensional con-
    stants) and the "physical laws" connecting them.

These four lacking elements represent the unitary epistemology,
the general unitary law, the unitary description of living systems,
and the unitary derivation of mathematical physics.

Index